Tibetan Diary

Tibetan Diary

*From Birth to Death and Beyond
in a Himalayan Valley of Nepal*

Geoff Childs

UNIVERSITY OF CALIFORNIA PRESS
Berkeley · Los Angeles · London

University of California Press
Berkeley and Los Angeles, California

University of California Press, Ltd.
London, England

©2004 by the Regents of the University of California

Library of Congress Cataloging-in-Publication Data

Childs, Geoff H., 1963–
    Tibetan diary: from birth to death and beyond in a
Himalayan valley of Nepal / Geoff Childs.
        p. cm.
    Includes bibliographical references and index.
    ISBN 0-520-24109-6 (cloth : alk. paper)—ISBN
0-520-24133-9 (pbk. : alk. paper)
        1. Ethnology—China—Tibet—Nubri.
2. Philosophy, Tibetan.   3. Nubri (Tibet)—Religious
life and customs.   4. Nubri (Tibet)—Social life and
customs.   I. Title.
    GN635.C5C45 2004
    306'.0951'38—DC22

                                    2004004204

Manufactured in the United States of America

13   12   11   10   09   08   07   06   05   04
10   9   8   7   6   5   4   3   2   1

The paper used in this publication meets the minimum
requirements of ANSI/NISO Z39.48–1992 (R 1997)
(*Permanence of Paper*).

Contents

Illustrations

Acknowledgments

Many people have contributed valuable suggestions, editorial advice, and various forms of encouragement that have helped bring this book into being. My father, Neil Childs, relished the task of critiquing my prose and pointing out inconsistencies. More importantly, he deserves gratitude beyond measure for giving conspiratorial winks and nods to those youthful endeavors that eventually led to my career in anthropology. My mother, Peggy Childs, has always shown her love by never letting on how terrified she was every time I disappeared into the heart of Asia. By surviving so many bouts of cancer with dignity, courage, and grace, she remains a remarkable source of inspiration and a continual reminder of the strength that comes from the family. Lily, the personification of patience and understanding, helped turn hovels into homes on the three continents where the research and writing of this book were accomplished. Curt has stood as a paragon in my life for how positive motivation and clear-minded resolve can lead to the fulfillment of dreams. Steve Clingan, an avid reader with a broad range of interests, merits recognition for the numerous suggestions he made and for helping me gauge where this work stands in relation to an educated lay readership. Zsuzsanna Gulacsi selflessly contributed as a judicious sounding board for ideas and as a reliable editor during the formative phase of this project. Parts of this book, especially the ethnographic portions, derive from my Ph.D. dissertation at Indiana University. Credit goes to George Alter, Christopher Beckwith, Emilio Moran,

Elliot Sperling, Michael Walter, and Richard Wilk for their guidance and intellectual stimulation. Bryan J. Cuevas, Gregory Price Grieve, and an anonymous reviewer made insightful suggestions that resulted in a vastly improved end product. John Powers provided valuable advice on the presentation of topics relating to Buddhist philosophy. Many thanks are due to Rachel Kaul who compiled the index. Reed Malcolm, Colette DeDonato, Stephanie Fay, and Erin Marietta at the University of California Press were especially patient and helpful in making sure this project never stalled, and the contributions of the copyeditor, Anne Canright, led to significant improvements.

In Kathmandu several people deserve special mention. Kunga and Chökyi opened their home and culture to me in 1984, and thereby provided an initial impetus to follow the unconventional career path of anthropologist. They also introduced me to Karma Lama, who in turn introduced me to the people of Nubri. Tsetan Chonjore, my language teacher and close friend, continues to influence my thoughts about Tibetan society in many small yet significant ways. His contributions are far from negligible. Tsering Dorje and the late Kalsang Tsering helped transcribe many of the interviews for this book.

I would like to thank Keith Goldstein, K.P. Kafle, Sabra Jones, Nick Lederer, Esther Lev, Barb Secrest, Peg Swift, Donna Warrington, and Frank Weinstock, the board members of SEEDS (www.nepalseeds.org), who helped transform the empirical findings of ethnographic research into practical projects with tangible benefits for the people of Nubri. The experience of being stranded in a Nubri snowstorm and listening to an anthropologist's droning monologue (which experience is more harrowing?) failed to deter them from taking an active interest in the lives of people less fortunate than ourselves. Sabra Jones, a physician, deserves special mention for deploying her healing skills in a most altruistic manner. Her untimely death in the summer of 2002 has left a void in all our hearts.

Fieldwork in 1995 and 1997 was made possible by grants from Fulbright-Hays and the Wenner-Gren Foundation. A subsequent trip in 2000 was supported by a fellowship from the Andrew Mellon Foundation. The current manifestation of this book came to fruition while I was employed as a postdoctoral fellow at the Australian National University and during my current position at Washington University in St. Louis. I would like to thank all my colleagues at both institutions for sustaining such a supportive intellectual environment.

Those who deserve the most credit for this book are the people of Nubri and Kutang. They opened their homes, shared their friendship, and tolerated my frequent excesses. Lama Gyatso kept my spirits high through laughter; Rinpoche kept my spirits from flagging through a daily dose of sanity. Tsogyal, the consummate matriarch, never let me forget the importance of family. Rigzen Dorje shared texts, explanations, and grandfatherly compassion. Chimi could always be counted on for off-color humor. Dawa and Angjung kindled our hearth and filled our cups with warm tea after long trips throughout the valley. Lama Karma helped me get settled, then had the courtesy to refrain from casting me out from the community like a malevolent spirit after I nearly plugged his spouse with the arrow that won the 1997 long-distance shooting contest. I thank Tenzin and his wonderful family for so many nights of hospitality and revelry, and even forgive him for not warning me that a particular batch of arak had been double-distilled. I thank Hritar, Amji Dorje and Tsewang Buti, Khamsum and Dorje, Dorje Lama, Dawa Sangmo, Dokdok, and all the others who allowed me to share the warmth of their fires while away from my home base in Sama. Thank you, Lama Jigme, the new incumbent of Pema Chöling, for bringing clear leadership and fresh ideas to religious and secular affairs in Sama. And thank you, Purbu Tsewang, for your compassionate decision to return home and provide hope for Sama's children, and also for the selfless care that you now provide for Tashi.

This book is dedicated to Lienne and Pema. You know who your father is; now you know who he was. It is also dedicated to Tashi Döndrup, the *agu* (uncle) whom Lienne and Pema have never met, but who will always be an integral member of our family in spirit if not in presence. A long life of hard knocks dampened neither Tashi's incisive wit nor his congenial demeanor. His example of forbearance in the face of adversity is truly inspirational. Words can never express the gratitude for the innumerable ways in which Tashi Döndrup continues to exert a positive influence over my own life, and the lives of my little girls.

Prologue

The Genre and the Purpose

Interest in Tibet and Tibetan culture has risen exponentially during recent decades. One tangible result has been a proliferation of publications, the majority of which center on Tibetan religion, or more specifically, Tibetan Buddhism. As perhaps the most salient and visible feature of Tibetan culture, Buddhism has captivated the imagination of the general public such that it now figures prominently in many people's preconceptions about Tibetan society. Many now believe, and some openly state, that the key to understanding Tibetan culture is to explore the esoteric teachings of Buddhism. The logical extension of this argument is that the study of religious philosophy represents the most direct means of comprehending how individual Tibetans think and act. As an anthropologist who has lived and worked in various Tibetan societies since the mid-1980s, I find such a perspective far too simplistic, laden with logical fallacies; it lies at the root of an antiquated and naive stereotype that has cast Tibetans as a people incarcerated in an eternal past. Rather, I concur with the thinking of another anthropologist, Charles Ramble:

> If Buddhism is defined in terms of a set of sectarian precepts, then anyone who wishes to understand the doctrine and how it regulates the lives of its followers might as well stay at home and read the scriptures, since the behavior of Buddhists will correspond precisely to these bookish standards. . . . Familiarity with Buddhist literature equips the researcher to understand Buddhism; by itself it cannot enable him to know how the religion is incorporated into the tradition of a particular community.[1]

Few besides the most ardent materialists deny that religion is integral to Tibetan society. Buddhist philosophy exerts a profound influence on the lives of ordinary Tibetans. An awareness of the core principles of a religious philosophy, however, should never be equated with an understanding of how people think, act, and react within a complex matrix of cultural values. Anthropologists see the creation and reformulation of sociocultural systems as an interactive and dialectical process among and between individuals. Everybody in a society knows its basic rules, yet continually confronts situations where a conflict between individual aspirations and social expectations can make bending or reinterpreting those rules advantageous, or even essential. To portray Tibetans as people who act in strict accordance with the ideological underpinnings of their religious philosophy is to construct them in the image of the noble savage who exists in a timeless dimension of social and ecological harmony, lacking the initiative to change because of the restraints imposed by traditional culture. Such a view contradicts everything we know about the creative nature of individuals and much of what we have learned through diligent ethnographic research.

This book is a collection of stories, observations, and analysis culled from several research trips I made between 1995 and 2000 to the Nubri Valley in Nepal. By weaving together vignettes in villagers' everyday lives, I hope to provide insight into what it is like to be a Tibetan struggling for fulfillment in an unpredictable environment. Buddhist philosophy, which dominates most writings about Tibetan societies, pervades many of these stories. Instead of engaging in an ad hoc interpretation of people's thoughts and actions in light of an overarching religious philosophy, however, I allow the actors to speak for themselves, to unveil to the reader their rationales and attitudes in their own way. Like the sublime mountain scenery, religion here thus becomes a prominent constituent of the backdrop to the stories in this book.

Nubri society, like any society, is laden with tensions between cultural ideals and individual aspirations. The creative manner in which people negotiate their way within, or around, the boundaries set by social conventions tells us far more than any exposition of the rules of expected behavior ever could. As the personal narratives in this book convey, the actors described here are not trussed in cultural straight-jackets that inhibit creative development.

The assumption guiding this book—that people's actions, though influenced by cultural norms and expectations, are not predetermined— leads to various questions that, while straightforward, are not always easy to answer. In this particular Tibetan society, how much autonomy do individuals have in making the most important decisions in their lives? How do age, gender, economic standing, and pedigree affect a person's options? In what ways do familial obligations conflict with individual aspirations, and how are such conflicts resolved?

This work highlights the search for meaning in daily existence, whether in the pursuit of eternal truths or in the mundane struggle for survival. Because the choices that individuals make, and the consequences of those decisions, make far more sense when viewed in an ethnographic context, I have included considerable cultural, social, and historical detail, while simplifying the theoretical foundations. In addition, I have tried to present the ethnographic detail in a way that is lively and entertaining, and that does not require either training in anthropology or access to Tibetan society to understand. Finally, the footnotes have the dual function of relating the ethnographic descriptions of Nubri to the academic literature on Tibet and of directing the reader to further sources of information. The accompanying bibliography is by no means exhaustive, and is naturally more inclusive of works in some disciplines (e.g., anthropology) than in others (e.g., religious studies).[2]

STRUCTURAL APPARATUS

Anthropologists study everything from culturally specific symbolic systems to the ways in which group identities are formed and maintained. The main purpose of my own field research was to investigate the relationship between population dynamics and resources.[3] Such an endeavor involves far more than simply enumerating humans and households; after all, demographic events such as births, marriages, and deaths occur and acquire meaning in a specific cultural and social context. Tabulating births and deaths is the task of the demographer; interpreting these events is the work of the anthropologist. Although the collection of empirical data was a vital part of my study, I quickly came to realize that true understanding required situating the quantitative, demographic side of the analysis within an indigenous perception of the life cycle.

The life cycle, in anthropological terms, is a series of social statuses that an individual passes through during a normal life span.[4] As the individual grows and matures, he or she will undergo certain rites of passage, a symbolic transformation from one status to another. Marriage, for example, marks the departure from adolescence and entrance into adulthood. In Tibetan societies, too, the quest for sacred knowledge through pilgrimage often signals a transformation in status from mundane householder to spiritual adept. Even death can be considered a rite of passage, for the Tibetans believe in reincarnation and therefore perform ceremonies to help the deceased person find a suitable rebirth. However, anthropologists do not see the life cycle as something that is programmatic or predictable; in that sense, it is distinguishable from the life course—the diversity of experiences that set people apart from one another. Not every individual undergoes the same series of passages that contribute to a full and meaningful social life. Circumstances at birth can inhibit a person's ability to marry, leading to the socially ambiguous status of bachelor or spinster. Personal ambitions may lead an individual to reject the career of householder in favor of a life as a solitary hermit living at the very margins of society. In this book we will examine the cultural rules that define the normal succession of life cycle events, as well as the flexibility that permits and even accepts, though not always without conflict, life courses that depart from the norm.

From birth to death and back to birth again: that is the inevitable and interminable progression of existence according to the tenet of reincarnation that is so central to Buddhism. This book examines the life cycle in one enclave of Tibetan culture, and is oriented around the life course experiences of humble people whose stories would normally slip into obscurity. The first two chapters provide an introduction to the people and landscape of the Nubri Valley. Thereafter, the book is organized according to stages in the life cycle, commencing with birth and concluding with death and reincarnation. Each chapter is dedicated to one stage in the life cycle, such as adolescence or old age, and the rites of passage associated with that stage. Concerns specific to each juncture of the life cycle, for example a desire to attain religious knowledge through pilgrimage or to generate sufficient merit in old age to assure a fortunate rebirth, are highlighted in relation to individual life trajectories, and contrasted with social obligations and familial expectations. Taken as a whole, the vignettes of everyday life present a picture of a complex society in which cultural ideals and individual aspirations often collide.

The search for meaning in any society is often guided by historical precedence. For Tibetans, actions of the ancestors offer a model of behavior that can be used to assess people's conduct in the present. In this book, temporal depth is provided by contrasting events in the present with tales from the past. The deeds and accomplishments of the ancestors resonate through time, kept alive in the collective memory by written records and oral transmissions. Tibetans have a distinct sense of history and continuity. Nowhere is this more evident than in the stories they tell each other while sitting around the fire on a cold, snowy night.[5]

QUALIFICATIONS

Although it would be tempting to call this book an accurate portrayal of Tibetan village life, a few cautionary remarks are in order. First, it is nonsense to generalize about "Tibetan culture" based on information gathered from a single setting. Although unified to a great extent by a common language (or dialects thereof), a common religion (with all its localized idiosyncratic manifestations), and to a lesser extent by a common ethnic identity (or interpretations thereof), Tibetans are a diverse group whose social practices and cultural beliefs vary from region to region, from valley to valley, and in some cases from village to village. The details of social life contained in these pages describe life in one specific Himalayan locale, and should not be interpreted as a universal statement on Tibetan society.

Another caveat involves the authenticity of representation. Bear in mind that observers of human behavior, myself in this case, are prisoners to some extent of their own life experiences. Observer bias is the tendency for a researcher to see more of what he wants to see the longer he stays in the field. Quite simply, a higher degree of involvement in the daily life of a community can lead to greater subjectivity. Because I was interested in specific research problems, I tended to focus on certain aspects of Nubri society at the expense of others. A Tibetan or even another ethnographer describing life in a highland village would certainly emphasize aspects that I have glossed over, and perhaps not even mention many features of social life that I find so significant. Some of my personal predilections will no doubt become obvious to the reader. Then again, this book is in many respects as much about gaining insight into the workings of another culture as it is about a particular Himalayan society. The ethnographic endeavor is truly an adventure, both as an intellectual exercise and in the traditional sense of an exciting or dangerous experience. My perceptions were molded by social interactions that were heavily conditioned by my status as a male anthropologist working in an alien environment far from home, where, initially at least, I was an outsider and an unknown entity. Excluding my own voice from the narratives would be misleading, perhaps even dishonest.

Similarly, my status affected the ways in which people interacted with me, both positively and negatively. The ability to read Tibetan placed me in the advantageous position of being considered an intellectual peer of the high-ranking lamas of the community. Literacy in traditional Tibetan societies is generally reserved for the clergy and nobility, not for the commoners and especially not for women, except for nuns and a few privileged members of the aristocracy. My interest in historical texts, administrative documents, natal horoscopes, and other types of literature eased the process of establishing rapport with many of the prominent male figures in Nubri society. At the same time, being male meant that some female domains of knowledge were beyond my grasp. Although I was able to obtain data on reproductive histories, I was often prevented by notions of propriety from asking questions centering on the culture of childbearing. For such topics I generally had to rely on information from men, whose perspectives differ radically from those of their wives, daughters, or sisters.

The task of writing a book that appeals to a broad audience entails a bit of creative license. Although I did take some liberties in the process of editing both written and oral accounts, I can and will vouch for the authenticity of the narratives. I have strived to maintain the integrity of the narrators' voices and to faithfully convey the thoughts and emotions expressed to me by the speakers themselves.

Finally, a note on Tibetan names. Most Tibetans do not have surnames but rather two given names, conferred by a lama shortly after birth. For example, two important individuals in this book are Tashi Döndrup and Pema Döndrup. These men, although their second names are identical, do not belong to the same family. They could, but the names alone give no evidence of relation: Döndrup is a given name, not a surname. Because of this naming custom I feel it is misleading to treat a second given name as if it were a surname. Therefore, in the notes and in the list of references I cite works by Tibetan authors using both of their names (e.g., Pema Döndrup 1979—see Pema Döndrup, not Döndrup, Pema). The same convention applies to high-ranking clerics who have honorific titles by which they are known to their disciples and which they use in their written works. I cite these works according to the authors' formal titles (e.g., Dudjom Rinpoche 1991—see Dudjom Rinpoche, not Rinpoche, Dudjom). Finally, I cite the works of those Tibetans who do have recognized surnames (generally members of the hereditary nobility) according to Western conventions (e.g., Taklha 2001—see Takhla, Namgyal Lhamo).

CHAPTER 1

Raising the Curtain

Attire yourself to be acceptable in another man's world,
Nourish yourself to be acceptable in your own.

Tibetan Proverb[1]

THE JOURNEY

As usual, the porters lagged behind. Weighted down by large packs bulging with reference books, reams of paper, and other "necessities" for my field research, they made slow and ponderous progress on the mountain trail. The footpath was often precarious, narrow and steep, with sections washed away in landslides caused by the frequent monsoon deluges. It was day nine on the trek from Kathmandu, the day that would bring me to my new home in the ethnically Tibetan village of Sama, a remote Himalayan settlement in northern Nepal's Nubri Valley—a place I had never visited and where I knew not a soul.

In contrast to the physical exertion expended by the two hardy porters, my own burden was more psychological, induced by nagging doubts of an uncertain future. I was an anthropologist entering the field for the first time, embarking on a rite of passage from graduate student to practitioner of the discipline. Until now, the sluggish pace of the trek had afforded a welcome postponement of the inevitable hardships to come, a reprieve from the unavoidable questions that lay ahead. How would I be accepted by the people of Nubri? Would I be embraced or shunned? Would I be able to handle the physical and emotional trials and tribulations that surely awaited me? More to the point, what was I getting myself into?

Eventually I crested a ridge. Stretching before me was a wide plain situated more than two miles above sea level and surrounded by lofty snow-clad peaks. At 26,760 feet, Mt. Manaslu, known to the valley's inhabitants by the Tibetan name Pungyen (Ornamented Heap), commanded the entire scene. A translucent plume of smoke arose from a distant hollow, marking the village of Sama. The moment of truth had arrived.

On reaching the fields bordering the village, I came across a coarse stone wall that served to separate the herds of ravenous bovines from the villagers' life-sustaining crops. I decided to wait for my guide, Karma, who was also my companion and confidant. He knew everybody here; I was a complete stranger. I slung my pack to the ground, happy to be relieved of the encumbrance for the moment, but also knowing that this would be the final respite before having to explain my presence to these isolated mountain people.

While I stood reflecting on my impending entrance to the village, an old man trudged into view. He carried a bamboo basket and a hand-axe, crude implements needed to cut and gather fuel for his hearth. His shoulders were stooped, and his face was creased and wrinkled by years of exposure to the high-altitude sun and perhaps by sufferings that I could only imagine. Ragged, home-spun woolen clothing indicated that he was poor, poorer than anybody I had ever known. Yet there was still a spring to his step and a jauntiness in the way his head swayed back and forth as he hummed a sacred mantra.

The old man spotted me and approached, obviously perplexed by my presence. Although tourists had been coming through the village since 1992, and mountain climbers before then, it was now late August, the monsoon season, when Sama was undisturbed by foreign intrusions. Besides, Westerners were always preceded by an army of Sherpas and porters as if to proclaim their self-importance. I was alone.

"Elder brother, are you well?" I called out in greeting. Immediately the man's face lit up as he heard Tibetan words formed by a foreigner's tongue. A broad smile revealed gaping holes where his teeth used to be. "I am well. Are you going to cross the pass?" he inquired, under the assumption that I was a transient trekker seeking high-altitude adventure. "No," I informed him, "I plan to stay here for a few months." He looked startled. This was a curious prospect to ponder, without precedence indeed, since no foreigner had ever spent more than a few days in the village.[2] Slowly his smile returned as he grasped the situation. "In that case you can stay with me. I have my own house and live alone." I thanked him for the offer, yet assumed this invitation to be no more than a social courtesy. Meanwhile, the withered old man with the stooped gait turned and strolled away to ascend a trail that wound through thorny shrubs to the forested hills above.

Karma arrived with the porters and immediately took me on a whirl-wind tour of the village, introducing me to all the movers and shakers of the community. During the barrage of rapid conversation in a dialect that was still unfamiliar, I managed to discern that Karma was arrang-ing for me to stay with the family of a high-ranking married lama. The next morning at the crack of dawn Karma abruptly left to return to his family in Kathmandu. Despite being surrounded by people, I had never felt more alone in my life.

At first the arrangement of living with the lama seemed perfectly suit-able, one rationale being that my relationship as his guest would bestow social status by association, a certain legitimacy to my presence in the village that is essential for successful research. However, practical reali-ties rapidly intruded in a most sobering manner. Houses in Nubri are single-room structures wherein privacy is nonexistent. This particular lama seemed more adept at perpetuating his descent lineage than at teaching his progeny fundamental social graces. He had numerous chil-dren and a wife stressed by the logistics of keeping the kids in line while providing for a continuous flow of visitors who came seeking audiences with her husband. My days were transformed into a continual struggle to keep research notes from being tattered and scattered by the grubby hands of toddlers. Constant vigilance was needed to thwart children from dispersing my underwear through the house and village, and to prevent my manual typewriter from becoming a keyboard for juvenile amusement. Indeed, the academic rite of passage called fieldwork was quickly transformed into an aggravating series of skirmishes with the children of my host.

The offer of the old man whom I met when first entering Sama kept creeping back to mind. I began to make excuses to visit him, and found his company to be most pleasant. His humble abode and warm hearth offered welcome breathing space from the din of battle in the lama's quarters. Sacrificing proximity to the learned lama was a small price to pay for assuring peace of mind, body, and possessions. I moved in with Tashi Döndrup.

LIFE WITH TASHI

Tashi is the illegitimate son of an impoverished mother and of a father who denied all paternal responsibility. He grew up poor and worked his entire life just to keep a roof over his head and food in his stomach. Lacking land and cattle, the critical assets of this rural economy that are

generally bestowed through paternal inheritance, he could never marry
and raise his own family. Despite such an unfavorable past, Tashi managed to cultivate a sharp intellect and immense capacity for generosity.
In addition, he is elderly and respected by his fellow villagers, not
because of wealth or any position of prestige that he happened to be
born into, but because of his friendly demeanor, solid work ethic, and
raucous sense of humor. People enjoy his company.

Tashi became my most important social link in Sama. He was more
than a mere friend or companion, for he guided me through the myriad
social gaffes and blunders that I was destined to perpetrate in this traditional society. Most important, he became my fictive yet ever so real
brother. Rather than referring to each other by our given names, he
called me "little brother" *(nuwo)* and I called him "elder brother" *(ajo)*.

Once the villagers accepted my presence and heard that Tashi and I
called each other by familiar kinship terms, we naturally became the
butt of local jibes. Our male neighbors wondered aloud, "How could
two able men, guys who call themselves brothers, live as celibate bach-
elors in their own home?" Friends chided us to take a common wife, an
accepted practice for brothers in Sama and in scores of other Tibetan
communities where fraternal polyandry is customary. As part of the
sexual innuendo so common when men congregate, elderly spinsters
were suggested as potential spouses who could bring a semblance of
marital bliss to our bachelor quarters. We were content, however, to be
alone.

Becoming the target of jokes was gratifying, since it implied a degree
of familiarity with fellow villagers—people far too polite and reserved
to ridicule a stranger to his face. Yet the villagers' acceptance came by
no means automatically. It had to be earned. At first people had no clue
what I was doing in their midst, which of course led to rampant specu-
lation about precisely who I was and for whom I was working. The fact
that anthropologists tend to poke their noses into all aspects of life and
ask scores of inane questions, all the while frantically scribbling cryptic
notes in an indecipherable script, only fueled the villagers' suspicions.
They began to talk about me.

Within a few weeks of my arrival a funeral procession took place in
Sama. In my ignorant naiveté, I envisioned tagging along and interviewing the lamas performing the last rites in order to better grasp local
conceptions about life and death. Tashi was mortified at this suggestion
and reprimanded me with a reminder of how gossip can act as a social
regulator within the community. "Don't you dare follow that funeral

procession to the cremation grounds!" he admonished. In response I reasoned, "But Tashi, how else can I learn about the customs here?" "Ask the lamas anything you want, but don't follow them to the burning place. If you do, people will wonder why you are obsessed with death. They will *talk* about you," he warned.

Tibetans believe that gossip can have negative repercussions. At the individual level, becoming the subject of gossip can trigger physical, mental, or economic misfortunes, while at the societal level the unabated spread of gossip can upset social cohesion. Tibetans even have ritual texts at their disposal that are designed to thwart the negative effects of gossip.[3] In my case, social survival in Sama meant that my instincts as an academic voyeur needed to be tempered by a bit more sensitivity. Tashi was there to steer me clear of conflicts and to assure that I refrained from activities that would make me the target of malicious talk. (For the record, he did not always succeed.)

Suspicion that I worked for the Nepali government was a major impediment during the early weeks of fieldwork. Nubri is inhabited by Buddhist highlanders living at the geographical, social, and economic fringe of a Hindu state. Their opinions of outsiders were overwhelmingly prejudiced by negative experiences with government officials, usually high-caste Brahmins and Chetris. Wariness that I was somehow linked to the government did not help matters at all. It took the fortuitous, albeit inadvertent, assistance of an itinerant government official to dispel such a notion.

This government peon, a man whose level of arrogance was inversely proportionate to his menial position, came strutting into the village one day. At the time I was observing a ritual at the *gomba* (village temple), where most of the male members of Sama had congregated for the day. The official spied me in the crowd (indeed, I did stick out) and jumped to the conclusion that I was an illegal alien who must be dealt with using the full force of his petty rank. Nubri is a restricted area and I was the first outsider to receive permission to live there for an extended period. Naturally I asserted the legitimacy of my credentials and offered to show him the permits that had been issued in the capital and approved by the local police. Yet the numbskull refused to be swayed by facts, or perhaps he was holding out for a bribe. A harsh exchange of words nearly turned to blows as we argued heatedly in a crude admixture of Nepali and English, neither of which local villagers understood well.

As if on cue, the ritual within the temple ended and a throng of lamas and monks spilled outside and formed a circle about us two combatants.

One man blurted out, "Hey, Gyemi [Foreigner], what's the fighting all about?"[4] I turned to the gathering and explained the nature of our disagreement, at which point an elderly monk stepped forward and enveloped me in his red robes. "Don't worry," he said, "we'll pretend you are a monk and hide you in the temple!" His suggestion was greeted with a burst of laughter from the crowd. Men began to jeer, and finally the official skulked away in defeat. The fight was proof positive that I was not in cahoots with the government. To this day I thank my good fortune for sending an obstinate official to the village just when a social breakthrough was sorely needed.

Later that day my adversary crept sheepishly into my makeshift office at the gomba to extend an olive branch. He turned out to be a nice man, perhaps one who could have become a friend under different circumstances. In his defense, he had been warned by higher officials to be on the lookout for illegal aliens in the valley. Foreign travelers are always seeking ways to enter the most remote and hence most romanticized areas of Nepal. He had just been doing his duty, albeit with minimal tact and far too much zeal.

We chatted for a bit, avoiding any mention of the previous confrontation. He then asked me about my motivations for wanting to live among and study the lifestyle of *bhotay,* a derogatory Nepali term for Buddhist highlanders of Tibetan extraction.[5] To high-caste Hindus, Tibetans occupy the lowest rungs of the social order, and the government official was truly perplexed. "Why," he asked, "do you want to study these bhotay? Look at the food they eat. They are so dirty, and they smell bad," he said, pinching his nose to emphasize the point.

He had a valid point from the perspective of a lowlander, and in fact from the perspective of anybody who values the occasional scrub. The Tibetans of Sama do exude a very distinct odor, for their bodies are saturated with the combined smells of smoke from the hearth; yak butter, which oils their hair; sweat from their daily toils; and the bovines with which they are in constant contact. People very rarely bathe, in part because of the cold weather and in part because there is no cultural prohibition against having a veneer of grime coating the skin. The perplexed official could not understand why a foreigner would ever volunteer to live with these Tibetans, learn their language, eat their coarse food, and allow his personal hygiene to plummet so drastically. To him these people were the antithesis of civilization, whereas I was supposed to represent all that was modern, progressive, and socially desirable, according to the development discourse that had enveloped Nepali society. He no doubt considered me, with my soiled jeans, tobacco-stained teeth, and tangled locks of hair, as somehow disparate from the squeaky-clean foreigners who came through Nepal in droves, sporting spandex trekking pants and Gore-Tex parkas.

My degeneration from cleanliness did not happen overnight, but was an inevitable result of prolonged existence in a place where showers do not exist and clothing is scrubbed by hand on rocks beside a frigid stream. Tashi and I washed our hair each Saturday morning without fail, yet the rest of the body gradually acquired a layer of filth that would be removed only on my return to the temperate lowlands. Washing clothing was an especially disagreeable task, so I became content to wear an outfit that had a liberal coating of dirt and soot with a discernable tinge of yak droppings.

Eventually the vermin moved in. During my early weeks in Sama I routinely walked through the village each morning, calling out greetings or jokes to my neighbors. To those whom I saw picking lice from each other's hair I would customarily shout, "Save a few for me!" This joke boomeranged when people noticed me battling the first colonies of critters that had germinated within the seams of my underclothing. The women clucked their tongues and shook their heads in sympathy, whereas the men with characteristic lack of subtlety grasped their bellies and stumbled about in fits of mirth.

Providing levity in the village was far preferable to being the object of suspicion. I quickly learned to pick lice from my body and perform the emphatically non-Buddhist act of crushing them on a stone. Through tenacious effort and enhanced dexterity I eventually mastered the art of capturing the ever-elusive fleas from the lining of my sleeping bag. Even the occasional rat running across my legs at night ceased to be a matter for concern. A capacity to adapt to adversity is a prerequisite for an anthropologist. The less I obsessed with a diminishing standard of hygiene, the more I could focus on the work at hand.

While undergoing the travails of adapting to village life, I found myself bonding to Tashi Döndrup like a brother, and he to me. He took great pleasure in watching my progress, and boasted to fellow villagers that here was a foreigner who was willing to put up with vermin and eat the local food without much complaint. Knowing that I would be there for a while, we devised a system for dividing labor within our humble household. He insisted on doing all the cooking, so I took it upon myself to be the dish washer, food purchaser, and water fetcher. The latter caused poor Tashi some embarrassment, since it is typical in Nepal for locals to do the manual labor for foreign visitors. Each time I passed through the village bearing a large plastic jug filled with water from the cold stream nearby, villagers would derisively call out, "Hey, Gyemi, are you now Tashi's servant?"

Matters relating to physical chores reached a crisis point one day when I announced my intention to accompany Tashi on a wood-gathering mission. He doggedly resisted my attempt to tag along, but finally was swayed by the reasoning that I needed to see where villagers got their fuel supply. As we made our way toward the forest, groups of people harvesting barley in the fields laughed when they saw me with a bamboo basket slung, with self-conscious bravado, over my shoulder. Correctly surmising that I was unaccustomed to bearing heavy burdens without the aid of a modern backpack, some men shouted out, "Better come back with a full load!"

We climbed high, eventually reaching a stack of wood sheltered beneath an overhanging rock. After a brief rest we loaded as many logs as possible from Tashi's precut stash into our baskets. I then sat down, balanced the basket against my back, and fixed the long leather strap against my forehead. With knees wobbling and Tashi pushing from behind, I struggled to attain an upright position. So far so good, but merely standing with a basket supported on one's back is far easier than traversing a steep and grassy slope. With mislaid confidence I took a tentative step forward, which shifted the weight in the basket. The abrupt and radical challenge to equilibrium sent me tumbling down the steep slope amid a cascade of airborne logs. Tashi was mortified. He rushed to my side saying, "Forget it, forget it, and don't try this again!" I, on the other hand, was in need of some redemption—a resurrection of vanquished pride—and thus, through trial and error, eventually got the knack of carrying the basket. The crowning moment came when I swaggered through the village bearing a man-sized consignment of firewood. After that experience, however, rather than telling me he was off to gather wood, Tashi always devised a less than convincing ruse that he was visiting the neighbors (with axe in hand and basket over shoulder?) and slipped away without me. He did everything in his power to ensure that no misfortunes came my way.

And so the days in Sama began to slip by without much drama. Although the life of the anthropologist has been romanticized as a continuous series of adventures, the reality is more along the lines of coping with tedium while fending off ever-encroaching bouts with insanity. In the midst of the physical and psychological stress one must persist in systematically recording an unending stream of trivial observations and tidbits of data about everything from household economics to protector deities.

Devising a daily routine was essential. Most days began with a leisurely breakfast of roasted barley flour and butter tea followed by a stroll to my "office," an uninhabited house on gomba property. The gomba is situated on elevated ground about fifteen minutes' walking distance from the village. It is a quiet place inhabited by nuns, a few monks, and several elderly householders who have retired to this place of relative solitude. My office was unoccupied, for the nun who usually lived there had recently passed away. Gomba homes are built in rows, so I shared common courtyard walls with others. To the west lived Ani Kunsang, an ancient nun who walked with a stoop. Her face was shrunken from years of exposure to the withering sun, and her voice was enfeebled by age. Each day she puttered about gathering small sticks and other scraps of wood that could be used to heat her humble abode and cook her meager fare. When the sun shone she sat in her courtyard spinning a prayer wheel and chanting mantras in a nearly inaudible voice. I liked Ani Kunsang, in part because she appreciated my desire for solitude during the working mornings. Although we rarely conversed, we shared a special bond of understanding.

Usually the only sounds on gomba property are the soft murmurings of prayer flags fluttering in the wind and the squawking of ever-present ravens. Each day the ravens, unperturbed by the clatter of my type-writer, seemed to mock me with their incessant clamor. Like the smell of butter lamps in the temple and the sight of Pungyen towering high above, the sound of ravens is indelibly stamped in my mind as a reminder of life in the Tibetan village of Sama.

WHO'S WHO

The characters in this book all live or lived in a high valley that runs parallel to the Tibetan border in Nepal's Gorkha District. The upper part of the valley is called Nubri and is settled by people of Tibetan stock, while the lower section of the valley is named Kutang and is inhabited by a hybrid population of Tibetans and Ghales (a people who are linguistically and culturally related to Tibetans, yet quite distinct). Despite their many differences, Nubri and Kutang are inextricably linked through intensive economic, religious, and social interactions.

The main characters you will soon encounter include Pema Döndrup (1668–1744) and Pema Wangdu (1697–?), two men whose exploits are recorded in biographies written in their native villages of Kutang. Unlike most Tibetan biographies, which deal primarily with religious training, spiritual advancement, sermons to disciples, and esoteric insights, the biographies of Pema Döndrup and Pema Wangdu contain a wealth of information about daily existence and the social context in which their struggles for spiritual insight transpired.[6] Even though they lived long ago in a world that was profoundly different from today's world, their stories illustrate some of the tensions inherent in the choice of forsaking domestic sociability for a solitary existence in the pursuit of enlightenment. And even though both lamas passed away centuries ago, reminders of their presence are everywhere. Scattered across the physical landscape are sacred sites where Pema Döndrup and Pema Wangdu encountered deities, caves where they meditated, and stones inscribed with their images.

The other characters in this book live in the present. You have already met my intrepid companion Tashi Döndrup, who by the way was born in 1929, the Year of the Snake. In addition you will read stories narrated by Tashi's contemporaries and fellow villagers from Sama, prominent men such as the married lamas Tashi Dorje, Rigzen Dorje, and Tsewang Gyatso and the celibate cleric Lopön Zangpo. Not only were these remarkable men invaluable sources of knowledge, they also were close companions to whom I owe a debt of gratitude for putting up with my ceaseless inquiries. Allow me to introduce them.

The venerable Tashi Dorje is one of the most highly respected men in all of Nubri. Born in 1919 as the younger of Sama's head lama's two sons, he was destined by the rule of primogeniture to be second in command to his brother in the spiritual hierarchy of the village. When his elder brother, the head lama, died at a young age, Tashi Dorje presided over religious affairs as regent for two decades until his brother's son and rightful successor came of age. Tashi Dorje now lives in Kathmandu at a monastery headed by his grandson, a reincarnate lama. Most of his days are spent in his living quarters, an immaculate room containing a sofa that doubles as his bed, several shelves packed with books, and a small alcove housing statues of the Buddha to whom he makes daily offerings. His face, weathered with age, is always graced with a kindly, grandfatherly smile. Despite having attained the ripe old age of eighty, Tashi Dorje possesses a mind that is still remarkably nimble, his voice is clear as the mountain air, and his memory of past events unfailing.

Rigzen Dorje, born in 1918, is Tashi Dorje's cousin. The two journeyed together on many occasions to seek teachings from some of

Tibet's most prominent lamas. In his prime, Rigzen Dorje was a bold and contentious man, ready to seize initiatives and unwilling to let others stand in his way. These days he is mellowed by age and failing health, and as a result his political prestige has waned to the point of being inconsequential. In matters of religion, however, Rigzen Dorje is much sought after. He is one of the few lamas in the village who understands the art of divination, so when people fall ill he is called upon to determine which malignant force in the spirit world has caused the malady. Now nearly completely deaf and chronically ill, the elderly lama is far less active, to the detriment of his fellow villagers. Nevertheless, Rigzen Dorje still possesses the agility of someone half his age and retains a sense of humor that transcends cultural boundaries. One time the two of us walked up to Nubri together from the steamy lowlands. As we strolled through the inundated rice paddies of a village the local inhabitants were astonished to see a foreigner conversing with this dignified Tibetan lama in the latter's vernacular. They inquired, "Old man, who is this white person with whom you speak?" A sly grin, partly veiled by his wispy mustache, broke across his gaunt face. "This is my son-in-law. He is married to my daughter," replied Rigzen Dorje while jabbing me in the ribs with his bony elbow. The slack jaws and incredulous looks of the locals exposed their gullibility. We still joke about this incident today.

Tsewang Gyatso, born in 1938, is known simply as Lama Gyatso. Reputed to be particularly skillful at performing rituals and scrupulously fair in political and economic matters, he wields much authority in the village. Since his home adjoins the house that Tashi Döndrup and I shared, we were considered to be *kyimse,* a term reserved for those special neighbors one calls on for help in times of crisis or when additional workers are needed for labor-intensive tasks. Lama Gyatso proved to be an invaluable ally, sticking up for me whenever I inadvertently made a social blunder or political gaffe. One striking feature of his personality is his aptitude for role changing, shifting with agility from jovial friend to solemn lama whose voice of authority commands respect.

The man known as Lopön Zangpo is a reclusive monk whose expertise in religion is unparalleled. Born in 1929, the same year as Tashi Döndrup, he was sent by his parents to Dagkar Taso Monastery in Tibet; there he became the most capable disciple of the monastery's abbot.[7] When the monastery was destroyed by marauding Red Guards in the early 1960s, Lopön Zangpo returned to Nubri where he established a series of training centers for monks. Although he rarely ventures outside the valley, Lopön Zangpo is renowned throughout the Tibetan world for his sharp intellect and devotion to the Buddhist teachings. These days, at age seventy, he spends most of his time reading, meditating, and performing rituals of the Dagkar Taso tradition in his private chapel in the company of his son and spiritual successor.

These are the main characters you will read about in the pages ahead. Before turning to their stories, however, I must say a few words about the landscape, history, and society of the Nubri Valley.

CHAPTER 2

The Lay of the Land

Fortunate friends of Nubri,
Keep not flowers upon the ground, but proffer them to the gods.

Tibetan Proverb

From the deep gorges and impenetrable forests to the high pastures and glorious peaks, the environment of the Nubri Valley does not lack for scenic splendor. But what makes Nubri so intriguing is the layers of meaning inscribed on the physical surroundings by human inhabitants. This is not a pristine and untouched landscape, for it bears all the marks of long-term human intervention: terraced fields shaped and molded to mimic the natural flow of the slopes, southern-facing hillsides intentionally denuded of trees to create winter pasturage, and eroded gullies where cattle have grazed too intensively. More significantly, from a cultural standpoint at least, the landscape is immersed in sacredness by being connected with the deeds of mythical creatures and historical predecessors. A rock bearing the indubitable image of male genitals is said to have been the work of the eighth-century saint Padmasambhava. A temple perched high above a village on a rock outcrop bears witness to the meditation site of a famous lama. A row of stones inscribed with religious messages lines the path to a ridge where Pema Döndrup met a white bear three centuries ago. And all the major peaks are considered to be abodes of protective deities and their retinues. The people of Nubri enliven their landscape in ways that transcend mere physical beauty and lend a timeless quality to the entire valley. By ascribing meaning to the natural environment, they cause the past and present to converge and become inseparable.

The Nubri Valley comprises the upper stretch of the Buri Gandaki (River) in Gorkha District, Nepal. Geographically and culturally the valley is divided between the lower section, called Kutang, and the upper section, called Nubri. The entire valley has long occupied a

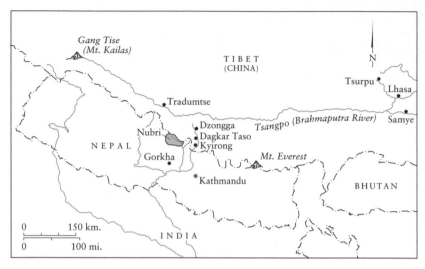

Nubri in Relation to Nepal and Tibet

special place in the sacred geography of the Tibetan Plateau and Himalayas, and was described by a famous Tibetan lama six centuries ago in the following terms:

> It is a good place, one which is near to Tibet and easy to reach. At a future time, the Buddhist teachings will spread here. At that time devout yogis, a religion protecting king, and virtuous people must lay claim to this valley. Happiness will result when people go there. The valley consists of innumerable cliffs, forests, and small ravines uninhabited by humans. It is called Fortunate Realm of Snow, for it is surrounded by mountains. The ridge to the east is small and beautiful. The mountain to the south is smooth and lustrous. The mountain to the west is lofty and pure. The valley is not plagued by the heat and poisoned water characteristic of the lowlands. Fruit and vegetables are abundant, as is firewood. Tibetan barley grows in the upper part of the valley; rice grows in the lower areas. In the center, there are provisions for making a town, iron for constructing irrigation channels, and various grains. There are rocks containing the five precious jewels. Wild animals are unaccustomed to people.
>
> Upon reaching this land, build a palace for a king and a temple for the Buddhist teachings in the upper part of the valley, and establish a settlement for the general populace in the lower part of the valley. Institute the ten laws of virtue [no murder, theft, sexual misconduct, falsehood, slander, irresponsible chatter, verbal abuse, covetousness, vindictiveness, holding wrong views]. Avoid singeing meat in the hearth, for it will offend the deities who dwell upon the mountains. If blizzards and fierce rains occur, perform white yak and white sheep rituals for the lords of the

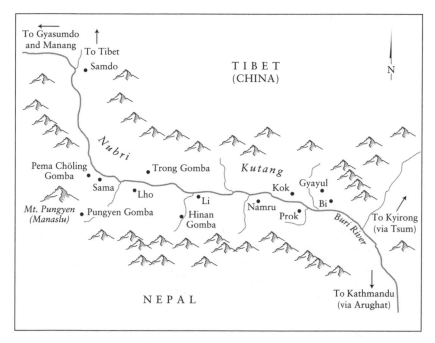

To Gyasumdo and Manang
To Tibet
• Samdo
TIBET (CHINA)
N
Nubri
Pema Chöling Gomba •
• Trong Gomba
Kutang
Kok • • Gyayul
• Sama
• Lho
• Li
Namru •
• Bi
Mt. Pungyen (Manaslu) • Pungyen Gomba
• Hinan Gomba
Prok •
Buri River
To Kyirong (via Tsum)
NEPAL
To Kathmandu (via Arughat)

The Nubri Valley

mountains. If human diseases, cattle diseases, floods, or crop failures occur, the consort of the white serpent deity must be appeased through rituals.[1]

KUTANG

Situated between the warm, humid lowlands and the frigid highlands, Kutang is a place where crops grow abundantly on the steeply terraced terrain. Deciduous forests give way to pine on the higher slopes, before the mountainous topography becomes too precipitous to support any trees whatsoever. The land is renowned for its towering cliffs, imposing crags, and plunging ravines, making access to the small hamlets perched on the hillsides a truly rigorous task.

Kutang was probably settled more than nine centuries ago, though no firm evidence exists to bolster this claim. The current inhabitants are an admixture of Ghales, an ethnic group of hill dwellers who mainly inhabit Central Nepal,[2] and Tibetans who migrated from Kyirong and other areas to the north. Through time and intensive contact with their neighbors, the people of Kutang became somewhat Tibetanized. That is, they wear Tibetan clothing, their literary language is Tibetan, and they practice Tibetan Buddhism. Nevertheless, they are quite distinct from Tibetans in many ways, most notably in their unique dialect. The term Kukay literally means "Language of Kutang," but it has a double meaning in that the first syllable—*ku,* for Kutang—is a homonym of the first syllable in the Tibetan word for thief, *kuma.* Therefore, Kukay is also interpreted to mean "stolen language," since it incorporates words and phrases from several neighboring languages, including Tibetan. Nobody but those who live in Kutang understands Kukay, so it acts as an important mark of ethnic identity to the fifteen hundred speakers of this distinctive vernacular.

In the past, travel to the market center of Arughat, several days' walk below Kutang, was especially hazardous owing to the lack of bridges and the crude footpaths, which often required one to progress on wooden posts stuck into cliffs overhanging raging torrents. People recall traveling under those conditions, a mere two decades ago, in terms of high adventure and continual peril. Despite the risks involved in getting about, however, the people of Kutang have never remained in isolation. To the contrary, they have always been intrepid travelers who supplement their agrarian economy through trade with neighbors.

The sheer hillsides of Kutang are farmed intensively, yielding an impressive array of vegetables in addition to the staples of barley, wheat, corn, and potatoes. The fact that two New World crops (corn and potatoes) are keys to the subsistence economy attests to Kutang's connections with the outside world. To augment farming, small herds of cattle and a few chickens are kept for domestic consumption. The residents of Kutang are notably industrious, ranging throughout all vertical zones of the valley in pursuit of a highly diversified, and hence more secure, economic base. Families are rarely together as a single unit, since members are routinely sent to satellite settlements to exploit seasonal resources. Nearly every piece of land that is not too precipitous to plow is put into cultivation. Steep and grassy slopes are communal property used for herding domesticated animals.

Villages are small, consisting of no more than thirty to forty houses clustered in distinct neighborhoods. Houses are two-story structures; the upper is the living quarters for the family, and the lower is a stall for bovines.[3] To reach the upper floor one must climb a makeshift ladder— a tree trunk with hollowed-out steps. Walls are constructed by piling flat stones on each other. No mortar is used to solidify the structure, nor is plaster used to keep the wind from seeping through the chinks. Living quarters consist of a single room where everybody eats, socializes, and sleeps. Privacy is never much of a concern. All activity centers on the hearth situated along the midpoint of one of the walls. Since homes do not have chimneys, the dimly lit interiors are congested with smoke that permeates everything, depositing a layer of soot on walls and the bodies of inhabitants alike. Lining the inner walls of the house are storage chests where grains and household implements are kept. The natural consequence of storing food within the home is pest infestation. Rats have the run of the place, especially at night when their carousing can prevent even the soundest sleeper from enjoying more than a fitful rest. Needless to say, neither indoor plumbing nor electricity is a feature of these rustic homes.

Kutang, like many transitional areas between Buddhist and Hindu culture, is famous for a rather unsavory reason. Every time we ventured to Kutang, Tashi would repeat a stern warning: "Watch me at all times. Do not drink if I do not drink, and certainly do not eat unless I do so." You see, Kutang has gained notoriety as a place where "poison thy neighbor" is something of a local sport. During one visit, our hostess tearfully related the demise of her four-year-old daughter. The girl fell ill one day and continued to lose weight, turning a morbid grayish-black hue over the course of the next month. She eventually succumbed to a malady that her mother insisted was inflicted by poison. Although she believed the culprit was her neighbor, convincing proof of the deed was impossible to garner—and irrefutable evidence is required if a poisoner is to be forced into exile.

The art of making and intentionally afflicting somebody with a locally concocted toxin, a craft passed on from mother to daughter or from mother-in-law to daughter-in-law (like witchcraft in medieval times, the administering of poison is considered to be the exclusive domain of women), is shrouded in mystery. As a consequence of this tradition, however, highland-dwelling Tibetans have always approached journeys to these lower gorges with trepidation. I spoke with elderly Tibetans who passed through Kutang more than forty years ago, and still their most vivid memory of the area was the threat of being poisoned.

One such encounter has been recorded for posterity, that of the famous female pilgrim Ani Lochen (1865–1951), who came to the area nearly a century ago:

> I went to the village of Kok [in Kutang, near Bi] where there was a very
> small nunnery to ask for alms. A young nun there gave me a round lump of
> butter and milk. I drank the milk first, but the next day I became very ill

because poison was mixed with the milk. There was no other solution, so I prayed to the Lama and repeatedly performed a breathing exercise. The color of the vomit was like milk. I vomited a lot, and it resembled actual poisonous snakes moving about. Then my religious companions reported this to Chime Dorje, the chieftain of Namru [a nearby village]. The chieftain summoned this nun and was able to prove her guilt. He said, "If Ani Lochen dies, then it is your fault!" At that time I thought that that nun was also affected by the poison. Then I recited prayers, as an unbearable compassion towards all female poison-givers and sentient beings was generated within me.[4]

In an area of exceptionally high mortality, I always suspected that many natural deaths were used as a pretext to accuse a rival of performing this unspeakable deed. Tashi would be mortified to hear my skepticism. He was nervous about staying in Kutang, but understood that our work demanded at least brief visits.

NUBRI

The crags and cliffs of Kutang gradually open into a wider valley as one ascends to Nubri. Nubri is separated from Kutang by a dense forest of immense trees thriving within a deep and sunless gorge where the water has carved a narrow passage through solid rock. After emerging from the gorge one enters a different environment where varied species of pine, birch, and rhododendron dominate the lush forests. Sandwiched between steep drops to the river and the sharply rising slopes leading to snow-capped peaks, small hamlets encircled by fields are perched on relatively flat tables. The surrounding landscape is dominated by high summits, most of which tower to 20,000 feet and above. Side valleys that penetrate deep into the realm of snow peaks and glaciers are used for grazing during the summer months.

At Sama, the largest village in Nubri and my home base for research, the valley widens into a flat plain and takes a ninety-degree turn to the north. The weather pattern is different here. Clouds that rush up through the narrow lower valley suddenly begin to swirl in a lazy clockwise motion, resulting in a constant afternoon cloud cover and substantial precipitation. Winters are harsh in Sama. Following the frequent snowstorms, the valley echoes with the sound of avalanches thundering down from the sheer slopes above. Long ago, village leaders recognized the threat posed by such natural calamities and imposed a ban on cutting trees from the slopes immediately above the village. In this way they assured the maintenance of the forest as a natural avalanche barrier that protects the village from snow slides.

As in Kutang, the economy in Nubri is based on the triad of farming, herding, and trade. However, agricultural production is somewhat constrained by the altitude and cold weather, so trade is a far more critical component of each household's economy. In Sama the crops are limited to barley, which is parched and then ground into a flour called *tsampa*, the staple food for most Tibetans, and potatoes that are boiled and eaten with chili peppers or made into a stew. Herders follow a transhumant annual cycle. Yaks and various bovine hybrids are taken to the high pastures during the summer, then moved to a winter pasture near the village during the cold and snowy season. Since the village is situated at an altitude of 11,000 feet, snow in the winter is a constant threat to livestock. Not only can an avalanche wipe out an entire herd in a matter of seconds, but significant deposits of snow can prevent cattle from getting to the grass on the ground beneath. As a consequence, winter pastures are always on nonforested southern-facing slopes so that the sun's radiance can quickly remove the snow cover. Herders maintain small huts at the winter pasture that are well stocked with fodder, allowing the cattle to be stall fed in an emergency.[5]

To the untrained eye, life in the villages of Nubri appears to have a timeless quality, as if historical processes somehow bypassed the place. Tourist brochures now entice Western visitors to visit with promises that they can experience first-hand "authentic Tibetan culture" in "ancient" villages imbued with a "rich cultural heritage." This perception, however, is perhaps guided by a modern tendency to equate poor and rural communities with a traditional and unchanging character. Once we begin to dig below the surface, social, economic, and cultural transformations are evident in even the most remote Himalayan settings, as we will see when we examine the history of the Nubri Valley.

THE ESSENTIAL DOCTRINES OF BUDDHISM

Nubri residents are without exception devotees of Buddhism, a religion based on the teachings of a man born about 2,500 years ago as Prince Siddhartha of the Shakya clan in Lumbini, a small kingdom on the northern plains of the Ganges River.[6] Rejecting the extravagant lifestyle of the royal palace, he set out to solve the eternal questions surrounding the nature of suffering, bodily decay, and death. Through a lifetime of contrasts, from living in sumptuous luxury to austere denial, he came to realize a middle way to spiritual progress that is achieved through balancing the extremes of material pursuits and severe asceticism. After his

awakening, accomplished by perfecting his wisdom through meditation, this man came to be known as Shakyamuni Buddha, or "awakened sage of the Shakya clan."

Shakyamuni Buddha's analytical approach to the human condition is
rooted in what he termed the "Four Noble Truths." In summary, these
state that (1) suffering characterizes the lives of us all; (2) suffering
stems from our own desires, which in turn are rooted in ignorance—in
particular, our inability to recognize the impermanence of things; (3) the
cycle of suffering can be broken by removing its root cause, which is
desire for things that are impermanent; and (4) one can overcome suffering by cultivating wisdom, nurturing positive thoughts and actions,
and developing insights into the nature of existence through meditation.

Buddha's teachings are grounded in the interrelated concepts of
karma and cyclical existence. Accordingly, life is characterized by an
unceasing continuum of birth, growth, decay, death, rebirth, and so on.
The circumstances of one's current life are not random or arbitrary, but
are conditioned by karma—positive, negative, or neutral actions perpe-
trated in previous lives. In other words, a preponderance of harmful
thoughts and actions in the past will result in a high level of suffering in
the present. By this tenet, it is possible to simultaneously rationalize one's
current plight (the present effect of previous actions) and take measures
to ensure that one does not suffer as much in future lives (the future
effect of today's actions). Far from being fatalistic concepts, karma and
cyclical existence are based on the recognition that humans are active
agents who shape their own outcomes in life. Through ignorance of the
basic workings of karma and rebirth, however, most sentient beings
remain locked within the sufferings that come with cyclical existence.

Depending on actions in previous lives, rebirth occurs within one of
six realms of existence. Those who lead immoral lives accrue negative
karma and subsequently end up in one of the three lower realms—the
animal world, the hells of extreme heat and cold, or the domain of the
hungry ghosts (so called because of their voracious appetites that can
never be satisfied). The cumulative effect of positive actions leads one to
be reborn in either the paradise inhabited by the gods, the lesser paradise of the demigods, or the human realm. Of these, the human realm
represents the penultimate existence, at least in theory, since humans
alone have the capacity to become fully awakened and thereby break
the chain of cyclical existence.

The understanding that desire and ignorance serve to perpetuate
cyclical existence, and that only humans are capable of escaping from

incessant suffering, together represent the foundation for leading a life of compassion. Through eons of cyclical existence the laws of probability imply that each individual is somehow related to all other sentient beings. By virtue of the belief that we have been reborn innumerable times, in all possible bodily forms and manifestations, it is more than likely that we have had close ties of kinship or acquaintance with every other being on earth. In the process we have been subjected to, or subjected others to, myriad forms of abuse, whether by accident or intention. As a human it is thereby imperative to treat every living creature with sympathy and empathy born of experience. Compassion is not just a philosophical ideal but a moral imperative, an approach to life that can alleviate suffering in the present as well as in the future.

BUDDHISM IN TIBET

Buddhism arose in India and then rapidly spread to other parts of the world, including places as culturally diverse as Afghanistan and Japan. In the seventh century, well over a thousand years after the death of Shakyamuni Buddha, the teachings began to trickle into Tibet from various sources, most notably India, China, and Central Asia.[7] At the time Tibet was an emerging empire, contesting for power with Chinese, Arab, and Turkic armies along the ancient Silk Route.

As a court religion during Tibet's imperial past (roughly 640–842), Buddhism enjoyed royal patronage and began to develop an infrastructure that included temples, monasteries, and a full-time clergy. With the collapse of the empire in 842, religious practice apparently devolved to household-level traditions that, according to Tibetan sources, corrupted the essential teachings of the Buddha. A spiritual renaissance, referred to by Tibetan historians as the "later diffusion of Buddhism," occurred during the eleventh century when Indian masters were invited back to the Tibetan Plateau. Since that time religious development has been characterized by the rise of powerful monasteries that often had competing doctrinal as well as political-economic interests. Monasteries became land-owning institutions that were funded by various systems of taxation. Sectarian splits often resulted in some noticeably non-Buddhist activities such as internecine warfare. Far from there being a separation of church and state, religion and politics became intimately entwined in Tibet.

In addition to the political aspects of monasticism, the institutions became cultural repositories where men (nunneries were rare and generally underfunded) could pursue the most fundamental philosophical questions concerning human existence. Monasteries became centers of literacy as well as places where systems of knowledge that could benefit all of society, such as medicine, were actively subsidized and developed. Monks acted as spiritual advisors to the general populace, and performed rituals to ensure that the rains would fall on time and crop-destroying hailstorms would be averted. Religion eventually infiltrated nearly every aspect of Tibetan society.

Today there are five major sects of Tibetan Buddhism: Gelugpa, Kargyupa, Nyingmapa, Sakyapa, and Bön. The most prominent is the Gelugpa, whose political leader is the Dalai Lama. Since the Fifth Dalai Lama claimed governmental authority through the aid of his Mongol allies in the seventeenth century, the Gelugpas have dominated the political scene of Tibet. The Nyingmapa, or "Ancient Ones," were often at odds with the Gelugpa overlords and were sometimes pushed to the geographic fringes of Tibetan society, to places such as Nubri.

One key difference between the two sects is the way in which succession is determined. Gelugpas consider celibacy to be a prerequisite for spiritual attainment, which means that succession through direct patrilineal descent is impossible. The solution to the problem is rule through incarnation. When a teacher, abbot of a monastery, or political leader such as the Dalai Lama passes away, the reincarnation of that person— his bodily manifestation—is recognized as the legal heir to his title. Rather than being a mere offspring, the new head of a monastery (or the state, in the case of the Dalai Lamas) thus represents a cognitive continuum with all who came before him. Nyingmapa lamas, in contrast, not only are permitted to marry, but are even expected to procreate their own successors. In this way teaching lineages and biological lineages are often one and the same in Nyingmapa circles.[8]

Like any religion, Buddhism is transformed and adapted by human agents to fit the diverse cultural milieus where it takes root. Religious practice in Tibetan settings represents a convergence of traditions. Buddhism, the relative latecomer on the scene, melded with a pre-Buddhist belief system that emphasizes a symbiosis between humans and the deities who both inhabit and animate the harsh physical surroundings. Spiritual forces permeate the landscape and must be treated with deference to assure health and well-being. Although many spiritually advanced Tibetan lamas, as well as Buddhist practitioners and scholars in the West, analytically separate Buddhism from "folk religion," most Tibetan laypeople make no such distinction. While the lamas seek perfection through meditation, they also assist the laypeople in their quest for material sustenance by performing rituals to appease potentially malevolent forces. By the same token, although the highest esoteric teachings of Buddhism remain far from the grasp of the ordinary villager, the beliefs in karma and cyclical existence—the links between actions and future consequences—most certainly exert a powerful influence on the behavior of most individuals.

THE SOCIAL REALM OF RELIGION

Sectarian affiliation in Nubri is predominantly Nyingmapa with a discernable Kargyupa undercurrent. With the exception of one institution tucked away in a remote corner of the valley, monasteries staffed by full-time celibate practitioners do not exist. Rather, religious practice is a complex, village-level affair involving various specialists with distinct ritual roles. As mentioned above, one characteristic of the Nyingma sect is the fact that celibacy is not considered a prerequisite for spiritual advancement. At the pinnacle of Nubri's religious hierarchy are hereditary householder lamas, called *ngagpa*s. The prestige of such lamas is rooted in attributes that are both achieved through birthright and acquired by training. Only males born with the requisite pedigree have the potential to become a ngagpa representative of their lineage. But ancestry alone is not sufficient. One's recognition as a religious authority also entails considerable training with one's father as well as other spiritual masters. In the case of Nubri's ngagpas, their spiritual and biological lineages can be one and the same, albeit not all males within a ngagpa family become lamas.

A ngagpa lama of a Nyingma community like Nubri is the hereditary incumbent of a village temple. Such a temple is the spiritual focal point of the community and is considered the property of the lama. Religion and economics are inseparable in such a setting, because householders are obligated to pay tax (usually grain) to the temple and contribute labor to the lama's family (that is, help harvest his fields or cut fodder for his herds) in order to maintain membership within the community. In return the lamas provide essential services for their kin and neighbors, such as performing household purification rituals, life empowerment ceremonies, funeral rites, and a host of other rituals meant to mediate between the human and supernatural realms and thereby assure health and prosperity for all. Far from being removed from the community, as is the case with many celibate monks, hereditary lamas in the Nyingma tradition are part and parcel of village life.

Married lamas are not the only religious practitioners in Nubri. There are also a few celibate monks who, for the most part, remain secluded within their private chapels and do not engage in mundane affairs such as farming and herding. Further down the religious hierarchy are the *chöpa*, literally "those who make offerings." Chöpa are married householders who do not have a pedigree but who voluntarily undertake rudimentary liturgical training so that they can participate in the ritual life of the community. These part-time practitioners spend most of their time in the economic and social activities required to maintain a family, and only engage in religious practices during major festivals when large numbers of community members are required. At the low end of the religious spectrum are nuns *(ani)*. Unlike monks, who are generally revered and accorded great respect, nuns are devalued in the eyes of villagers. Most receive only elementary liturgical training and are relegated to the background at communal rituals, thus holding a symbolic position below even that of the part-time chöpa. Nuns are technically full-time practitioners, as indicated by their close-cropped hair and red clothing. However, one is more likely to find them engaged in worldly activities, such as weeding fields, than in spiritual endeavors such as prayer and meditation. Quite simply, Nubri society restricts the level of spiritual attainment open to nuns.

The village of Sama is divided between the village proper and a monastery complex. The village is a conglomeration of nearly one hundred houses divided into distinct neighborhoods located on both sides of a small stream. Perched on slightly higher ground is the house known as Labrang (Lama's Palace), the hereditary home of Sama's head cleric who by the right of primogeniture is the top-ranking ngagpa in the community. Tashi Döndrup, my host and good friend, lives in the neighborhood called Gangbala, which people interpret to mean either Filled [with People] or [Situated] On the Spur of a Ridge. Other descriptive neighborhood names include Yurdrung (Beside the Water Conduit), Kaniwa (Below the Kani—a structure marking the entrance to the village), Godun (Seven Doors), and Drongdö (Upper Village). The village is the site of intensive economic activities and a place where social events such as weddings and funerals transpire. It is the place where people are born and die, where young people flirt while threshing grain, and where political quarrels sometimes erupt into brawls. As such, the village is referred to as *jigtenpey yul,* or the Realm of Worldly Suffering.

Life to these Tibetans mired in jigtenpey yul is characterized in great part by sin and atonement. Each and every action has an effect that may or may not be immediately apparent. Take the seemingly innocuous act of plowing, an essential task for subsistence in an agrarian community. Metal-tipped plows are harnessed to two *dzo,* the male crossbreeds between yaks and cows. One man holds a ring connecting the noses of the bovines and pulls them forward, while another stands behind whipping the buttocks of the beasts as he guides the plow. Each time a furrow is completed and the team is turned, the man holding the plow shouts the mantra "Om mani padme hum," the purpose being to counteract the negative consequences incurred by plowing. Plowing is considered to be a sinful task, since it exposes those insects that dwell within the soil while burying those that live above ground. All sentient beings are worthy of compassion, including those that are inadvertently sacrificed in the human quest to procure food.

Pema Chöling Gomba (Lotus Island of Dharma Monastery) is known as *chöpey yul,* the Realm of Religious Practitioners, and is situated on level ground above the village. The main temple and adjacent houses are surrounded by grassy pastures punctuated by tall juniper trees that gradually give way to a forest. The backdrop is dominated by magnificent peaks, most notably Mt. Pungyen, the residence of Sama's protector deity.

In the West a Buddhist monastery evokes images of temples with gilded pagoda roofs surrounded by stately white buildings inhabited by shaven-headed devotees of the ancient teachings. Yet the Tibetan word *gomba* (conventionally translated as monastery) is a multifaceted term. At its most basic meaning it signifies "a place of solitude," which according to Buddhists is the preeminent setting for pursuing spiritual activities. In this sense a gomba can be a clearing in a forest or a cave inhabited by a solitary yogi. In the Tibetan world a village temple complex, such as Pema Chöling, is also referred to as a gomba. As the focal point of a community's religious life, situated within close proximity to the village, such a gomba is not necessarily a solitary place of meditation, but functions as a center for the ritual activities through which communal cohesion is achieved. There are ceremonies to be performed for the deceased, annual festivals to be held in honor of the local protective deities, and daily prayers to be recited in order to assure prosperity and health for all those who dwell in the immediate environs. Villagers and village life regularly impinge on the solitude of Pema Chöling Gomba.

Nevertheless, Pema Chöling is a place of relative peace and quiet. While the village continually teems with people and bovines tromping along the muddy paths, and resonates with the cries of children and the

chatter of neighbors conversing across the low stone walls separating
their courtyards, the gomba is comparatively tranquil. Monks and nuns
reflect on Buddhist teachings about the nature of existence. Old folks in
their waning years of life spin prayer wheels and mutter mantras, hoping
for a positive influence on their impending rebirths. The contrast between
the gomba and the village is stark: solitude versus communal engage-
ment; contemplation versus bustling activity; spiritual pursuits versus
mundane concerns. The gomba is where people retire for peace of mind.

In terms of spatial arrangement, the central point of Pema Chöling
Gomba is Pema Chöling Lhakhang (Temple), a three-story structure
capped by a golden roof. Inside, the smell of burning butter lamps is
pervasive, an aroma that is familiar and unforgettable to all who have
visited a Tibetan temple. Light filters through a pair of windows on
either side of the door. Opposite the door is the altar, dominated by a
dimly illuminated statue of Padmasambhava, the famous eighth-century yogi who helped establish Buddhism in Tibet.[9] Painted wooden
planks line the walls on either side of the altar. Some of the paintings
depict ferocious deities who wrathfully defend the faithful, purposefully
(and some say, compassionately) destroying those who are guided by
ignorance, greed, and ill will toward others. Others portray Buddhist
masters, spiritual predecessors of the lamas who now officiate over the
ceremonies at Pema Chöling. One painting, which many locals point to
with pride, depicts the genealogical descent lineage of the Ngadag
lamas. This visible link with the past is on display for all to see.[10]

There is far more to the monastery complex than Pema Chöling Temple. The main temple itself is set amid private chapels with attached
houses. Some of these are inhabited by elderly monks, men whose religious careers were interrupted by China's destruction of monasteries
across the border in Tibet. Several chapels are owned by householder
lamas as places to keep their cache of sacred texts and to periodically
spend time in retreat from village life. In addition, many small, single-
story houses cluster about the temple. Some are inhabited by old folks
who have bequeathed the management of land and herds to their sons
and renounced village life through retirement. Often they live with a
daughter who takes care of them. Other houses are inhabited by elderly
nuns, women who never lived in convents but rather were retained in
their natal homes by parents who anticipated one day needing somebody to take care of them in retirement. Pema Chöling is thus an odd
blend of religious institution and geriatric settlement. On the one hand,
it is where full-time religious practitioners, such as monks and nuns, are

expected to live. On the other hand, it is a place where elderly house-holders quietly dedicate their twilight years to accumulating merit for subsequent lives. Pema Chöling Gomba may be physically removed from Sama Village. Nevertheless, it is an integral part and in many ways a focal point of village life.

REGIONAL AND LOCAL HISTORY

No firm evidence exists to fix a precise date for the settling of the Nubri Valley.[11] Nevertheless, several Tibetan sources allow us to engage in some well-founded conjecture. According to oral accounts, the people in the upper part of the valley migrated long ago from the Tibetan Plateau, while the people of the lower part of the valley came from Tibet and from areas to the south that are currently inhabited by Ghales. Based on a count of people in terms of clan affiliation, people of Tibetan ancestry are more numerous. Today, the inhabitants of Nubri claim Tibetan ethnicity *(mirig)* yet state that they are subjects *(miser)* of Nepal. Such has not always been the case, for Nubri is no exception to the rule that political and ethnic boundaries fluctuate through time.

In former times Nubri was part of the Gungtang Kingdom, centered in the town of Dzongga, Tibet. Gungtang was ruled by descendants of the medieval Tibetan emperors and was a local power to be reckoned with for many centuries. In the eighteenth century one Tibetan historian wrote, "In the middle of Gungtang is lofty and rugged Nubri. The mountain to the right resembles a king seated on a throne. The mountain to the left resembles a queen pregnant with child." Nubri was incorporated into the Gungtang domains sometime in the eleventh century, judging by a quote from the same historian: "During his reign, Lhachogde (late eleventh century) extended his realm beyond its extent of former times. In Nubri, the rugged mountainous area in the center [of his realm] which resembles a great highland wrapped in a silk curtain, he built a palace." Around 1280 Gungtang's hold over Nubri was solidified during the reign of Bumdegon, a ruler who built a series of forts to protect or control the boundaries of the kingdom. Accordingly, "In order to suppress the barbarous border region of Nubri, he [Bumdegon] built Dragdzong Nagpo (Black Cliff Fort) at Rö (Sama)."[12] The garrisoning of this fort—remains of which are still visible today—may represent the first expansion of ethnic Tibetans into Nubri.

Prior to that event the settlement history of Nubri is somewhat vague. Tibet's intrepid yogi Milarepa (1040–1123) journeyed to the area during the late eleventh century. His biography specifies that he went to a "land of a different language," meaning that the residents of Nubri spoke a vernacular that was not Tibetan. Milarepa then denigrates Nubri as being an "uncultured realm of darkness" and its inhabitants as "bovines."[13] His statements can be interpreted to mean that Nubri at the time of his visit was inhabited by a non-Tibetan people who did not practice Buddhism. Perhaps it was the expansion of Gungtang power into Nubri that brought the first ethnic Tibetans to the region.

According to one source that may date from the late 1300s (but certainly no later than the 1600s), "Tibetan is spoken in the upper part [of the valley]. In the lower part, there are many dissimilar languages."[14] This statement mirrors the current ethno-linguistic division of the valley alluded to above. Pema Döndrup, who was born and raised in Kutang, confirms that the division existed during his lifetime. As he was about to embark on a journey to Tibet in 1688, some people expressed concern over his inability to speak an intelligible dialect of Tibetan. Furthermore, residents of Sama referred to him and a companion of his as "valley dwellers" (rongpa), a generic term used by Tibetans to describe those non-Tibetans inhabiting lower areas. The linguistic references suggest that the first wave of ethnically Tibetan settlers (as opposed to troops garrisoning the fort) may have been present in the upper stretches of the Nubri Valley as early as the late fourteenth century, but no later than the seventeenth century.

In 1620 the Gungtang Kingdom was eradicated by the rulers of Tsang, Central Tibet, and then in 1641 the former Gungtang domains were subsumed by the Fifth Dalai Lama and his Mongol allies. The Fifth Dalai Lama then commenced to reorganize the entire Tibetan administration, to take in newly united territories. Dzongga, the former seat of Gungtang power, was made the center of a Tibetan administrative district. Subsequent tax documents list Nubri as a division of Dzongga District, and thereby a place controlled by the Tibetan government centered in Lhasa.

Around 1640 a married lama from Tradumtse Monastery in Tibet moved to Sama. He was a genealogical descendant of Tibet's medieval emperors, most notably Songtsen Gampo and Trisong Detsen, who ruled Tibet and much of Inner Asia during the seventh and eighth centuries. According to legend, the lama from Tradumtse stuck a magical dagger into the ground in a pasture near the present village of Sama. A well of water gushed forth that flows to this day, even during droughts and the coldest days of winter. The miraculous event tamed the environment and made it fit for human habitation, or more precisely, for the cattle on which the locals depend.

The lama's claim of imperial pedigree is not spurious, but is attested in the historical record. Referred to by their lineage name Ngadag ("Possessing Power"), his descendants now occupy the loftiest position in the local social hierarchy. Being linked to the Tibetan emperors of yore gives these lamas a family background that is well recognized throughout the entire Tibetan world. Several of the men whose stories you will hear shortly, such as Tashi Dorje, Rigzen Dorje, and Lama Gyatso, all belong to the prestigious Ngadag lineage.

When an Indian pundit employed by the British to clandestinely scout routes into Tibet passed through Nubri in 1861, he stated that the area south of the Himalayan divide was considered to be Nepali territory. Only after crossing the pass to the north of Nubri did he enter an area administered by Tibet. The current border between Tibet and Nepal was only recognized and formalized in 1856, following a war between the two nations, at which time a local lord was appointed by the Nepali government to act as *subbha,* a position that obliged him to collect taxes and administer Nubri under the name of the central government. For most of Nubri's history, therefore, the inhabitants of the area lived under various Tibetan administrations. After 1856 and until this day the residents of Nubri have held the dual distinction of being ethnic Tibetans who are subjects of Nepal. This new designation has had many ramifications.

While carving out borders during the eighteenth and nineteenth centuries, the kings of Nepal incorporated a multitude of different ethnic groups within a nascent state structure. To provide order, they devised a legal code in which all ethnic groups and castes were ranked according to Hindu concepts of ritual purity. Tibetans, referred to by the derogatory term *bhotay,* were relegated to one of the lowest categories in the hierarchy. They were classified as "enslavable alcohol drinkers," due to their adherence to Buddhism, their fondness for drink, and their propensity to eat cows—a sacred animal in the Hindu worldview.[15] Today Tibetan highlanders resent being considered low-caste ne'er-do-wells. But as a minority population in a remote corner of Nepal they lack the political power, economic resources, and social stature to do much about it. While development funds flow to many areas of Nepal, those in positions of power ignore the people of Nubri, who are considered impure and inferior. The politics of ethnicity and foreign aid contribute to Nubri's image as an untainted and timeless residue of

Tibetan culture, an image that now attracts Western trekkers to the area. On the positive side, the residents of Nubri have been spared the havoc brought upon their brethren in Tibet through the abuses of Chinese occupation. Being in Nepal has had some advantages.

Until recently the village of Sama was an intermediary point for the thriving trans-Himalayan trade.[16] Products from Tibet such as salt, wool, dried cheese, and sheep were bartered for lowland grains such as rice and millet. For centuries the people of Sama prospered through this trade, which provided more than an adequate supplement to the meager yields from their fields. Trading has always been a male occupation. Men routinely traveled far away to Tibet and Kathmandu. Some even ventured to Calcutta to buy precious stones for sale back in the highlands. The men of Sama still enjoy the adventure of trading, yet their activities are somewhat curtailed by recent political and economic shifts. Trade with Tibet, now a part of China, is more restricted and less lucrative than before, mainly because rice is trucked in from mainland China and hence is cheaper than rice brought by yak over the passes from Nepal. Meanwhile, the salt market in the hills of Nepal has been undermined by imports from India. Nevertheless, each year from spring through autumn, friends and neighbors throughout Nubri form caravans to cross the treacherous passes in quest of commodities for profit, but more so for subsistence. A common refrain throughout the valley is "We trade or we starve."

Nubri is not, nor has it ever been, insulated from regional political and economic trends. Change, to Buddhists, is inevitable—which makes it somewhat ironic for outsiders to view highland Buddhist communities as being locked in a timeless existence. Today the people of Nubri are subjected to many vectors of intervention, from nongovernmental organizations (NGOs) intent on improving their lives, to a government intent on strengthening control over the area and weakening local autonomy, to Maoist guerillas devoted to transforming the political consciousness of the residents through conviction or coercion. Perhaps the pace of change has intensified in recent years, a trend that is evident throughout the world. But the main point remains irrefutable: Nubri society is anything but static.

· · ·

Every morning majestic Mt. Pungyen is clearly visible from grassy pastures surrounding Pema Chöling Gomba. Soft morning sunlight highlights every rocky precipice and twisted icefall on the flanks of the mountain, and illuminates the soft plume of snow blowing from the summit. On most days the clear view of the summit lasts only until noon, when clouds from below eddy slowly but surely up the valley to enshroud the peak. During crystalline mornings it is easy to see why the Tibetans of Sama designated this magnificent peak as the seat of their omniscient protector. Let us now move on to explore the life cycle of those who live in the shadow of Pungyen.

CHAPTER 3

Life Begets Death, Death Begets Life

The Life Course Begins

Without climbing the cliff of adversity,
One cannot arrive at the meadow of happiness.

Tibetan Proverb

To Tibetans life does not begin at birth, but rather at conception. After death, a being's consciousness *(namshey)* wanders in an intermediate realm until impelled by the forces of its own karma to enter a womb at the instant of conception. Gestation is a hazardous time when women try to consume nutritious foods and seek spiritual means to prevent any harm coming to their growing baby. Once born, the child must fight for survival against daunting odds. Infancy is fraught with more hazards than any other stage of the life course, and the infant mortality rate in Nubri is frightfully high. Nearly one in every four children born alive does not live to see his or her first birthday. In this chapter we will explore the circumstances of birth and the means people take to ensure that their children will grow to become members of the family and community.[1]

WHY DID THIS CHILD DIE?

Tashi and I sat side by side in the semidarkness illuminated only by diffuse sunlight struggling to penetrate the smoky gloom of the house of our hostess. Teetering precariously on unstable blocks of wood in front of us sat chipped and stained ceramic cups filled to the brim with a steaming clear liquor, *arak,* the local whiskey distilled from corn. We were engaged in our usual question-and-answer routine in the midst of a door-to-door demographic survey.

We usually preferred to conduct questionnaires outside on the portico to avoid the social obligations of drinking arak. Once inside the house, we were guests and obliged to imbibe. Outside, however, we remained in a socially enigmatic position: visiting, yet not really visitors, since proper etiquette dictates that offerings of food and drink transpire only within. Citing the need for sunlight to see what I was writing allowed us to avoid becoming guests and evade the obligatory liquor consumption that would compromise the work at hand.

Our current respondent was a good friend; refusing her hospitality was the equivalent of a social rebuke. Initial resistance to the woman's invitation to enter her home was countered by a laugh and mocked incredulity. Her sinewy hands, hardened through a lifetime of toiling in the fields, gripped Tashi's upper arm as she pulled him toward the door. He conceded defeat, and we climbed the wooden ladder and ducked our heads through the low entrance. This is the Tibetan way; it's part of the social game. One always declines the first offer of food and drink so that the hostess has an opportunity to coerce and cajole the visitor. To accept immediately shows too much eagerness and perhaps greed on the part of the guest, yet to refuse altogether implies that the offered refreshments are inadequate or that the hostess occupies a rank of social inferiority. As with so many aspects of this Buddhist culture, proper etiquette requires finding the middle ground.

The interview continued as I attempted to ascertain details of her reproductive history. "My next child died after only three months," said the woman, whose weathered appearance belied the fact that she was only in her mid-thirties. "What did the child die of?" I asked. "Who knows?" exclaimed the mother, obviously irritated at my intrusive inquiry. "Do I look like a doctor?"

She lifted a soot-blackened kettle from the iron grate resting above the flittering embers of the fire and shuffled toward us, weighted down by her heavy woolen clothing. Having to recall the heartbreaks of motherhood could only add to this woman's burden. Tashi and I were used to such outbursts to our questions. We had visited hundreds of homes throughout the valley seeking data on births, deaths, and migration. Our task was not easy. In Nubri, as everywhere, deaths are recalled reluctantly and with considerable anguish. I persisted. "What type of symptoms did you observe?" She stooped before me and motioned to my cup, silently indicating that I should speak less and drink more. I placed my pen and writing pad on the gritty, rough-hewn floorboards beside the hearth, grasped the cup with both hands, and peered sideways at Tashi. I always felt a bit uncertain in this social situation, for as my elder, he should drink before me. But as the foreigner, I was a guest of honor, and therefore my companion deferred the first move to me. A deep slurp of the corn whisky filled my chest cavity with welcome warmth. Arak is thought to have healing powers and is used to relieve daily aches and pains. It is also a coveted elixir in that it allows one to escape, however briefly, the reality of existence in this harsh locale. The people of Nubri drink a lot. Perhaps they have a lot to forget.

I drained half the cup and set it carefully back on the wooden block, knowing full well but not really caring that today's productive activities were bound to suffer. A muffled cry from a child, swaddled in layers of woolen clothing and placed within a makeshift crib in the corner, blended with the crackling of the open fire and the hissing of the wind as it penetrated the many fissures in the walls. Our hostess refilled my cup and turned to do the same for Tashi.

Returning to her seat across the hearth from us, she placed the kettle back onto the iron grate, adjusted her garment, and resumed her cross-legged seated position beside the cooking implements. Struggling between a desire to blot out past adversity and an inclination to share her misery, she eventually exhaled audibly and said, "My son was weak from the beginning. With each passing day, he lost energy and began to wither away. By the third month of life he quit eating, and even refused liquor. He stopped eating and drinking arak. That is why he died."

I stole a furtive glance at Tashi, but he merely gazed down into his cup, his head shaking slowly, almost imperceptibly. Nearly every woman whom we interviewed had lost at least one child. One woman had even witnessed the passing of eleven of her twelve children; the only one who managed to survive is both deaf and mute. I could not help but note that the cumulative effect of these interviews was beginning to desensitize me and Tashi to the emotions evoked by recalling individual tragedies.

PROTECTIVE MEASURES

The people of Nubri, like their Tibetan brethren elsewhere, are by no means passive when it comes to childcare. In one sense an infant's death can be rationalized as the workings of that individual's karma. From afar we might then assume that parents are fatalistic, since after all a child's destiny is determined at the moment of conception. Why try to intervene with fate? Such a facile assumption misses an important behavioral detail: Although a child's fate may be preordained, parents can and do take extensive measures to enhance their offspring's chances of survival. They most emphatically attempt to influence outcomes.

Tibetans believe that the natural environment is filled with potentially harmful agents that are willing to let loose death and disease when provoked or when not sufficiently propitiated.[2] Infants are especially vulnerable. One way to prevent infants from coming to harm is to smear soot on their foreheads and cheeks before taking them outside. The custom, like so many others in Nubri, is embedded in the folklore of the region. I once asked Tsogyal, Lama Gyatso's wife, the reason for this custom. She related the following tale:

> Long ago there were two villages separated by a river. Many evil spirits lived on one side of the river and continually sowed strife among that village's inhabitants. No evil spirits lived on the other side, so those villagers lived in harmony. One day two spirits decided to cross the river and make trouble. They agreed that one would go to the home of a happy couple and cause them to quarrel, while the other would wait at the bridge and toss the woman into the torrent of water when she fled to her parents' home. The plan worked, and discord erupted in the happy household. When the couple's fight became unbearable the woman picked up her child and started to leave. But then she remembered that there were many harmful spirits across the river, so she bent down next to the hearth, took soot from three stones in the fire, and smeared it on the forehead and cheeks of her infant child. She then took soot from the bottom of the skillet and made a black mark on the tip of the child's nose. Ever vigilant, she remembered to mutter aloud a prayer to Dolma, the savioress, while crossing the bridge. She returned safely to her parents' home. Afterward, the spirit who went to the house came and asked the spirit guarding the bridge whether he had thrown the woman and child into the river. "What woman," he replied, "I only saw a skillet go by saying a prayer."

Noticing a somewhat perplexed look on my face, Tsogyal chuckled and explained. "The soot from the skillet had made both mother and baby invisible to the harmful spirit, and since that time we have followed her example to protect our own children."

Protection from the spirit world is also bestowed through life-empowerment ceremonies *(tsewang)* performed by lamas shortly after the birth of a child. The intent of the ritual is to promote longevity and freedom from illness. Such rituals are performed far more often for boys than for girls, which is a strong indication of the role that gender plays in the valuation of children in Sama.[3] Despite the best efforts of both parents and clerics, infancy is a tenuous period of life through which many individuals will fail to pass.

TUBTEN AND PURGU'S FIRST SON

My introduction to infant mortality—not the abstraction that is culled from massive surveys and then quantified in academic accounts and government statistics, but the stark reality—occurred a few weeks after I had entered the village of Sama. Early one morning in my new neighborhood, a baby boy took a final sip of milk from his mother's breast. Nobody knew that this would be his final attempt to suckle, yet everyone recognized that the child was in grave danger. Born two months previously, he was the first grandson of Lama Gyatso, one of the most prominent men in the village. Purgu, Lama Gyatso's daughter-in-law and the mother of the child, was a strong woman, both physically and emotionally. She needed to be, for she managed a household consisting of her two in-laws as well as her two husbands, Tubten and Lhundrup.

Two husbands? Indeed, the form of plural marriage known as polyandry is common throughout the Tibetan world. In a community where arable land is scarce, brothers frequently take a single bride between them to avoid partitioning their inheritance.[4] Such is the case with the two sons of Lama Gyatso. As the elder brother, Tubten is expected to be the progenitor of the first child. The reality of this arrangement was made obvious each morning when I awoke at dawn, laced my boots, tightly zipped up my jacket, and ventured outside for some bladder relief. I always made sure to shout out a greeting to Lhundrup, Tubten's good-natured younger brother, who was relegated to sleeping on the outside balcony. Invariably he returned my salutation by popping his head up from behind the railing. There was always a grin on his face, which would no doubt fade to a bashful smirk when it was finally his turn to sleep inside.

The infant boy, the couple's first child, was Tubten's pride and joy. As the father, he was especially concerned about the baby's deteriorating condition. He implored me to help. The locals had yet to understand that I was definitely not skilled in the art of healing, even finding it a struggle to keep myself healthy. People in this part of the world often assume that all Westerners carry medicines that effect miraculous cures. Although I could not refuse Tubten's request for help, it was only to lend moral support; I steadfastly refrained from attempting any cures in the fear that my cursory knowledge of medical practices would jeopardize the child's valiant attempt to rally.

Tubten's child had not been able to escape the wrath of the spirits. As the day wore on, the infant became more enfeebled and anemic. Late in the afternoon Lama Gyatso called on his uncle, Lama Rigzen Dorje, to perform a divination ceremony. By this means, the family would at least know what type of pernicious spirit had unleashed the ailment on the child.[5] Rigzen Dorje scurried down from his monastery home. On this day, the elderly lama's customary mirth was absent. A human life was at stake.

Rigzen Dorje would attempt to ascertain what was wrong with the child by performing a drum divination ceremony. As he sat in Lama Gyatso's home sipping tea, he shouted instructions to his assistants who were outside on the balcony preparing the drums. One drum was suspended from the rafters, while another lay horizontally on the coarsely chiseled planks of the balcony. On the oiled surface of the lower drum the lama had drawn two concentric rings, which were divided into sixteen sections by four lines radiating from the center. The name of a malevolent spirit was written in each of the sections. Grains of barley, the life force and dietary staple of the village, were then carefully placed in the center of the drum, the last seed, positioned in the exact center, representing the ailing infant. Rigzen Dorje pulled a weathered piece of brown paper from the recesses of his cloak. The parched manuscript was a ritual manual that he had hand-copied years ago from a version kept by his father. The tattered edges of the paper attested to its frequent use.

The lama began to recite from the text in a voice hoarse with age yet clear with conviction. At first the tone of the recitation was subdued and methodical. Gradually, as the eyes of the onlookers swelled in concentration, so too did the power of Rigzen Dorje's voice, building by the moment in tempo and amplitude. Upon reaching a crescendo, he grasped a curved stick and began beating the drum suspended from above. Immediately the grains of barley sprang to life on the lower drum, dancing with the vibrations triggered by the reverberations overhead. The drumming slowed, and the potency of the venerable lama's voice trailed off once again. Everybody was silent; all attention was riveted on the barley.

The stillness was soon broken by the resumption of Rigzen Dorje's chants. Suspense again built in harmony with the rising force of his utterances. He began to chant more rapidly, with more ferocity, and then, as the spectators scrutinized his every gesture, Rigzen Dorje clutched the bent stick and beat the drum anew. The rhythm of the drum matched the cadence of his voice, sometimes increasing in intensity, sometimes droning off into the distance, until finally, with a burst of energy, he hammered the drum furiously while shouting forth the words written by his forefathers on the rough paper. When the drumbeats stopped, everybody became still and attempted to discern the meaning of the pattern the barley had left on the drum's surface. Comprehension slowly dawned. His eyes bulging, Rigzen Dorje pointed to the section on the drum where the grain of barley representing Tubten's child had come to rest. He proclaimed, "It is Mamo! You see, it is Mamo who has sent the disease!"

Mamo is depicted in the local temple as a hideous, dark-skinned female deity who is stripped to the waist to expose sagging, emaciated breasts. Mamo is considered to be one of the most loathsome forces in the region, for she has a tendency to unleash a variety of ailments on unsuspecting villagers, especially helpless children. A grave look crossed the face of Lama Gyatso as he huddled in conference with Rigzen Dorje about the portents thus revealed. Knowing the cause of the ailment is the first step toward remedy. If the malefactor from the spiritual world can be identified, it is possible to appease the deity through appropriate rituals. The two men made their judgment and immediately set about preparing incantations and offerings in the hope of sparing the infant's life. "Hopefully it is not too late," Lama Gyatso murmured as he entered his home to prepare an altar to honor Mamo. His words did not encourage Purgu, the mother, who desperately clutched the child to her breast, hoping and praying that her firstborn would attempt to feed.

Later that evening Tashi and I sat at home in silence eating our corn mush. Suddenly the tranquil night air was splintered by a piercing shriek, followed by uncontrolled sobbing. The vigil was over; the child had died. His life force was at that very instant dissipating into the bitter night winds, having been extinguished before his universe could expand even beyond his mother's nurturing breast. I made a motion to get up, but Tashi extended his hand and said, "No, not tonight. We pay our respects tomorrow." Such is the custom in the village. Throughout the night our sleep was disturbed by the mother calling out in agony for her beloved child.

In the morning, after a breakfast of butter tea and parched barley flour, we went to console the bereaved family. The hearth, the center of all social activities in Nubri homes, sat at the far end of the rectangular room. Seating arrangements in the Tibetan home are dictated by gender and social status. To the right of the hearth, installed in an alcove at chest level, is the altar devoted to the male-lineage deity. Below the altar sits the senior-most man in the household; across the fire from him sits the woman in charge of domestic duties. Beside her rests a collection of household cooking implements, an assortment of soot-blackened pots and rough wooden utensils for stirring. Male visitors sit on the male side, females on the female side.

Lama Gyatso sat at his usual place to the right of the hearth and below the altar. On this day it was not Purgu but her mother-in-law, Tsogyal, who directed the preparation of tea for the flow of visitors who came to offer sympathy. Purgu huddled in a corner, her faint sobs muffled by the woolen blanket wrapped around her body. She peered out from her protective covering to see who had come. Tashi and I offered a vessel containing arak to Lama Gyatso. I handed Purgu a flower picked that morning and said, "Do not grieve, for it was the child's karma to die when it did." Over breakfast Tashi had drilled this phrase into me—it is the customary verbal offering to those who have lost a family member. Afterward, as we sat sipping tea, the phrase was repeated like a mantra by a string of visitors coming to help assuage the grief caused by the child's premature departure.

Can a mother, one who grows up in a village where infants die all the time, ever resign herself to the heartbreak of losing a child? Can the frequency of infant deaths ever accustom one to such cruel events? Purgu's lamentations could soften the hardest of hearts. Her grief was palpable as it filtered from house to house, and seemed to echo from the narrow valley walls and the clouds above. Heads hung low in the neighborhood that day. People spoke in hushed tones across the stone walls separating their courtyards. Everybody in Nubri lives under this cruel regime of mortality, watching their own children and siblings die prematurely, sometimes inexplicably. According to the Buddhist worldview, nothing is accidental, for contemporary occurrences are conditioned by past events. Regardless, no rationalization can erase the emotional burden of losing a child. Anyone who has heard the tortured laments of a grieving mother will attest to this.

FORECASTING THE FUTURE

To Tibetans the life course is sketched out in rough form at birth, and can be ascertained in part through astrological reckonings. One's path through life's trials and tribulations is greatly influenced by the accumulated actions of previous lives. The key to understanding one's life course is in the stars.

Three days after an infant is born, a lama is summoned to the home to select a name and to perform a life empowerment ceremony, intended to ensure a childhood free from illness. The village astrologer *(tsipa)* is then called to the home. Using the date and time of birth as reference points, he consults his charts to compose a *kyekar*, or natal horoscope. The calculations are written on a piece of paper that is carefully folded and kept in a safe place by the child's parents. When a person dies, his or her *kyekar* is tossed into the hearth. Until that time it is regularly consulted, since it contains guidelines for leading a successful life.

People in Sama do not always recall the precise ages of their children and in some cases are even confused about their own ages. This may seem odd, yet to many Tibetans it is far more crucial to know one's astrological birth sign (Horse, Ox, Snake, Dragon, etc.) than the precise number of years that have elapsed since birth. In a very large family, parents may have trouble recalling all of their children's astrological birth signs; the recourse to written records can help jog their memories. (If the parents themselves are not literate, they obtain assistance from the several people in the village who are.) During the course of my demographic survey, I had the opportunity to read several natal horoscopes that were brought forth when parents could not recall the birth signs of their children.

During one interview, the elderly father of ten children—six of whom are still alive—struggled to remember the birth sign of one daughter. He reached behind his seat by the hearth into a wooden storage chest, extracted a weathered piece of locally produced paper, and handed it to me to read. Not only did the kyekar resolve the issue at hand, revealing the birth sign of his daughter, but it also contained a wealth of cultural information, both as to how Tibetans view the life cycle and their perspective on the interconnections of past, present, and future. I asked the man if I could copy this and his other children's kyekars, and he kindly consented.[6]

One of the natal horoscopes starts as follows:

Born on a Friday during the 12th month of the Male Fire Horse Year [January/February 1966]. A strongly passionate girl, she will live to be seventy-eight. In this time she will bear two sons and have seven setbacks in life. She will enjoy traveling. She will be a selfless person, thinking always of benefiting others. She will express great anger, crave happiness, and have a good heart. Her economic fortunes will rise and fall. She will have no thought of harming others. Her pride will be great. As a youth she will be afflicted with headaches. In her elder years it will be proper for her to wear red clothing. All of her cattle and horses will be of the finest quality. She will become learned in writing and mathematics. She will show anger toward family members and kindness toward others. Early and late in life she will be happy. If she does not wash and maintain religious purity, the defect of mental retardation will appear.

I know this woman; she is Tashi's neighbor in Sama. At present she has a devoted husband and several children, most of whom have survived infancy. At some point, however, a family tragedy may occur, for the horoscope clearly states that she is destined to wear red clothing in later life—which can be interpreted to mean that she will become a nun. In most cases, women who enter the clergy late in life do so because of divorce or the death of a spouse. Will she one day become a widow and don the red robes? Only time will tell.

Her brother's horoscope reads as follows:

> Born on Friday, the 22nd day of the sixth month of the Female Fire Sheep Year [July 28, 1967]. Although strong of body, he will have a confused intellect. He will like food. Although he will not harm other people, he will not help them either. His thoughts will be morally just. He will live to be seventy-eight. He will have seven setbacks in life and many grandchildren. Occasionally he will be wounded by insults. Death will come quickly in the end. Moles will appear on his chest and back unless he gives food offerings again and again to the deities. He will wear clothes made from the pelts of horses and cattle. Although he will not find religion until his twentieth year, he will even then realize benefit from it. In the future his blessings will increase. He will achieve wealth and his reputation will be great. He will have wealth, merit, and cattle.

Not exactly a flattering depiction, for, to put it bluntly, he is slated to be strong yet not especially bright and rather useless. Yet he will have a predilection for the religious life and can expect fame and fortune with the passage of time. Perhaps guided by the horoscope, his father sent him as a young boy to a distant monastery. Today, as a mature young cleric, he has proven to be an entrepreneur in the monastic setting. Although some question his devotion to spiritual pursuits, his parents boast about the large remittances that he regularly sends back to the village. One vexing question remains: as a celibate monk, how will he fulfill the prediction of having many grandchildren?

CIRCUMSTANCES OF BIRTH

In early April 1997 Tashi and I took a trip down the valley to Kutang. The balmy weather of this relative lowland was a relief after months huddling close to our hearth in snow-packed Sama. Traversing a path that clung to a denuded slope, we arrived at a vantage point above the village of Bi. Below us stretched the hamlet consisting of several houses clustered into small groups, separated by soft carpets of newly sprouting barley and corn. Bi is perched on a gently sloping table, wedged between a steep incline above and a sharp drop to the river hundreds of feet below. Smoke filtered through the roofs of the chimneyless houses. The silence was occasionally broken by a woman calling out to her neighbor or by a child crying out in distress. Bi is a rough-and-tumble village where Tashi knows everybody and feels right at home.

Before ever coming to Kutang I had read with fascination the biography of Pema Wangdu, who lived in Bi about three hundred years ago. As we rested on a ledge above the village, Tashi extracted a filterless Bizuli-brand cigarette—one of Nepal's cheapest and most coveted toxins for the impoverished masses—from within the recesses of his robe and placed it between his nicotine-stained fingers. As he stuck a match and held it to the cigarette, I began to recite from memory details of Pema Wangdu's childhood, a story my companion knows well from oral versions that have been passed down from generation to generation. The following events transpired around the year 1700.

> My father's clan is Gyemi, which stems from the string of births following the minister Gar. My mother's clan derives from the descendants of the monkey and the rock ogress. Once her family was firmly ensconced as lords of the Kyung clan, she was born at Kyirong in Mangyul [Southern Tibet].[7] My father's name is Hrungshing, and my mother's name is Yogchog. Previously, by virtue of their karma, they came together at the sacred site called Drolmapel [below Kutang]. The eldest of their three boys is named Ngawang Tsering, the middle is Ngawang Dargye, and I, the youngest, am Ngawang Döndrup [Pema Wangdu is his religious name]. The names were given by a lama.
>
> At that time, having acted as a translator between Bhutan and the Gorkha king, the lama Thugje Chenpo and my mother's brother Tashi became wealthy and powerful men.[8] Although we were of the same family, and although they were compassionate men, one time my father said, "From the beginning I have wandered about as a beggar. Now as an old man I yearn for my natal land just as an old stag wants to ascend to the top of a cliff." Having said this, we returned to Kutang, his place of birth.

Thus far we have learned that Pema Wangdu's father was from Bi. He married a woman from a wealthy and powerful clan from Kyirong, the neighboring region in Tibet. Consequently, Pema Wangdu and his siblings were raised in a Tibetan sociocultural environment. Eventually his father wanted to return to his natal village, and so uprooted the entire family to fulfill his longing. Pema Wangdu, unfortunately, was totally unfamiliar with the language and culture of Kutang. Furthermore, by migrating outside of the community, Pema Wangdu's father had apparently relinquished his right to any property. The family was destitute, and the hardships of Pema Wangdu's childhood are evident from the following passages of his biography.

> We moved back to Bi. Eight or nine months elapsed. At that time immeasurable misery welled forth. We had neither a house to stay in nor any fire in the hearth. During the day I ate vegetables soaked in warm tea. At night I slept in the structure containing the water mill. Although I was born of a pure clan, the Kyung, I ate people's leftovers. I was not accustomed to the people and their language. Setting out hither, they cursed me. When I went to the doors of wealthy families in order to borrow food, they scorned me, saying, "He is the son of a beggar. Who has a boy who is a beggar?" I received nothing. My family did not get food or clothing. My body took on the appearance of a dried fish.
>   At the time there was a prolonged drought; two years of famine ensued. My mother thought, "This cannot go on for a month or even a day longer. My own son has no food or clothing whatsoever. As the year passes he babbles incessantly." A girl who noticed that I had no food or wealth offered me some greens foraged from the hills. My speech was obstructed when she gave them to me, only dribble and tears gushed forth. I went mad.[9]

Pema Wangdu was eventually cured of his affliction by a lama who performed purification rituals to exorcise the insanity from the suffering boy. Perhaps the hardships of youth steeled him for life as a mendicant, since later in life Pema Wangdu developed a proclivity for meditating in remote and nearly inaccessible places. He survived the torments of a deprived childhood and went on to achieve respect and a modicum of fame in this particular corner of the Himalayas.

When I finished narrating the struggles of Pema Wangdu, Tashi's eyes became glossy as he gazed absently at the craggy peaks rising above the river. His mood was distant, as one would expect from a man far removed from the rigors of a harsh childhood yet who feels close to the end of his present life. In moments like these I found it best to leave my companion undisturbed so he could freely ponder his own past privations. We were in no hurry.

Eventually Tashi began to speak. Born in 1929, he was raised at a time when Nubri was politically part of Nepal and neighboring Tibet was an independent land. This is the story of Tashi Döndrup's childhood.

Pema Wangdu is just like me. As a child I had nothing. You know, I am a *nyelu,* a bastard. My parents never married, and my father never even claimed me as his legitimate son. So my mother and I lived alone, without a home, without fields, and without cattle. Oh, how I suffered as a child! You can never imagine the hardships! But let me start from the beginning.

When I emerged into the world after spending nine months in my mother's womb, there was nothing to eat, nothing to drink. Food was scarce, so we often ate just boiled vegetables with our tsampa. When mother worked for other families, they would make corn mush for us. She would eat half, and I would eat half.

Even though my mother worked hard, I didn't have proper clothing to wear. I wore the old, cast-aside clothing of other people. I wandered about the village looking for whatever scraps could be worn. When it came time for sleeping, I had nothing to cover me beyond the rags that I wore. I didn't even have shoes, so I would pull my knees into my chest and sleep curled up like a ball. Even during the winter I often had no shoes. If I found only a single shoe, I would wear that. It snows a lot during the winter, so my feet were always blistered and cracked. I suffered very much when festering sores developed and bled. With my feet in such a condition, it was difficult to carry salt and barley up and down the valley. But I did so anyway, for this little bit of trade gave us some food.

We stayed at other people's homes, sometimes working as their servants, sometimes living alone if a house was empty. One time we even lived beneath a house in the stable for cattle. Mother was a good weaver, so while she did weaving for other people we would get a place to stay. But living in the homes of others meant that my mother and I always had to sit farthest from the fire, farthest from the warmth. It was not our home, after all. We had no home of our own.

My father gave me no inheritance, and beyond that he would not even look at me when we met. When I got older things gradually changed. He told me I was a good worker. Everybody knows this, I always have been. I asked him for money, barley, or even salt—anything that could be used for bartering. I told him, "If you give me something to trade with, I can do business. How can I do any business without any wealth?" One day he promised to give me some inheritance.

My mother and I never saw the coming of the other woman into his life. When I was seventeen or eighteen, my father married another woman. They had a son, you know him, he is the guy we call Balang [Ox]. When Balang was four, his mother died, and when he was eight, our father died. I felt sorry for him, so from that time onward I did much for Balang. Despite my help I still got none of our father's estate. All of the fields, all of the animals, the house where he still lives—all of it went to my half brother. I received nothing!

In addition to these bitter recollections, Tashi did have some fond memories from his childhood. He recounts,

You know Lopön Zangpo? He and I were close friends as children. He comes from a prominent family. We are *nyeldang*, meaning we have a special connection because we were born in the same year, the Year of the Snake. I stayed at his house as a servant for three years, so we often ate together when we were young. His mother would serve us corn mush on a single plate. The two of us always made sure that neither devoured all the food. When finished, I used to draw a line through the remnants sticking to the bottom of the plate. He would then lick the plate clean on one side, and I would lick clean the other side. This is how we ate together. We were the closest of friends.

One time we went to cut wood. Zangpo went to load his basket, while I stayed behind playing in the forest. When he came back carrying a heavy load of wood, I danced about making fun of him. Zangpo got angry and turned red. He dropped his basket, picked out a large piece of wood, and hurled it at me. Later, when we arrived home, he said, "Come here, my dear friend." All was forgiven. Another time we snuck into his parents' food repository where we knew there were sweets stashed deep in one of the storage chests. Since the storage chest was so deep, I held his legs while he reached down inside, grabbed some sweets, and ate to his heart's content. Then it was my turn, so he held my legs and I reached down inside. Suddenly my mother came and startled Zangpo so much that he let go of my legs. I fell with a thud, and then acted like I was dead. Boy, did we get in trouble that time!

The two of us were like brothers, we worked together, ate together, played together—we were inseparable. Later he became a monk and went to Dagkar Taso Monastery in Tibet. While he was at Dagkar Taso he told people of his friend back in the village. I also went to the monastery one time and had an audience with his teacher, the abbot. When the abbot heard where I was from, he exclaimed, "You must be the friend that my disciple often talks about!"

Those were some of the good memories from my youth. Most other memories are of hunger, hard work, and uncertainty. If only you knew how much I had suffered. Everybody used to say, "Poor Tashi, he is such a good person, but he is so unfortunate." I learned how to work hard, that is why things got better with time.

Despite his poverty, Tashi Döndrup is respected throughout the Nubri Valley because of his work ethic and honest, no-nonsense approach to life. He is a man who can clearly discern impure intentions behind the camouflage of public posturing, and who uses his razor-sharp intellect and innate sense for satire to poke fun at others, even those who hold positions of high status and prestige. An engaging personality has made Tashi Döndrup a popular man in Nubri and beyond. Yet Tashi was not born into a position commanding respect. From birth he occupied a socially ambiguous status. He was a *nyelu,* an illegitimate child. His father refused to recognize him as his son, and thus Tashi and his mother grew up in abject poverty working for others in exchange for food and shelter. Without land or animals, there was no prospect of Tashi getting married. How could he support a wife, let alone children? In the absence of the usual status markers—wealth, pedigree, or the red robes signifying a clerical vocation—Tashi overcame life's obstacles by virtue of his personality, moral fortitude, and solid work ethic.

The stories of Tashi and Pema Wangdu illustrate the importance for children in the villages of Nubri and Kutang to have some social standing. Pema Wangdu was a legitimate child, but somehow his father either never received an inheritance or was dispossessed by relatives because he married outside of the village. Whatever the case, Pema Wangdu's first years in his father's village were far from easy. He lived as a beggar, scorned by neighbors and forced to commandeer the water mill as a shelter at night. His high pedigree, asserted through clan affiliation, was useless under such circumstances. Perhaps it was poverty that turned him to a life of religion.

Tashi Döndrup's circumstances were quite different. His mother was a poor woman whose parents did not manage to arrange a match for her. The reasons behind her spinsterhood are vague—Tashi merely attributes it to poverty. In Nubri many women never have a chance to marry. Some remain single because of monastic ordinations, whereas others are excluded from the marriage market by the excess of available females resulting from the practice of polyandry. When two brothers take a single wife, simple arithmetic tells us there will be some women who will never find mates. The marriage market is made more competitive by virtue of dowries, whereby a bride can bring a much-needed infusion of land and animals into her husband's household. The poorer the woman, the less substantial her dowry, and the less chance she will have of getting married.

Unwed women lead lives of uncertainty. Working for others can put food on the table but provides no long-term security. Nevertheless, unwed women do have children, and they make many sacrifices for the well-being of their offspring. These were the circumstances into which Tashi Döndrup emerged from the womb.

In Nubri, no legal or social mechanisms require paternal support for children born out of wedlock. Thus, illegitimate children do not come in direct competition with their legitimate counterparts over scarce resources. Curiously, when Tashi was born, his father was not married but was living as a bachelor in his own home. Perhaps there was a large status difference between Tashi's father and mother, making marriage socially unacceptable. Regardless, the father's attitude toward his son was ambivalent, wavering between disdain and occasional affection. At one point the enterprising Tashi almost convinced his father to give him some property, but the proposal was eventually scuttled by the entrance of another woman into the equation and the birth of Tashi's legitimate half brother.

Although Tashi can joke about his status as a nyelu, deep inside he harbors some resentment. Growing up under his circumstances would embitter anyone, and he occasionally speaks about how unnecessary it was to endure so much pain and insecurity throughout his life. Most of the anger is reserved for his younger half brother, nicknamed Ox because his physical prowess contrasts so conspicuously with his limited intellectual capabilities. Boys inherit houses, fields, and cattle from their fathers, whereas girls inherit their mothers' jewels and some cooking implements. Balang, an only child, ended up with everything his father and mother owned, including a sturdy house, enough property to raise his own family, and long strings of semiprecious stones worth a lifetime of wages on the local market. He never married, however, and through time and mismanagement he ended up squandering most of his assets. He is now poor like Tashi.

A TEMPLATE FROM THE PAST

Tashi's tale reveals the hardships faced by a boy who has no father. But what happens when a child has no mother? Childbirth is especially hazardous for Nubri women. Birth, the dramatic and dangerous moment when a child enters the world, is anticipated with much trepidation. Complications can occur, often resulting in the tragic juxtaposition of birth causing death. One woman related to me the horror she experienced when her child's arm emerged first through the birth canal, and the trauma she endured as eventually the lifeless infant's body was manipulated until it could finally be brought forth. She survived, unlike many other women, yet since then she has been unable to conceive and is destined to remain in the socially ambiguous position of a childless wife. Such stories are common in Nubri, where medical facilities are next to nonexistent.

I had heard that my old friend, the venerable Tashi Dorje, was orphaned as an infant. So one day while visiting him in Kathmandu I asked him to tell the story of his birth and early years. The following events took place beginning in 1919:

My mother died just after I was born. I never even knew her. I was breastfed by the wives of my father's two brothers, both of whom had young daughters my age. For a month I would suckle from one of my aunts, then for a month I would suckle from the other aunt, and in this way I was able to drink milk for over a year.

I had one elder brother and four elder sisters. Our father was the community's head lama and patron of Pema Chöling Gomba. He had many hardships. My father said to his brothers, "I am going to have many problems raising these children." So he took another wife, a woman of advanced age. If he took one younger than him, many more children would have been born. Previously, this woman had been married to another man and bore him a child, but it died. After that she and her husband separated. She was free to become the wife of my father.

At the time there was a great lama from eastern Tibet staying in our village. He was my father's primary religious teacher. The lama asked, "Do you have any sons?" My father replied, "Yes, I have a son who is now staying with my brother." The lama advised, "Do not leave the child at the home of another family. Keep him at your own home once he has reached one year of age. If that child must suckle from a breast, it is best if he suckles from the breast of a *matsab* [substitute mother]. You should give him such milk, or the milk of a *dri* [female yak]. In my homeland, if a child has no mother, we feed him the milk of a dri."

Accepting the advice of his lama, my father brought me home, where he performed the first hair cutting ceremony. The lama performed the purification and life empowerment ceremonies, and my stepmother, the matsab, nursed me. It is said that they gave me the milk of a dri as well. For the first month or so, the milk of the substitute mother was weak and thin. After two or three months, her breast swelled like the breast of a real mother and she gave forth much milk. Although my relatives all called her matsab, I simply called her *ama*, or mother.

One of the noblemen in our village had to see for himself what kind of milk my substitute mother's breast produced. He came to her and said, "Squeeze that breast of yours." When she did as instructed, milk flowed forth. He proclaimed, "The mother who gave birth is the Chinese princess, the mother who did not give birth is the Tibetan princess." He then related the following tale about my ancestor, the great emperor Trisong Detsen [740–c. 798].

"Long, long ago, Trisong Detsen was born to the Chinese princess, one of his father's wives. Trisong Detsen's father also had a Tibetan wife who did not give birth to a son, so she stole the child and claimed it as her own. Several years later the Tibetan queen decreed that he was to be the lord of the land. One day many relatives and ministers came from China to meet the Chinese princess, so the king organized a great reception. Trisong Detsen's father was seated on his throne, with his wives to his right and left. The uncle of the Tibetan princess sat in one corner, while the uncle of the Chinese princess sat in the other corner. Trisong Detsen performed a miraculous deed, pouring *chang* [barley beer] into a large container and making the silver contained therein turn to gold. Everybody remarked, "Trisong Detsen, you are of the highest human form and have the most exalted name. You are the son of a most pure father and mother." His father said, "By performing such a miracle with that chang, you must now pour for our guests. Who is your real maternal uncle? Take that chang and serve your real maternal uncle first." From within the container of gold, Trisong Detsen scooped out a cup of chang and served the Chinese uncle. His father proclaimed, "From this day forth, your real maternal uncle is the Chinese one." Thus it became clear to all that the birth mother was the Chinese princess, and the substitute mother was the Tibetan princess. After telling this story, the nobleman of our village gave a white scarf and a coin to my substitute mother. "Take good care of this boy," he said.

Raising the motherless Tashi Dorje became a family affair. Members of the Ngadag clan in Sama are always ready to find parallels between their own lives and the lives of their famous predecessors. The past is a model for the present. Unlike Tashi Döndrup, Tashi Dorje had a relatively easy childhood, for he was, after all, a male member of the most prestigious clan in the entire valley. The importance of his survival extended beyond his immediate family to the community at large. In contrast, Tashi Döndrup had to fend for himself.

•   •   •

Many people born in Nubri never make it beyond infancy or childhood owing to misfortunes that lurk at every turn. Those who do survive are resilient and tenacious, boys and girls who through good fortune and a robust constitution begin to develop ambitions and plot out future courses of action. But in a society where family obligations often consume personal aspirations, the potential for disputes between parents and their children, or even between siblings, is everpresent. This is especially so when a boy wants to become a monk against his parents' wishes, as we shall see in the next chapter.

CHAPTER 4

Adolescent Discord

Family Needs versus Spiritual Deeds

A sore in the mouth must heal in the mouth,
A dispute in the house must be settled in the house.
Tibetan Proverb

RELIGIOUS ROLES AND THE INTERGENERATIONAL DILEMMA

To marry and procreate or to pursue the celibate lifestyle of religious renunciation—that is an age-old dilemma in the Tibetan world. Critical decisions such as these are firmly situated within the social and economic realities faced by a family and household. In some cases the interests of parents and children coincide. In others they clash, with disruptive consequences for all involved.

The following stories illustrate the theme of conflict between individual aspirations and social expectations. Three centuries ago Pema Döndrup fought vigorously to lead a life of celibacy and seclusion, a life dedicated almost exclusively to spiritual pursuits. His parents and uncle had other plans, however, for they envisioned him as a householder whose life would be devoted to the mundane activities of farming, herding, and fathering the next generation. A couple of centuries later Lopön Zangpo had no problem fulfilling his desire to be a monk. His parents were fully supportive, for they were wealthy and already had two sons who could manage the fields and herds. Ironically, Lopön Zangpo did not remain celibate for his entire life, contrary to the social expectations of a fully ordained monk. Lopön Zangpo's contemporary, Tashi Dorje, also wanted to become a monk. However, as a male member of the prestigious Ngadag descent lineage he had to marry to assure that the family line would remain intact for another generation. The three men had a common ambition—to become a monk—but they ended up taking entirely different paths along the life course.

PEMA DÖNDRUP RENOUNCES HIS HERITAGE

Pema Döndrup, you may recall, was born in Kutang in the year 1668. Under normal circumstances, his membership in a humble family of farmers would have rendered his vocation as a reclusive cleric virtually impossible, yet he managed his heart's desire anyway. Let's hear the story in his own words.

> My father's name is Pelchor, and my mother's name is Mani Kyid. I have two brothers and three sisters. I, Pema Döndrup, am the middle of the three boys. We lived in the village of Bi. Uncle Tsetan, my father's brother who lives in the village of Kog, did not have a son. When I was twelve, he came to our home and told my father, "I want an adopted son, so I really need this middle boy of yours." I replied, "I will not go, I want to practice religion." Then Father said to me, "You must go to Uncle Tsetan's home. If you do not go, you will not receive any inheritance of fields or other assets." Since my uncle was an influential man with possessions in both villages of Bi and Kog, I was powerless to refuse. I became his adopted son.
>
> Three years passed. One day I was tending Uncle's sheep at a place from where I could see Bi.[1] When I saw the village, I missed my mother and father; tears flowed from my eyes. But when I saw my other shepherd friends, I wiped the tears away and pretended not to cry. Another time I went to gather the sheep above Kog. Far down below in the settlement named Buryul, I could see my mother taking care of the cattle. I threw my basket from a rocky precipice, pretending that it accidentally fell down. As the basket rolled down, I followed behind pretending that I was looking for it. Eventually I reached a place on the cliff from where it was almost impossible to continue either downward or upward. I shouted until my mother and sister-in-law spotted me and came to the base of the cliff. Determined to be with my mother, I found a way down and went to Buryul with her.
>
> When I returned home to Bi, I came to realize that my very presence in Bi and Kog villages was the cause of my suffering. Therefore, I thought I should lead a life dedicated to religion.
>
> Once again I returned to Kog. I had been Uncle Tsetan's adopted son for three years. One day Uncle Tsetan's two son-in-laws said to him, "Your nephew is now fifteen years old, and you yourself are getting old. We must find him a bride." As they discussed this plan, I resolved not to engage in such worldly activities. I told them, "I will not live in the dreary world of suffering, neither in this lifetime nor the next. I will not take a wife." Uncle Tsetan replied, "What are you saying? Who will inherit my estate if you do

not become a worldly householder?" I told him that I felt no attachment to his estate. "Even if you wish to rejoin your parents," said Uncle Tsetan, "I prefer that you stay with me."

It is obvious that when one grieves, even the food one eats has no taste. When I was little I had great faith in anyone who put on red robes, thinking of him as a lama. As I recall the amusements of my childhood, they all revolved around religious themes such as reciting prayers, imitating the making of offerings, performing sacred dances, giving teachings while seated on a throne, making effigies, and giving instructions to many boys and girls. From my very childhood I imitated many religious practices. But now, when I was inclined to practice religion, I was powerless under the influence of my parents.

Once again I returned home to Bi where I stayed for four or five days. Father confronted me and said it was time to return to Kog. I declared, "I will not go! Doing so would go against my inclination. Since I am not a servant, and since my mind is not set on being there, I will not go." Father shouted, "Of course you are not a servant! You are the adopted son of Uncle Tsetan, and as such, you are the one who will receive his inheritance." I persisted, "Even if I am his designated heir, I will not go." Father then declared, "Since you are a son without a heart, you are no longer a resident of this house. If you do not accept Uncle's inheritance, you will receive nothing from the hands of your own parents, not even cups to drink from or plates to eat from."

Then Father accompanied me to the water mill. He screamed, "Get out of here!" So I departed feeling deep remorse. I came to the bridge at the edge of Bi. When my father came to look for me I had arrived at the far side of the bridge where I remained crying, unable to bring myself to walk further. Father became enraged when he saw me and yelled, "If you are going, then go!" When I did not budge, he threw a rock at me. He then turned around and left.

I turned my face to the ground and was reduced to tears. I thought about my father's wanting to send me to be another person's servant. If I received no good food whatsoever, then so be it. I would practice religion. If I received no inheritance, then so be it. I would practice religion and go on pilgrimage to the sacred realm of Tibet. I was young and unable to generate my inner strength. On the other hand, I simply dared not go back to Kog; but if I returned home to Bi, there would only be more quarrels.

My thoughts then turned to suicide, to seeking death in the river below. I rose, and after walking quite a long distance, I felt that somebody was holding onto the basket I was carrying and pulling from behind. I turned around to look, but nobody was in sight. Perhaps this was good fortune, for it gave me time to ponder my situation once again. I realized that even if I took my life in the river, regardless of whether the river carried me away or spit me out, suicide would not remedy my problems.

I returned to the edge of the bridge in a state of self-pity. By then Father had finished grinding grain at the water mill. He came out to see whether or not I had gone and saw me standing there weeping. Father then crossed over the bridge and commanded, "Don't cry!" He grabbed my hand and pulled me in the direction of Kog. I implored my father, "I don't think that you want to send me away to be another man's servant. Banish this thought from your mind." I realized that if this did not get through to him, then I would be powerless. Therefore I demanded that we not go back to Kog. Father was humbled and said, "Well then, let's go back home." He grasped my hand again and we returned to Bi. I was relieved once I was released from the obligation of being Uncle's adopted son.

In the same year, at the age of fifteen, I began to study religion. First of all, I went to greet the lama Orgyan Ngödrup, who gave me many teachings and initiations. I also received initiations and instructions from the lama Chökyi Gyaltsen in the village of Gyayul. When I was studying and searching for insight, I meditated during the day but understood nothing. Even though I gave up sleep at night and meditated in the cross-legged sitting position, I still understood nothing whatsoever. Thoughts of suffering kept arising spontaneously from who knows where. I just wasn't getting it. I came to realize that suffering is based on our failure to understand the true nature of existence. By clinging to our material existence we are locked in a continual cycle of suffering and fail to comprehend that everything is devoid of any enduring quality.

During the winter I remained in retreat at the village temple for three months. One day Pema Chöden, a religious friend older than I, said, "We should flee. The two of us will never obtain religious knowledge other than the practices of the householder lama if we remain here in the village." We discussed going to Central Tibet where we could seek teachings from a great lama. Otherwise, if we remained in the village, religious knowledge would always be beyond our reach.

My parents and relatives told me to work and practice religion at the same time. It seemed inevitable that I would be overpowered by the lust of attachment. During the day I went to work in the fields, and at night I stayed in the temple. Then one evening I said to my religious friend, "We must make up our minds to go. Everybody who truly wants religion goes to Tibet." My friend replied, "Although pilgrims are numerous in Tibet, no pilgrims from Kutang ever go there. You are still quite young. My father came from Tibet, so I do not have any inheritance. Your parents will say that I, the child of Tibetans, took you away to Tibet. This year I am twenty-three years old; the time has come for me to go." I told him, "Because I have reached twenty years of age, I am old enough to make my own decisions. It is not a moral offense on your part if we go to Tibet to acquire teachings. I didn't want to be the adopted son of my uncle, so I decided to choose the path of a religious life. As for provisions for our journey, we simply cannot ask our parents since they will not support us. We must steal food from them."

So we began to carry out the plan we had discussed. I did not go home, but stayed at the temple. When my parents went out to work during the day, I would steal a small measure of tsampa or wheat from their house and store it at the temple. When my parents and brothers admonished me for never coming to work, I told them that I received some morsels of food from performing religious ceremonies. They told me that there is no benefit in what I was doing; one cannot eat religion. Therefore, spending my time in such pursuits was just an empty dream. I did not reply and kept silent.

One day two friends approached us, wondering if we were ever going to depart for Tibet. We told them yes, that we were definitely going to see the great lamas. I told them, "If you two religious friends are going, then hide your provisions in the cleft of a rock." They asked if we could delay our departure for a day or two, and if we had any provisions. We replied that we had no money but did have a small amount of grain.

Since we had some chang (barley beer) to offer, we invited the lama of Gyayul to ask for his counsel since it was not right to hide our intentions from him. The lama gave us very good advice, saying, "Due to the vicissitudes of worldly suffering, I took the path of the householder lama. You two should go and study under the accomplished lamas in Tibet. By requesting teachings and wrapping yourselves in sacred garments, religious knowledge will come your way. Your parents will surely try to prevent you from going if they find out about your intentions. Therefore I will deny knowing anything about their sons." With this, the decision to undertake the journey was set. We were later joined by a fifth religious friend.

We prepared our small stash of flour. On the fifteenth day of the middle summer month of the Ox Year [1685], a date chosen according to astrological reckonings, we went to stay at the swampy area beside the bridge spanning the river. We were on our way to Tibet on a pilgrimage. Although we hadn't a single coin of money, we had some barley so we went to Prok where we ground the grain into flour at the water mill and dyed our clothing red like the monks do.

Since our journey was delayed for two or three days, word of the intentions of us five little monks got out and all the villagers began to talk about us. My elder brother caught up with me at Prok. "Don't go to Tibet!" he insisted. "You must return home! Mother and Father wept a lot, saying that you must come back." I remained firm and said, "I will not return home. Our parents have five other children to help them, so it really doesn't matter if I return or not. I will go to seek religion. My brother, you must return without me."

My brother observed, "You don't even have a woolen cloak." He then gave me a new blanket and said, "If you insist that you will not come home with me, then it is important that you go to Tibet. Here is a silver coin. I

want you to use it as a gift for the lamas so that you are able to acquire
religious teachings."

I knew then and there that I would miss my brother dearly. Tears flowed
from our eyes as he grasped my hand, joining it with his own, and bit his
lower lip. After wiping away his tears he said, "Little brother, be wary of
robbers and dogs. There is no need to be worried about your parents. We,
your brothers and sisters, can take care of them. But please return home
before our parents die." He turned and left, sobbing all the while. I also
grieved, for I was already beginning to miss my family.[2]

The story of Pema Döndrup's childhood illustrates the tension
between parental expectations and an adolescent's ambitions. In this
case the young Pema Döndrup opted out of the householder lifestyle
altogether. Instead of aspiring to become a married lama, a compromise
that he considered to be an inferior option, he set out to become a celibate monk. Once a man takes a vow of celibacy, he embarks on a life
course that is, ideally at least, removed from the distractions of everyday
life. The ultimate goal is to attain enlightenment, an achievement that
takes years of meditation in seclusion.

Throughout the Nubri Valley, and in fact in most Tibetan societies,
sons inherit their fathers' estates, which include land, animals, and
houses. If there are no sons in the family, a common solution is to adopt
a "substitute son" *(butsab),* who is generally a nephew. Pema Döndrup
became his Uncle Tsetan's adoptive son, an arrangement that was advantageous for his parents as well. Yet Pema Döndrup had his own ambitions, which led his father to state quite bluntly that if the boy renounced
his uncle's estate he could not return to his natal home and expect any
financial support. Part of his reasoning was perhaps that, with one son
out of the way, he needed only divide the family assets between the two
remaining sons. Pema Döndrup then caused a further scandal by refusing
to marry. Without a son of his own, that left poor Uncle Tsetan in a bind.

The final outcome of this dilemma is not found in the biography, but
is evident in land ownership and ritual sponsorship found in Kutang
today. The biography informs us that Pema Döndrup stood to inherit
his uncle's fields in Kog Village. It also describes how Pema Döndrup
later founded a temple in his natal village of Bi. During one of my visits
to Kog locals proudly pointed to some fertile, gently sloping fields situated in a prime location close to the houses of the village. These were
referred to as "Pema Döndrup's fields," and are owned by his descendants who reside in Bi. One of these descendants, a man nicknamed

Dokdok (Chubby) in reference to his plump face and wobbly gait as a toddler, took me on a tour one day of the temple founded by his forefather. The temple, managed exclusively by members of Pema Döndrup's clan, contains a small yet strikingly detailed image of the renowned ancestor. Kog and Bi are separated by difficult terrain that takes several hours to traverse. Nevertheless, as Dokdok informed me, the annual rites celebrated at Pema Döndrup's temple are still funded by the grain produced on Uncle Tsetan's former fields in Kog. Sharecroppers in Kog farm the land, keeping half the grain and giving half to the temple in Bi, where it is distilled into arak to be imbibed by the ritual participants. Since nobody else stood to inherit Uncle Tsetan's land, this remarkable legacy means that the fields would either be inherited by Pema Döndrup or given to the temple he founded. Pema Döndrup's fields in Kog have remained in trust for nearly three centuries.

The story does not end with Uncle Tsetan's inheritance. As you will see in a subsequent chapter, the misfortunes of Pema Döndrup's family continually intruded on his quest for a solitary existence. Both of Pema Döndrup's brothers died. The elder brother left behind a widow and two young children. Afterward Pema Döndrup's parents approached him at his meditation retreat and begged him to take his brother's widow as his own bride and live the life of a married lama. The narrative alludes to the fact that Pema Döndrup spent time in the village household with his sister-in-law, but is ambiguous about whether or not he acted as her husband. He had taken a vow of celibacy, but did he break that sacred commitment? What, indeed, are the consequences of breaking a vow of celibacy?

CELIBACY AND SUCCESSION

Tibetan society, like any other, is permeated with cultural contradictions. Whereas nuns who become pregnant are summarily expelled from the order, monks who are exposed for having amorous trysts often carry on without serious repercussions. To a great extent this seeming contradiction is a reflection of gender attitudes in Tibetan society. Women are considered to be more intelligent than men, yet less able to control their passions and hence less suited for the life of contemplation. When a monk and nun have an affair, generally the woman is faulted for beguiling the man into abandoning his vow of celibacy.

In Nyingmapa communities like Sama there is a compelling precedent for male religious practitioners to procreate. Married lamas, after all, occupy the pinnacle of the social order, whereas female religious practitioners are not held in particularly high esteem. Therefore, it comes as no surprise that nuns in Sama who become pregnant often flee the village rather than face a future of shame and humiliation. Meanwhile, monks sometimes carry on open affairs, yet continue to wear the red robes with few consequences beyond exposing themselves to gossip. The advantages of being a male and of having a high social status are evident in the following example of a celibate monk who decided that, like his married lama counterparts, he needed a son and disciple of his own.

Lopön Zangpo, born in the Year of the Snake (1929), is blessed with an unparalleled intellect matched by a lively sense of humor. His life story is interesting in that he is a rare example of a child from Nubri who was permitted, even encouraged, by his parents to pursue the path of a monk. Unlike Pema Döndrup, Lopön Zangpo was born to a prosperous father who wielded considerable financial and political influence in the valley. Furthermore, he was the youngest of three children. Village regulations in Sama stipulate that no more than two brothers can marry a single bride. Therefore, the father of these three sons was able to remove one child from the inheritance equation by permitting Lopön Zangpo to become a monk. His elder brothers then married polyandrously, so their father's estate was passed on intact from one generation to the next. The parents thus succeeded in assuring that their household's affluent status perpetuated through time.

Lopön Zangpo is now known as Rinpoche (Precious One), a term of respect reserved for the most highly respected clerics in the Tibetan world. Most people act with tremendous deference in his presence, addressing him awkwardly in seldom-used honorific terms. His lofty position was achieved not as a birthright, as is the case with the lamas of the Ngadag lineage, but through years of dedication to Buddhist teachings.

Lopön Zangpo spends most of his time praying, reading, meditating, and performing rituals in his hermitage situated at Pema Chöling Gomba. He rarely ventures down to the village. Yet he took a curious interest in me, the resident foreigner. Every day, as I sat recording field notes in my makeshift office at the gomba, a young monk would appear at the entranceway to the courtyard. He would remain silent, perhaps intrigued by the clatter of the manual typewriter. Only when I looked up from the task at hand would he incline his head in the direction of Lopön Zangpo's residence, hold that posture for a few seconds, and then dash away. I correctly surmised this to be an invitation to have tea with the distinguished Rinpoche.

I quickly came to appreciate the daily dialogues with Lopön Zangpo. His exalted position and the official deportment during our initial encounter led me to believe that all of our interactions would remain formal. As time passed, however, his engaging sense of humor broke through his aloof demeanor. When in a good humor—which was most of the time—he would tell stories, sometimes mockingly imitating the voices of fellow villagers as he poked fun at their mundane bunglings. Lopön Zangpo's anecdotes often closed with a punch line, quite literally. As he neared the end of a story he would lean forward as if to impart words of wisdom in confidence, then his eyes would brighten with a roguish glint as he delivered a sturdy blow to my shoulder with the open heel of his hand. The knock would invariably unsettle my balance, causing me to roll about like an egg with folded limbs still tucked beneath me in the cross-legged sitting position. Lopön Zangpo's fondness for levity left me with a perpetually bruised shoulder. Retaliation was out of the question.

Lopön Zangpo was an important link to the outside world. He had a short-wave radio, which pulled in Tibetan-language broadcasts from the refugee communities in India as well as state-sponsored programs from Lhasa. It is one thing for a man to sit in a remote Himalayan valley and listen to world news. It is an entirely different matter for him to recognize the magnitude of momentous events in faraway lands. He spoke with competence about Middle East tensions after informing me of Yitzhak Rabin's assassination in November 1995. When the news came through of Deng Xiaoping's death in February 1997, he reflected on the immense economic changes that had transpired in China under the deceased leader's tenure. True to form, Lopön Zangpo was also fond of making jokes about the ethical flaws of world leaders. One time he summoned me to his home, greeted me with a disinterested grunt, and motioned with a curt gesture to my usual seat by the hearth. He sat down, adjusted his robes against the cold, and then leaned forth to gaze at me with his penetrating eyes. Without flinching, he asked in a solemn tone, "Tell me, who is this Monica [Lewinsky] woman?" Lopön Zangpo was then convulsed with hearty laughter as he punched my shoulder, sending me sprawling across the floor once again.

My reclusive friend had lived up to the ideals of a celibate monk, or so I thought. The young monk who shared his home and helped with daily chores was a mere disciple, or so I thought. One day Lopön

Zangpo confided the truth: "He is my son," said the venerated old man, with a serious face. He then revealed the mother's identity. I was shocked, for she was the wife of another disciple of his. Villagers confirmed that the seminal event had transpired surreptitiously while the husband was away pasturing his herd in the highlands.

One could easily conclude that this was merely an episode whereby a celibate man succumbed to long-suppressed temptations of the flesh. However, subsequent events contradict such an assumption and make it clear that Lopön Zangpo had made a calculated decision. As soon as the child was born, Lopön Zangpo proclaimed the boy to be his own. He openly admitted paternity and expressed a desire to raise the child himself. The aggrieved husband bore little if any grudge, perhaps because the perpetrator was his teacher and a man of superior social rank, or perhaps because the two had genuine affection for each other. The mother and her husband offered to nurture the boy at their home for a year or so until it came time to wean the infant. Afterward Lopön Zangpo, with the assistance of his sister, who is a nun, took over the task of raising his son. The toddler has grown into an intellectually gifted young man who has received the most direct and intensive religious training of any monk in the entire valley.

The case of Lopön Zangpo is interesting in part because of the widespread acceptance of his transgression against an inviolable vow of celibacy. Few people question his conduct; after all, he is the most highly respected religious figure in Nubri, a man known throughout the Tibetan world as a formidable intellect and master teacher. Undoubtedly, the fact that Sama is a place where married practitioners are the norm rather than the exception moderates how people view celibacy in a religious context. One day the child will inherit his elderly father's temple, residence, and collection of religious texts—an event that could never transpire if Lopön Zangpo had not recognized the boy as his own flesh and blood, and if villagers had not accepted this turn of events with typical forbearance.

"MY FATHER MADE ME MARRY"

Tashi Dorje, who is a few years older than Lopön Zangpo, was denied the opportunity of becoming a monk. In his case, the decision was rooted in the necessity of assuring that a prestigious lineage, the Ngadag, remained intact. You may recall that his mother died when he was born, so he had been raised by a substitute mother.

"Did you ever want to become a celibate monk?" I asked Tashi Dorje during one of our frequent discussions about the history of his descent lineage. The elderly lama with tightly braided gray hair was dressed in the red and yellow garments of a religious specialist. We sat in his light and airy room at a monastery situated on a hill overlooking the Kathmandu Valley. The setting seemed a perfect metaphor for the division envisioned by Buddhists between the realms of spiritual practice and worldly suffering. Tashi Dorje lives in relative serenity, surrounded by the sounds of monastic chants and the smells of ritual incense. The profusion of foul odors from the floor of the valley does not penetrate to the monastery level. Here there is no squalor, only thatched-roofed houses and a footpath winding between terraced fields, a reminder of this valley's agrarian roots. The air circulating through the monastery is relatively pure and the vegetation green and lush, in marked contrast to the squalid scene below where the streets, mostly pitted alleys, teem with life—vendors hawking their wares, dilapidated vehicles noisily spewing noxious fumes, and myriad stray animals (sacred cows, mangy dogs, rodents, clouds of insects) all foraging on mounds of rotting refuse that litter the neighborhoods and marketplaces. Kathmandu is no longer the quaint and tranquil town that attracted hippies and adventure seekers back in the 1960s.

Tashi Dorje removed the ornate silver lid from the top of his white ceramic cup, took a long sip of tea, and then chuckled as he recalled the distant days of his youth.

> When I was young, I wanted to be a monk. While watching our father perform rituals, my brothers, sisters, and our friends from the neighborhood got the idea to act out our own religious ceremonies. Behind our house was an overhanging rock. That was our temple! When a group of children gathered there, we would make offerings and recite prayers. All of the children took part in our game.
>
> I could not read or write before I was eight. Due to the death of my mother, I was kept at home under the care of my grandfather. He thought it was best that I wait a few years to see if any religious inclinations developed. Then one day my grandfather—he used to be the head lama of the village, you know—performed my initial hair cutting ceremony. This was my first step toward becoming a monk. My grandfather gave me a new name, Tashi Dorje. Tashi comes from Tashi Namgyal, one of my ancestors from long ago. He was the first lama in our lineage to settle in Sama. They say that Dorje was given to me because it was part of my grandfather's name. From age eight I began learning the thirty consonants of our alphabet and the system of spelling through recitation.

Then when I was sixteen [around 1934 or 1935], I went to Dagkar Taso Monastery together with my elder brother, Tinley Gyatso, and another relative. The monastery was in Tibet, on the other side of the mountains. It only takes a few days to get there from Sama. Our father sent us. Tinley Gyatso already had a wife; I was unmarried. At Dagkar Taso we requested teachings from the abbot, whose name was Rigzen Tinley Tsewang. I consider him to be my root lama. In the past he and my father used to exchange teachings. Sometimes my father was the teacher, and sometimes the abbot was the teacher. In this way they developed a very close relationship. Rigzen Tinley Tsewang taught my brother and me for about two months. After that we returned to Nubri, but from time to time we would go back for more religious instructions. I kept going until he passed away. He was not my only teacher, for my father and grandfather gave me many religious instructions. Both of them were married lamas, as I was later to become.

From the time I was young, I had a wish to be a celibate monk at Dagkar Taso Monastery. However, there was a nobleman from the village of Prok who had a daughter. My father was looking for a bride for me who was from a good family, so he urged the nobleman, "Please give us your daughter as a bride for my son." He agreed to do as my father requested, for all of the man's sons had died. Consequently, it was important for him to marry his daughter into a prominent family like ours. But there was a problem. A lama had already performed the first hair cutting ceremony for the girl, so she had been initiated as a nun. But this lama said to my father, "Although the headman's daughter has become a nun, she does not practice religion. It is therefore acceptable for your son to take her as a bride." So we got married.

At the time I was twenty-one and she was fifteen. Many people came to the wedding; that is the custom of our land. Taking a bride is by no means easy. We must first make confessions to the lamas and give offerings at the temple. It is not appropriate to hold the wedding before completing certain rituals. This is our custom. Even householder lamas like me must observe these protocols. Fully ordained monks, on the other hand, do not have to go through all of this, for they are not supposed to get married!

He had a twinkle in his eye as he concluded his story.

Perhaps the passage of time has tempered Tashi Dorje's disposition toward the fact that his father would not permit him to become a celibate monk. Or perhaps he understands all too clearly his role in a genealogical continuum that links the illustrious emperors of Tibetan history with his Ngadag clan members in Nubri. Tashi Dorje's father was the head lama for the entire village, and therefore the highest-ranking member of the Ngadag clan. According to the rule of primogeniture, Tashi Dorje's elder brother, Tinley Gyatso, was destined to assume the position of head lama on his father's death. Just as critical, Tinley Gyatso was expected to fulfill the duty of procreating the next generation of lamas. Nevertheless, as we have seen, mortality is a force to be reckoned with in Nubri. Parents must consider the very real threat of premature death, both their own and those of their children, in their long-term strategies for assuring family continuity. If Tinley Gyatso were to die before producing an heir and if Tashi Dorje were to become a fully ordained monk who had sworn an irrevocable vow of celibacy, the family line would be threatened with extinction. To a certain extent Tashi Dorje's marriage was a contingency plan for perpetuating the lineage.

As it turned out, Tashi Dorje's elder brother did die prematurely. He passed away three years after his wife gave birth to Karma, a male successor and the next in line for succession. Karma, however, was a mere child when his father passed away, in no way capable of managing the complex religious and economic affairs that were required of Pema Chöling Gomba's head lama. Therefore, Tashi Dorje stepped into the breach and acted as regent for twenty years until Karma came of age. If Karma had not survived, the Ngadag lineage would have been in trouble.[3]

NUBRI AND THE TRANSNATIONAL WEB OF BUDDHISM

Impediments to becoming a monk inevitably arise in a society where household labor and the perpetuation of one's descent lineage are primary concerns. Parents normally are the ones who decide who among their children will become religious practitioners and who will remain as worldly householders. In bygone days many parents in Nubri were reluctant or even unable to send their sons to distant monasteries in Tibet, since doing so required substantial donations to the lamas in exchange for religious instructions. That is not to say that the monasteries were the exclusive domain of the wealthy. In traditional Tibetan society many commoners had to send a son to join the religious order as one of several obligations incurred by leasing a monastery's agricultural land. Monasteries would also accommodate illegitimate children or orphans who had no other means of support. Nevertheless, those children who had the financial backing of their parents were probably more likely to excel in the institutional setting, given their enhanced ability to gain access to the teachings of their masters.

The institutional center of the Tibetan religious world shifted in the 1960s when China began systematically to dismantle most features of organized religion in Tibet. Many famous teachers fled across the Himalayas and reestablished their monastic traditions in exile. This coincided with a time when interest in non-Christian religious traditions was on the rise in the West, and cheap air travel suddenly made Buddhist masters accessible to a new host of spiritual seekers. Many of the monasteries rebuilt in exile were made possible by funds from various sources, including affluent Tibetan carpet merchants and pious Western Buddhists searching for merit and meaning in their own lives. One such institution, Ngedön Öseling Monastery, is where Tashi Dorje now lives.[4]

Tashi Dorje's wife passed away after giving birth to their only daughter. She was raised in a religious milieu and eventually became the second wife (after the first had died) of the famous Tibetan lama Orgyan Tulku, one of the preeminent masters of the Nyingmapa school. She bore a son, Tsoknyi Rinpoche, who was recognized as a reincarnate lama and who founded Ngedön Öseling on a hill overlooking Kathmandu. Tashi Dorje is not the only Nubri resident to grace the halls of this monastery. A large number of the young monks who cavort on the grassy hilltop were dispatched from Nubri by their parents.

The recent proliferation of monasteries in exile has led to the emergence of new connections between the highlands of Nepal, Tibetan religious institutions, and the West, connections that are strongly influenced by emerging demographic trends. When many of the exile monasteries were founded Tibetan refugees were having numerous children, enough to supply the burgeoning monasteries. Today, however, the exile birthrate has plummeted concurrently with rising education and economic prosperity. Young Tibetan parents now seek secular education for their children. The combination of a low birthrate with the evolving ideal that monasticism is a matter for individuals and not their parents to decide means that the exiles no longer supply the transplanted monasteries with a requisite number of monks.

Meanwhile, birthrates in the ethnically Tibetan enclaves of highland Nepal remain high. To illustrate the fertility discrepancy, consider that Tibetans in exile are now experiencing on average 1.2 births per woman, whereas in Nubri the fertility rate varies by village from 5.3 to 7.0 births per woman.[5] The declining birthrate among exiles has led to a recruitment drive in the ethnically Tibetan hinterlands of Nepal, in places such as Nubri where secular education is not an option and where the economy is based on agro-pastoral activities, such that having many children still makes sense. With the rise of well-endowed exile monasteries, a new option has arisen for managing family sizes and compositions after children have been born.

Today the Tibetan monasteries in Nepal and India are more egalitarian. Sending a son to a monastery does not require that parents make a large donation, in part because much of the child's education is being underwritten by donations from Western devotees. Nowadays parents from Nubri cite cultural reasons, such as the accumulation of merit and good fortune, for sending their sons into a clerical vocation. In addition, they make it quite clear that economic concerns fare prominently in the decision-making process. For one, in a social setting where all brothers have an equal right to inheritance of the parental estate, designating one son to be a monk removes him from the inheritance equation. The cost of his upbringing is subsidized by the monastery, which in turn is subsidized by foreign patrons. To further sweeten the deal, through proper training a child can eventually start to generate income of his own by performing rituals for the benefit of wealthy refugee householders in Kathmandu. Much of this cash ends up back with the parents. Today more than ever, social and economic life in places such as Nubri are linked with the rest of the world in subtle yet surprising ways.

BUDDHISM IN NUBRI: CONTINUITY OR DEGENERATION?

Not all aspiring clerics end up in the refugee monasteries of Kathmandu. Many of those who remain behind represent a special type of religious figure in Nubri society: physically or mentally disabled monks and nuns. I remember my first meeting with one such individual. As I strolled through the forest behind Pema Chöling Gomba, a young man approached me. A woven bamboo basket dangled from a rawhide strap slung over one shoulder. His body swayed from side to side in exaggerated motions, evidence of his misshapen legs. I had already noted the shaven head and the red robes of a monk; when he came closer, a childlike grin crossed a whiskered face, which drooped curiously to one side as if he had suffered a stroke. He held out his hand and implored, "Shim shim?" This is the term used by children when begging sweets from foreigners. He exhibited the maturity of someone half his age, underscored by the fact that he was out collecting dried dung for fuel—a task performed exclusively by children.

Despite his disabilities, Gyaltsen was capable of reciting sacred formulas from texts, and hence could fulfill the most fundamental duties of a religious practitioner. One day I saw him sitting on a neighbor's porch chanting rhythmically as he read aloud from a text positioned on a low table in front of him. Such competence afforded him a modicum of respect in the village, and assured that he had a place in the social order. Although understandably he was never anybody's first choice to perform such duties, people were happy to give him a chance when most other ritual practitioners were unavailable.

Mentally and physically disabled monks and nuns are individuals who did not choose the religious vocation on their own but were placed there by parents. Tashi Dorje once explained to me, "Parents derive benefits by giving their children to the monastery because monks and nuns perform religious deeds. They pray for the good of all sentient beings. This includes one's parents, so their prayers can bring many benefits to their families. No religious blessings whatsoever are gained by parents who choose householders' lives for their children. Such children will never achieve peace of mind, since they engage in worldly, as opposed to religious, activities."

The explanation makes sense, but it still puzzled me that nearly every disabled child in Nubri wears the monastic robes. I asked Tashi Dorje to explain this social phenomenon. He said,

> Well, when such a child is young, people believe that he will not survive. Many feel that giving him to the monastery will cause the disabling affliction to be driven away. But even if you teach these children religion, how will they ever know what is being taught? Many people rationalize that even if a disabled child cannot perform manual work, at least he or she can be beneficial to the family by serving in a religious capacity. Sadly, no matter how many times they bow before the feet of the lama, most disabled children never get better. But there is another reason. In our village the lamas who perform the hair cutting ceremony for initiating monks and nuns can then compel those children to work for them. This is the lama's right as the one who performs the initiation ceremony.

Tashi Dorje's response underscores the pragmatic side of Tibetans by alluding to an economic dimension of relationships between masters and their disciples. Monks and nuns who are initiated by a lama in Nubri enter into a lifelong economic contract with their spiritual advisor. In exchange for basic training in reading, writing, and liturgy, they are obliged to work in the lama's fields or help herd his animals for a specified number of days each year. This old custom of corvée labor, called *ulag,* is a relic of past times. One outcome is that lamas have a distinct economic advantage over their worldly householder counterparts.[6] By virtue of ulag, lamas are able to command much larger labor forces than their household sizes would otherwise allow. The additional hands mean, for instance, more grass can be cut for winter fodder and hence a larger herd of bovines can be sustained. In all Tibetan societies, both past and present, religion and economics are closely intertwined.

All of these considerations may tempt one to conclude that today's somewhat relaxed attitude toward monks and nuns in Nubri indicates a long-term degeneration of local religious culture. Outside observers generally have an idealized version of what Tibetan Buddhist culture is supposed to look like. When social realities do not conform to such expectations, many people have a tendency to assume that processes of modernization and globalization have somehow encroached on and eroded a more pristine cultural past.[7]

Historical evidence, however, suggests that religious practices in Nubri have perhaps never lived up to the high standards set by the philosophical and rational ideals of formal monastic Buddhism. Commenting on Nubri's religious milieu nearly three hundred years ago, Pema Döndrup lamented:

> Religious practitioners who attain the threshold of their abilities are uncommon. Although I have many male and female disciples who are as numerous as the throngs of people encountered in a nomadic encampment, faithful disciples are as scarce as stars in the day. On the other hand, disciples who desire material things and new friends are as plentiful as stars in the night sky. Disciples who face difficulties and bear the burdens of hardships are few, whereas disciples who are inattentive and who fool around are abundant. Rare are the disciples who are willing to sacrifice their own lives for religion or who faithfully guard the pledges to their lamas as fervently as they guard their own lives. Male students disregard the lama's instructions and instead aim to please their sponsors in order to get food and clothing. As for nuns, they listen to whatever their parents say in order to get food and clothing. There are none here who practice religion to its fullest extent.[8]

A few years later, Pema Döndrup's disciple Pema Wangdu expressed concern over the continuance of what he considered to be heretical practices in these highland communities. Around 1730 he initiated a campaign to prohibit animal sacrifice, a custom considered by Buddhists to be about the most sinful means to appease a deity. Pema Wangdu commented,

> All practice in the area is heretical. People hunt the wild animals in the mountains. In the valleys all the goats and sheep are given to the knife. Even the pure protectors of this realm have succumbed to the power of the

cutting of life. In each part of the valley there is a practitioner of the black arts. Through evil thoughts, everybody—males, females, young and old—have adopted the heretical views. During festivals people sacrifice animals to the local deities. Although we live in the sacred region of Kutang, this narrow gorge resembles the barbarous edge of darkness.[9]

Animal sacrifice in a Buddhist community? This of course sounds positively antithetical to the compassionate stance of the Buddha's philosophy. "Thou shalt not kill" is after all a central tenet of the religion. Yet the Nubri Valley is a place where Buddhism and indigenous traditions have coexisted for centuries in a relationship exemplified by compromise. Assuming that sociocultural transformations in Nepal's hinterlands have commenced only recently, with the opening of the country to a global world system, is misleading. Such conjecture projects an unchanging past onto a society that is characterized by persistent and dynamic change. Ironically, those actions envisioned as efforts to preserve Tibetan culture—for example, by subsidizing a monastery—are having an immense impact on Nubri culture. The fact that monasticism is an option that is more accessible and coveted than at any time in the past changes many aspects of Nubri social life, from village-level religious practices to postnatal strategies for managing one's family size and composition. In contrast to the past, when men such as Pema Döndrup had to take considerable risks to embark on a life course as a monk, today as many as one in five children from Nubri have that option decided by their parents.

• • •

Whether born rich or poor, robust or disabled, individuals are confronted with social roles that, at least in the early years, are dictated by parents. Despite the obstacles of familial obligations and cultural expectations, individuals do rebel against the system, as in the case of Pema Döndrup. In some cases these nonconformists end up achieving remarkable deeds that become part and parcel of a communal memory. For some it is necessary to leave home, embark on a heroic adventure, and then return a changed person who can transform society. Expulsion, ordeal, and reunification: the epic quest in search of redemption is a common theme throughout the world. For Tibetans, pilgrimage in search of sacred knowledge and timeless truths—the focus of the next chapter—represents the ultimate rite of passage, the journey toward achieving a secure and respected position within society.

CHAPTER 5

Growing Through Travel

The Pilgrimage for Knowledge and Prestige

Better to drink arak with a heart of good intention
Than to go on pilgrimage with a heart of evil intent.

Tibetan Proverb

THE PERILS OF BEING SPIRITUALLY UNPREPARED

"Taaa-shi! TAAAAA-SHIIIII!" I bellowed with all the force my lungs could muster, scolding myself for having gotten lost in this forsaken corner of Nepal. The vegetation on the steep hillside ranged from tangled, impenetrable thickets to widely spaced fir trees, their gnarled roots protruding from the thin soil. Immediately above loomed a rocky precipice that was beyond my capability to scale, especially with a full backpack, while one hundred feet below me the slope seemed to drop off into an abyss. On the other side of the river the clustered homes of a village looked like boulders strewn among the patchwork of fields. The sheer verticality of the landscape gave the illusion that with one giant bound I could easily land on somebody's roof in the village below. This was not turning out to be an idyllic stroll in the countryside.

Tashi and I were on pilgrimage to a temple sequestered deep in a side valley of Nepal. According to legend, this valley was concealed long ago by Padmasambhava, the eighth-century saint who helped introduce Buddhism to Tibet.[1] Foreseeing that future calamities would engulf the land, Padmasambhava enshrouded several valleys and decreed that they could be opened only in the future, when war and social upheavals brought forth the need for refuges where Tibetan society could be safeguarded. Only people with pure motivation and highly developed spiritual capacities would be able to gain access to these sacred locales. All others, blinded by their own spiritual ignorance, would consistently fail to find the doorways to the hidden valleys.

Tashi and I were venturing into one such hidden valley, a place for which a devout frame of mind and the purest of intentions are prerequisites for entry. While stumbling about, lost and forlorn, I could not help but wonder if obstacles had been erected in my path due to a combination of my own obstinacy and lack of piety. Locals believed that those who are not mentally prepared for the journey are destined to flounder about dazed and confused, never able to find the entrance to the hidden valley. Was this to be my own fate?

At the last resting spot Tashi and I had had one of our frequent spats. Like brothers, we were devoted companions yet had a tendency to annoy each other. We had argued over the fact that he'd caught me flirting with a local the night before, a woman he considered to be of ill repute. Always the protective elder brother, he did not refrain from expressing his opinions about my behavior. When our verbal dispute began to wane I arose in a fury, hefted my pack onto my shoulders, and stalked off, vowing to continue the conversation at our next resting place. In retrospect this was a very bad idea. The seldom-used path to our destination split off from the main trail and was well concealed by foliage. I ended up following a seasonal herding trail that dead-ended on the slope where I now found myself.

Two hours had passed since I'd left Tashi's company. The situation was becoming a bit nerve-racking. "TAAAAA-SHIIIII!" I yelled once again. The only reply was a sequence of echoes receding in the distance. I sat down somewhat apprehensively to contemplate the next move. Suddenly, I heard Tashi's voice calling from above—faint and distant to be sure, but unmistakably his voice. I hollered back and awaited his response. Through trial and error I could pinpoint his relative position high above. I commenced climbing upward, skirted some cliffs, bashed my way through brambles, and eventually emerged on a steep, grassy plain. A trail, winding back and forth in a series of switchbacks to the summit of a ridge, cut a swath through the precipitous meadow. On the crest sat several white *chöten*, beacons for the weary (and in my case lost) traveler. These sacred objects marked the path into the hidden valley.

Tashi's willowy figure was silhouetted against the white cumulus clouds beyond the chöten. I could distinctly see his arm waving back and forth as he called out my name once again. The climb was steep, but at least the destination was now clear. Sticky with sweat, bleeding from numerous nicks, and out of breath, I eventually reached Tashi.

He sat near the edge of a vertical rock face that plummeted to a raging torrent a thousand feet below. I surveyed the surroundings and, as on many occasions, marveled at the people who manage to make a living in this rugged terrain. My musings were abruptly terminated. When he is agitated, Tashi's verbal invectives can be bitter. A litany of recriminations and rebukes now spewed through his toothless gums. The tongue-lashing seemed interminable, and had the desired result of whittling my ego down to its most self-effacing core. I knew that I fully deserved this scolding.

Finally, Tashi turned despondent. "What if you had fallen off a cliff?" he appealed. "I was on the verge of jumping off this cliff myself. I thought, what if Geoff is dead? Everybody back home will say that I killed you and took your money!"

"Tashi," I sheepishly implored, "everybody knows we are like brothers. Nobody would accuse you of committing such an act."

He turned to me with a glare that penetrated to the back of my skull and scorned with derision. "You don't know the people of Nubri. You know nothing of that place!"

Thus began our pilgrimage. As the anger and excitement of the moment subsided, we once again settled into our comfort zone as devoted companions. I extracted a plastic jug filled with arak from my pack and sloshed some of the clear fluid into our wooden traveling cups. We had distilled this particular batch especially for the trip. To the Tibetans of Nubri, a journey without arak is not a true journey. The liquid turned to fire in our bellies, bringing relief to my aching limbs and ego and smoothing the frayed edges of my friend's ornery disposition. Life was not as bad as it had seemed to be a mere hour ago. We still had another five or six hours of trekking to reach the evening's destination, but at least Tashi knew that he now had me on a short leash.

Before arriving in Nepal I had read a fourteenth-century account describing the divine qualities and natural beauty of the hidden valley we were now entering. As we discovered, the text did not exaggerate. In this sanctuary monkeys frolicked in the boughs of ancient fir trees that strove upward as if to compete with the grandeur of the surrounding peaks. We hiked through a forest of rhododendrons in full bloom, becoming immersed in pink and red blossoms that fluttered gently to the ground to form a soft carpet beneath our feet. The trail crossed over a rickety bridge uniting two sides of a gorge that plunges five hundred feet straight down to a river below. As we approached a temple sequestered deep within the hidden valley, the trail wound through an open pasture where wild mountain goats grazed unperturbed by the presence of humans.

Along the way we encountered images carved in stone of lamas who had sought, and found, solitude in this extraordinary valley. Through a veneer of lichen we could discern the figure of a bearded man on one large, flat stone perched against the hillside. The inscription read, "Homage to the root lama, Pema Döndrup." History was alive in this valley. Pema Döndrup had spent years here residing in various shelters, enhancing his spiritual capacity through solitary meditation, and in the process assuring his stature as the preeminent religious figure of the time in this corner of the Himalayas. Yet before Pema Döndrup could attain his position of prestige, he had to establish a foundation for his own spiritual practice. He needed to undertake a pilgrimage in quest of ordinations, initiations, and basic religious instructions from the most distinguished lamas in his religious lineage.

PEMA DÖNDRUP'S FLIGHT TO FREEDOM

Pilgrimages are undertaken by Tibetans for a variety of reasons.[2] Some people visit holy sites to pray for specific wishes, such as health, prosperity, or even the ability to conceive a child. Others have more pious concerns, seeking to advance their religious practice by tapping into the energy of a place that pulsates with spiritual power. Many people consider a pilgrimage to be the highlight of their life. One elderly man from Nubri proudly displays outside his home a poster of Bodhgaya, the site in India where the Buddha Shakyamuni attained enlightenment. The poster, carefully enshrouded in clear plastic for protection against the elements, is fastened to the end of a *mani* wall—a long structure made up of flat stones inscribed with images of deities, lamas, and sacred scriptures. Each day after his chores are complete, the man circumambulates the wall and the poster. The physical act and attendant prayers remind him of his pilgrimage undertaken several years ago, and reinforces the vow that he made then to refrain from smoking.

We left Pema Döndrup in the last chapter just as he was bidding his brother farewell before setting forth on his great pilgrimage to Tibet. By remaining in Kutang, he and his friend rationalized that they could aspire to no more than householder lama status. If they truly sought enlightenment, they would have to seek instruction from Buddhist masters who resided outside their remote valley.

Travel in Tibet has never been easy. Distances are immense and settlements widely dispersed on the vast plateau. To complicate matters,
the two young travelers came from the very fringe of the Tibetan cultural world, speaking only the Kutang dialect, which was (and still is)
unintelligible to Tibetans. The mere fact of being Buddhists did not
automatically grant them access to Tibetan society. In fact, Tibetans do
not consider people from Kutang to be their ethnic kin. Kutang is
described in eighteenth-century Tibetan sources as lying in Mon, a
name reserved for what Tibetans consider to be the barbarous intermediary realm between the refined civilizations of Tibet and urban Nepal.
People from Mon were derided in former times for being ignorant,
impudent, and uncouth. To the Tibetans, Pema Döndrup was a foreigner despite his claim of descent from a Tibetan clan. He was an outsider striving to gain entrance to a world that was at once familiar and
strange.

Another impediment for the young men was that they were paupers.
Religious mendicants in the Buddhist tradition are permitted, and even
expected, to beg for food; that is how many pilgrims sustain themselves
on long journeys. In past times, however, the acquisition of religious
teachings often required donations to the lamas. Tangible limits to religious advancement were prescribed in the hierarchal Tibetan social
system by wealth and status. Even so, the system was by no means
inflexible. Persistence and aptitude could pay off in the end, permitting
even those of the most humble origins to join the ranks of the clerical
elite. We now rejoin the narrative as the two travelers make their way to
the upper reaches of the Nubri Valley. The year is 1685.

> [After leaving Kutang] we arrived in Sama and went to greet the Ngadag
> Lama [i.e., the ancestor of Tashi Dorje, Rigzen Dorje, and Lama Gyatso].
> He asked what we were up to. We replied that we were on our way to
> Central Tibet. He then told us that the circumstances for travel were good
> and instructed us, "While in Tibet, don't say that you are from Kutang. Say
> you are people from a sacred valley in Ngari [Western Tibet]. When you
> arrive in Lhasa, you will come to know the language." We departed after
> he gave us some religious teachings.
>   Along the way the people of Nubri asked us where we were heading.
> When we told them that we were going to Lhasa, some people were totally
> surprised. Others with negative attitudes expressed disgust by asking,
> "How can lowlanders like you ever reach Lhasa?"
>   We crossed the pass and arrived at Nangzar, where a Tibetan government
> agent was stationed. He inquired about our destination, so we informed him
> that we were pilgrims on our way to Lhasa and asked about the traveling

conditions. The man replied, "These days both the timing and circumstances for travel are good. There are no diseases, and it isn't too hot. Also, the lamas are in good health." He then invited us to have tea and chang, and said, "My home is to the east of Lhasa. Please take this letter there for me." He then gave us the letter along with some butter and dried cheese.

The people of Nangzar also wondered how people from Kutang would ever get to Lhasa. The government official said, "It should not be a problem. If you recite prayers, and if the karma of your past lives is favorable, then you will reach your destination. You must say that you are from Kutang in Western Tibet." The people of Nangzar pointed out that we did not speak the language of Central Tibet, to which the government agent replied, "When you arrive in Central Tibet, by drinking the water and eating the food, you will gain knowledge of the language. You will then understand."[3]

We left and walked to a village called Tsangchung. A local official told us that some people had recently been robbed on the pass by seven bandits. When we pointed out that we had nothing of value, he said, "You have good clothing but few possessions. They will steal your clothing." So we stayed in Tsangchung village for seven days, during which time we said many prayers and sent burnt offerings to the mountain deities. Due to the compassion of the Buddha, there were no bandits on the trail.

The intrepid pilgrims then made their way to Lhasa via the holy sites of Western Tibet. They traversed vast stretches of the Tibetan plateau, an area of high-altitude desolation punctuated by cultivated river valleys and grassy plains. Their journey took many months of hard walking, sometimes through uninhabited deserts and mountainous terrain. At times the young men suffered from hunger and from lack of familiarity with the territory, prompting Pema Döndrup to comment, "Having no wealth is like wandering in the intermediary realm between death and rebirth." Hospitality was not always forthcoming for the young men. "When begging tea from the people of Tibet, we were often sent away even when their tea was boiling. Those who hadn't any tea never sent us away. On rare occasions we met people whose compassion surpassed that of our own parents. They expressed empathy for our plight and gave us tea to drink. Other times, not only did people refuse to give alms to us beggars, but they unleashed their dogs on us." Exposure to the elements was also an issue: "We had no protection from the rain. When it poured we sometimes huddled under the eaves of large gates, but other times there was not even a cave or overhanging rock for shelter. We were pummeled by the rain. Sometimes we could stay in horse stables, sometimes in donkey stables, sometimes in sheep pens. Our bodies began to stink like horses, donkeys, and sheep!"

Despite the obstacles, the two persisted on the journey, begging for food, greeting lamas, and visiting sacred locales. At one point they were guided by a wandering yogi. When the yogi eventually parted ways, Pema Döndrup lamented that he felt like an abandoned child. Yet one bit of advice from the yogi was to prove crucial. Pema Döndrup, like most practitioners in Kutang, was an adherent of the Northern Treasure teachings of Buddhism, a Nyingmapa subsect. On hearing of this affiliation, the yogi instructed them to go to Dorjedrag Monastery in Central Tibet, the main center of Northern Treasure tradition.[4] Henceforth, the young men's primary objective became an audience with the abbot of this institution. After going to Lhasa and visiting the Jokhang Temple and Potala Palace,[5] they headed to Dorjedrag. We rejoin the narrative at this point.

The lama of Dorjedrag was not in residence. He had gone to Samye Monastery to perform a ceremony for protecting the Tibetan administration.[6] So we went to Samye, where a great ritual was under way. As for the lama, he did not appear for an audience. We asked every monk that we met if we could have an audience with the holy man, but they told us there was no chance. Again and again we asked all the monks, both young and old, whether we could pay our respects to the lama and receive some oral teachings. They repeatedly told us it was not possible. I thought that perhaps their lama would never give oral instructions to foreigners like us.

We met an elderly horse steward at the lama's residence. I asked him, "Will the lama never allow people to greet him and receive oral instructions? Whoever I ask, monks young and old, they all reply that he will not greet us." The steward replied, "There is no point in asking the monks since they know nothing about this. At noon today, during the ritual, you will see a fully ordained monk, an old man whose hair has turned white. He will come to oversee the ritual. You should make your request to him."

When noon arrived the elderly monk appeared. To his right and left were attendants attired in religious garments, and in front walked a very young monk bearing incense. When they reached the ritual site, the elderly monk issued a command, so the two of us prostrated ourselves before him and said, "We are from a sacred valley in Western Tibet. We would like to request an opportunity to pay homage to Rinpoche and receive some oral teachings." The aged monk said, "Do not prostrate yourselves, I am not a lama." As he turned to leave, he said, "Come, come. I will arrange an audience with the lama without fail."

After a few moments a very young monk came to us and said, "You two, the treasurer sent for you to come up." We entered a small room where the treasurer of the monastery was seated on a three-tiered seat. He asked, "Where are you from? Do you have parents and siblings? What is your religious affiliation?"

I stepped forth and replied, "I am from Kutang, a sacred valley in Western Tibet. As for family members, I have several. My religious affiliation is the Northern Treasure branch of the Nyingma sect."

"Well, then," continued the treasurer, "who initiated you into the Northern Treasure teachings?"

I replied, "There is a householder lama in Kutang who initiated me."

The treasurer asked, "What type of grain grows in Kutang, the grain of the Tibetan highlands or the grain of the lowland valleys?"

I told him, "Lowland grains grow there. In all, there are about thirteen types of grain in Kutang."

He expressed surprise and commented, "Well, then, it is a bountiful place. Is there much gold and silver?"

I said, "Whereas grain is as abundant as the clods of earth, gold and silver are rare."

"Well, then," mused the treasurer, "which teachings would you like to request? Do you have gold and silver to offer to the lama?"

I said, "I have nothing whatsoever to offer. I came here after fleeing from my parents. I can only offer my body, speech, and mind. I have nothing else to offer." I then requested several teachings, but the treasurer informed me that nothing would be forthcoming unless I had something to offer to the lama. Ideally one should offer the lama nine items, and if this is not possible then five or at least three items should be presented. In fact he was trying to ignore me. When I prostrated myself before him from the left, he turned to the right. When I prostrated myself before him from the right, he turned to the left. I told him once again that I was impoverished. After thinking for a while, he told us that we could receive some initiations. He then asked whether we had robes in case we took vows and were ordained as monks. When we replied that we didn't have robes, he said, "Then what are you going to wear?" The treasurer then said, "Tomorrow morning Rinpoche will go to Dorjedrag. You two should first do the pilgrimage circuits at Samye and Chimpu, and then come to Dorjedrag. At that time you can have an audience with Rinpoche."

After finishing the pilgrimage of Samye and Chimpu, we went to Dorjedrag. For two weeks guards wouldn't allow us to enter the monastery, nor would anybody come out to help us. At that time we had nothing left to eat but porridge. We were running out of food. Some time passed, and then one day Rinpoche gave us permission to enter the monastery, where we received several initiations and teachings. On another occasion Rinpoche invited us in and gave us teachings pertaining to the community of novices. He assured us that he would meet us again in the future, and then said, "When you return to your homeland of Kutang, practice religion in a pure manner." After receiving his teachings and valuable advice, we went on pilgrimage to Yarlung.[7]

The young men had accomplished their objective, launching, in the case of Pema Döndrup, what would turn out to be a celebrated career. Gratified, the two continued their pilgrimage, visiting a host of sacred sites across Central and Southern Tibet. After passing a year and a half in Tibet, they finally returned home.

TRAVELING FOR MERIT

Tashi Dorje, the elderly lama of the Ngadag lineage, is an experienced pilgrim. During his younger years he undertook several trips to Tibet, and more recently he visited the venerated locales where the Buddha taught sermons in Northern India. As a veteran on the pilgrimage circuit, I sought out Tashi Dorje's opinions on the benefits of such a voyage. He explained,

> One can accumulate merit by going on pilgrimage and making sacrificial offerings at sacred sites. By circumambulating these places and performing prostrations, bodily sins and defilements are cleansed. Sins committed through speech are cleansed by reciting sacred mantras at a place of pilgrimage. By sins of speech I mean the sins that arise from dishonoring other people by uttering evil words about them. Such sins are absolved when you recite mantras. We Buddhists believe that if you cause misery to other people, for example by telling lies, stealing, and having thoughts of harming other sentient beings, then in a future life you will suffer as a beggar. Those who always consider ways to benefit other sentient beings will not experience the suffering brought about by having insufficient food, clothing, and housing. Retribution for those who kill and beat animals will be a future life that is short and riddled by disease. When sinful people die, they are reborn into miserable conditions. Those with pure thoughts will be reborn into a fine human body. All who are born must die—that is the nature of suffering for humans. Of the six types of beings, human birth is the best. This is because one receives the opportunity to practice religion in the human body. Those who practice religion will have an even better future rebirth. Those who do not practice religion will be reborn into a realm of suffering. Therefore, it is important to go on pilgrimage.

My friend Lama Gyatso also went on numerous pilgrimages, so I sought out his perspective as well. In a statement that recalls Pema Döndrup's motivation for traveling to Tibet, Lama Gyatso said,

> One benefit of going on pilgrimage is that you get the chance to meet many pure lamas. By requesting religious teachings from them you can eliminate

obstacles along the path of your life course. When you die, the road to your next incarnation will be especially good. You will not experience suffering. By internalizing religious teachings you attain a deep understanding of your own ignorance. Even when you die this understanding becomes an inclination for your next life. In the future you will attain a high rebirth—you will not be reborn in one of the lower realms [i.e., the hell realms or animal realm]. You will always experience peace of mind due to the good inclinations generated through pilgrimage. According to those disruptive Chinese, the Buddhist religion is based only on blind faith. So why do we practice religion? Why do we go on pilgrimage? In order to escape being stuck in cyclical existence, and to become enlightened like the Buddha.

Influencing future lives and mitigating the consequences of past actions feature prominently in these lamas' rationales for undertaking a pilgrimage. According to the ideal of selfless motivation, a pilgrimage is undertaken for the benefit of beings other than oneself. That is why, while on pilgrimage, some people offer prayers on behalf of recently deceased family members in order to counteract the sinful deeds they committed prior to death. The goal is to help the departed kin reascend to the higher realms of existence. However, one cannot discount more personal motives for undertaking the pilgrimage. The reckoning of past merits and demerits impels people like Tashi Döndrup to visit sacred locales in old age. Those who are closest to death, in particular the elderly, are more apt to undertake meritorious journeys. As death and rebirth inch ever closer they devote more time to adjusting their personal ledgers of merit and sin in hope of influencing their future existences. Pilgrimage is one of the most effective ways to accomplish this goal.

．　．　．

Earlier we witnessed the difficulties Pema Döndrup encountered on his quest for teachings in Tibet. Most of his problems stemmed not from a lack of aptitude or motivation, but from his poverty and lowly social status. To gain a contrasting view on pilgrimage from a person who was born into a position of prestige, I set forth one day to ask Lama Gyatso about a sacred quest he had undertaken years ago.

Lama Gyatso, born in the Year of the Dog (1934), was one of the first people in Sama I met. Karma, the man who first introduced me to the village, took me to Lama Gyatso's home the night of my arrival. At that time I was a complete outsider, an unknown entity, and had yet to prove myself as a person worthy of belonging to the community. Karma admonished me to stay on Lama Gyatso's good side, since he is a formidable political force in the village. If I got on this man's wrong side, he warned, chances were that my research would come to a grinding halt. Informal networks of power, such as the ability to sway opinions through public rhetoric and private gossip, must always be acknowledged in a village setting. I wanted to make a good impression on this highly respected member of the community.

I vividly remember the day when Lama Gyatso first invited me to have tea at his home. A few days after arriving in Sama, I was strolling down the path to the village from Pema Chöling Gomba, where I had consumed too many cups of butter tea with some elderly folks. Nobody was in sight, so I stepped to the side of the trail and into the bushes to relieve my bladder. Before I could conclude, I heard a throat clearing behind me. Craning my neck, I saw that it was Lama Gyatso decked out in his formal red garments. Because I had not yet figured out proper toilet etiquette in this community, thorough embarrassment ensued, on my part at least (I soon realized that public urination is nothing to be ashamed about). I quickly zipped up and proceeded to stammer through an awkward greeting that was probably incomprehensible and suffused with too much humility. Lama Gyatso merely smiled and invited me to his home for tea that afternoon. I graciously accepted.

Over the weeks, which turned to months and years, we have developed a very close rapport. Our main point of intellectual connection is an interest in local history. During breaks from fieldwork I would comb archives in Nepal and the United States for Tibetan historical documents relating to Nubri or to his Ngadag clan. I always made extra photocopies for Lama Gyatso. These texts became the basis for our discussions of historical matters. The knowledgeable lama filled lacunae in the texts with oral accounts. Lama Gyatso takes pride in his Ngadag ancestral line, so he greatly appreciated my endeavors as a participant in the writing of his family's history.

Prestige in Nubri manifests itself through symbolic interactions between individuals. When a villager greets a lama, he will customarily place his hands together and bend low at the waist to touch his forehead to the back of the lama's outstretched hand, a gesture of submissive respect. When two lamas meet, as men of equal social standing, they bump their heads together. Literacy in Tibetan and an interest in local history elevated my own social status in the village. Although an outsider, I was honored to be a head clicker with Lama Gyatso.

The skies were gray and threatening on the day I made the short climb from the village of Sama to Pema Chöling Gomba to ask Lama

Gyatso about his pilgrimage of bygone days. The clouds hovered so low that even the nearby ridges were veiled. It was late winter, a time of dark skies and persistent snow. Lama Gyatso was staying in his personal retreat, consisting of a small yet stunning chapel and a detached kitchen/living area surrounded by a high wall to lend some privacy. He often told me that village life is too hectic in the house that he shares with his two sons and their wife; to accomplish any serious study or meditation he needs a more reclusive environment. He and his wife, Tsogyal, retire periodically to the relative calm of the monastery complex. Relative calm is the key term here. As a popular lama, his services are always in demand, whether from householders requesting that he perform religious ceremonies, fellow clerics who want him to sort out political imbroglios, or the anthropologist seeking answers to frivolous questions. The efficient Tsogyal always has a kettle of butter tea warming on the hearth and an ornate wooden container adorned with brass fittings filled with arak for the special guest.

I knocked on the door leading into Lama Gyatso's courtyard. Tsogyal called out, asking me to identify myself. When she heard my voice, she scurried from the kitchen, unlatched the door, and pointed to the chapel, indicating that Lama Gyatso was within.

The chapel's interior was illuminated by light diffused through a white cotton cloth that serves as a doorway. Once my eyes adjusted to the dark, I could see Lama Gyatso sitting in the corner next to a small window, manuscript in hand, trying to discern the letters by the pale light filtering through the dust-covered panes of glass. All four walls were adorned with beautifully painted wooden panels depicting lamas and saints of yore, as well as the deities who protect both the teachings of the Buddha and the inhabitants of this valley. Most of the panels were commissioned by Lama Gyatso's father and painted by a man from the neighboring village of Lho. Although the lamas of Sama have commissioned statues from Kathmandu or even brought Newari artisans to their village to construct religious icons, most artistic needs continue to be met by local craftsmen who pass their knowledge on through family lines.

Lama Gyatso concluded his reading, then carefully wrapped the manuscript in a piece of silk before placing it back into a large, wooden storage chest. When he stood up his joints creaked with stiffness after sitting cross-legged for so long in the cold chapel. He shuffled with a stooped gait across the wooden floor to the door, flipped aside the curtain, and motioned for me to come along into the living quarters where Tsogyal waited.

We entered the warm, smoky room. Lama Gyatso sat in his usual seat beneath the altar dedicated to the protector deity of his patrilineage. I sat to his left on a thin carpet spread on the floor for visitors. Across the hearth from us sat Tsogyal. In contrast to the spacious interiors of village houses, the living quarters at Lama Gyatso's retreat are small, confined, yet ever so cozy on a gray winter day. The three of us exchanged a few jokes and engaged in a bit of village gossip while the tea was being prepared. Lama Gyatso's elongated teeth, yellowed and exposed by receding gums brought on by a lifetime with minimal hygienic care, revealed themselves every time he laughed. Elders here are often referred to as "long toothed ones" for obvious reasons.

Once the tea was served, I asked my friend to describe the pilgrimage to Tibet he and his fellow villagers undertook many years ago, in 1953. Lama Gyatso immediately turned serious, assuming his clerical demeanor. One aspect of his personality that I have always respected is his ability to switch adroitly between the distinct roles of friend and lama. As a friend, he is as casual and exuberant as the most heedless villager. As a lama, he is composed and highly dignified, indicating the serious nature of his rank in society.

"That was a long time ago, you know. I have difficulty remembering all of the details. First of all, I will tell you where we went, and then I can answer any specific questions you may have." Lama Gyatso then began to recite the itinerary of places where their entourage had stopped, greeted important teachers, and received initiations or religious instruction. At one point, he reached behind into a solid wooden box and extracted some small, carefully folded pieces of paper. "These are *tobyig,* confirmations of the teachings I have received," he explained while unfolding an example. The parchment contained a few handwritten lines of text stating what teaching was given, by whom, and on what date. All the lamas of Nubri collect these documents. They represent tangible evidence of a lifetime's endeavor to acquire wisdom and merit.

He continued:

> Eight of us went on the pilgrimage, including Tashi Dorje. I was the youngest of all; at the time I was twenty-one years old. We left during the eleventh month of the year, so it was autumn. We journeyed throughout Central Tibet, stopping in many places such as Shekar and Narthang, where we greeted the holy scriptures.[8] Eventually we came to Lhasa, where we saw the youthful Dalai Lama. He greeted everybody at that time. Since it was the time of Losar, the New Year festival, many pilgrims were in Lhasa, including several very important teachers from whom we requested religious instruction. During Losar, Lhasa was filled with monks. Some

were performing rituals, some were playing musical instruments, some were debating, and then there were these tall, strong ones who carried big wooden staffs. They acted as crowd control, always yelling at people to get back and striking them with their staffs.[9]

After the New Year ceremonies we went to Samye. Near Samye there are five chötens carved from large rocks. It was here that our ancestor Trisong Detsen met Padmasambhava for the first time. We then went to Mindroling and Dorjedrag, two monasteries that are famous among Nyingmapas like ourselves. We requested many teachings from the lamas. We went next to Tsurpu, the residence of the Lord Karmapa.[10] Afterward we went home, stopping at Sakya, Tingri, and many other sites on the way. In all, we were gone for half a year.

Unlike the ordeals endured by Pema Döndrup, Lama Gyatso's pilgrimage was a comparatively easygoing affair. While in Lhasa, they stayed at the home of a government official, a member of Tibet's nobility, whom they had known when he was stationed just to the north of Nubri. Still, I wondered how they made their way about Tibet, so I asked Lama Gyatso about the more mundane aspects of his journey.

Through our long association he understood that my research interests centered less on the spiritual aspects of Nubri society and more on practical concerns. Lama Gyatso's face became very animated as he got to his feet and dashed off into his chapel, beckoning for me to follow. By the time I had entered, removed my shoes, and allowed my eyes to adjust to the dark interior, Lama Gyatso was at his customary seat beside the small window. His arthritic fingers worked doggedly to untie the cords holding together a scroll on his lap. The scroll was unfurled to reveal a long piece of golden silk containing a text written in black ink. "This," he began with a chuckle, "is how we got around in those days!"

I sat down beside him and allowed my eyes to study line by line the beautiful calligraphy. My attention was drawn to the red seal at the bottom of the document and the accompanying inscription, "Issued from the Potala Palace in the Year of the Iron Ox." The seal was from the office of the Dalai Lama, and according to Lama Gyatso the document had been issued by the Fifth Dalai Lama, one of the most revered men in this special line of incarnations. The Iron Ox Year mentioned in the edict therefore had to be 1661. The document states that following the collapse of the Tibetan empire (which occurred in 842) one of the descendants of Trisong Detsen, Lama Gyatso's ancestor, moved to Mangyul, an area just to the north of Nubri. His heirs became the incumbents of Tradumtse Monastery, reputedly founded by the Ngadag ancestor Songtsen Gampo during the seventh century as a "border-taming temple" to extend the influence of Buddhism to the edges of Tibet and beyond.[11]

Lama Gyatso reiterated the history of his Ngadag lineage in Nubri, stating that a younger brother of the incumbent at Tradumtse came and settled in Sama thirteen generations ago. At the time the lamas of Tradum- tse had more prestige than their cousins in Sama by virtue of seniority. The hereditary lama of Tradumtse, however, failed to sire a son during the early part of the twentieth century, and so Lama Gyatso's father, a junior member of the Ngadag lineage in Sama, was asked to become the regent at Tradumtse. That is how my friend came into possession of this particular document.

"But how could you use this document to travel in Tibet?" I asked. Lama Gyatso smiled and explained:

> This is proof of our claim to being descendants of Trisong Detsen, who was the emperor of Tibet long, long ago. Nowadays it is useless, just a piece of silk. But in the past it was like a passport wherever we went in Tibet.
>
> When we took the edict to Tibet, sometimes people made fun of it. Sometimes it was greeted with disdain. It was not even sufficient to get us a personal audience with the all-knowing Dalai Lama when we showed it to the Tibetan government officials. But the Lord Karmapa and many lamas from Eastern Tibet asked to see our document. They were very interested to learn of our origins.
>
> I remember my grandfather telling me of the time he was traveling in Tibet with a servant. One evening after they made camp the servant went to cut wood. A local official recognized the servant to be an outsider, so he had him arrested. My grandfather went to see what was wrong. When the official asked who he was and where he was from, my grandfather showed him the edict. All of a sudden the official became very humble and released the servant. He then offered my grandfather tsampa, tea, and butter and said, "Because you have this edict, not only can you have anything you ask for, but please go ahead and cut whatever wood you need."
>
> At that time the edict carried influence. Since the document was issued during the time of the Fifth Dalai Lama, whoever carried it could receive whatever he wished and greet whomever he desired. In any event, it was useful for getting provisions along the way. The bearer of the document was entitled to horses for transportation and lodging at the rest stops.

Lama Gyatso's and Pema Döndrup's reasons for undertaking a pil- grimage were similar in many respects. They went to Tibet in search of religious instruction. To Tibetans, attaining religious knowledge involves far more than studying scripture. The decipherment of written materials is facilitated through the direct oral transmission from master to disciple of the subtle meanings behind teachings. By sitting at the feet of an erudite instructor, the aspiring student places himself within a stream of transmissions that dates back to the time when the Buddha roamed India giving sermons to disciples twenty-five centuries ago.

In the Tibetan world, acquiring religious instruction from famous lamas is the equivalent of acquiring prestige. For despite the readiness for Tibetans to accept in theory the egalitarian principles taught by Shakyamuni Buddha, Tibetan society has always been stratified. Contrasting the pilgrimages of Lama Gyatso and Pema Döndrup shows how status within Tibet's social hierarchy was an important factor that could either open or close doors standing between an individual and the knowledge of great Buddhist masters. Pema Döndrup hailed from the absolute fringes of the Tibetan cultural world. Not only did he speak a crude and nearly unintelligible dialect, but he was poor and dressed in rags. By the sheer force of his stubborn ambitions, however, he managed to gain admission into monastic circles, when a person with lesser will might have given up and gone home. Lama Gyatso, in contrast, was born with a pedigree verified through a document issued by no less a figure than the Fifth Dalai Lama. His entrée into the high Buddhist society of Tibet was assured.

A DIFFERENT KIND OF SACRED ENDEAVOR

Merit can be achieved in a variety of ways, for example by defending the Buddhist religion against any and all threats. In Tibet, the axis of the spiritual universe for the people of Nubri, such a threat came in the form of the interventionist philosophy of an atheist state. Under the leadership of Mao Zedong, China entered Tibet in the 1950s to reassert a long-standing territorial claim. Unlike previous periods when Tibet was subsumed within empires based in China that were ruled by ethnic Mongols (1279–1368) and Manchus (1644–1911), under Mao's guidance a systematic attempt was made to forcibly transform all aspects of Tibetan society.[12] As subjects of Nepal, the people of Nubri escaped the ravages of China's Cultural Revolution and other human-induced tragedies. Nevertheless, as border dwellers who had relatively easy access to Tibet, they became leading actors in some of the dramas that brought Buddhist teachers and precious icons into exile. The following narrative tells of one such event.

· · ·

It was early afternoon in the fall of 1998. The sun had ducked behind a thick layer of clouds as I made my way to the residence of Lama Rigzen Dorje, which sits in a grove of juniper trees below Pema Chöling Gomba. His modest residence consists of a small living area dominated by a hearth in the center of the floor, and an attached chapel, the interior walls of which are covered by paintings of the deities he venerates. I assumed he was home on that cold, cheerless day, for smoke could be seen filtering through his ceiling. These days Rigzen Dorje spends most of his time at home, making only an occasional foray to the village to visit one of his sons or when summoned to perform a religious ceremony.

I stood outside the entranceway and called his name, awaiting the invitation to enter. Within, his voice creaky with age, I heard him address the young nun, his granddaughter and caretaker: "Who is out there?" In past years Rigzen Dorje had immediately recognized my voice, but now he was nearly deaf. "It's Gyemi, the foreigner," she replied. "Ehey, come on in," he shouted through the open doorway.

I picked my way through the entranceway, cluttered with stray chunks of wood and some ragged felt boots, then allowed my eyes to adjust to the dim light for a moment before sitting at the customary spot by the hearth reserved for visitors. "Sit down, sit down. Hey, girl, pour him some tea," commanded Rigzen Dorje, who was just finishing his meal of cornmeal and potatoes. A few stringy morsels of partly consumed yak meat remained on his plate. The old man still enjoys flesh with his meal despite the fact that, at age eighty, his ability to chew is compromised by an absence of teeth. Tibetans consider meat to be an integral part of any meal. Giving it up is tantamount to denying one's cultural identity.

As I sat down Rigzen Dorje grasped my outstretched hand and pulled me to his side. We touched foreheads in greeting, and then with a surprisingly powerful stroke he delivered a slap on my back. We had become very close over time. He was the last person I visited before leaving the village after a long stint of fieldwork in 1997. At that time tears filled our eyes when he declared in a voice congested with emotion, "Perhaps we will not meet again. I wish you health and happiness." Walking slowly from his home I glanced back to see him standing where we had bade farewell, his hands held together in front of his chest in a gesture of prayer, a soft wind blowing through his long wispy hair. Imagine my delight when I arrived the following year to find that, although deaf and chronically ill, not only was he alive, but he still had that mischievous glint in his eyes.

His granddaughter, the twelve-year-old nun, sat on the female side of the hearth fully occupied in the task of preparing tea. Rigzen Dorje's wife had died about three years before, leaving him alone after over half a century of companionship. During my first visit to Sama the duty of caring for the elderly lama had fallen on the eldest daughter of his son, a nun whose mother had died while she was still an infant. To be a religious woman was not to be her calling in life, as I found out later when I encountered her in Kathmandu. Instead of the characteristic red robes and shaven head of a nun, she wore the clothing of a laywoman and sported shoulder-length hair. In her arms was a swaddled infant, her own child. She now lives far away from the reproving stares of her fellow villagers.

The girl now making tea had replaced her cousin as caretaker for Rigzen Dorje. She methodically churned the butter, tea, and salt within a wooden cylinder, then poured the steaming liquid into a metal kettle. Rigzen Dorje removed the silver lid from his wooden bowl and held it toward the girl. It is customary for the head of the household to first sample the tea before serving a guest. My elderly companion took a deep and noisy slurp from the cup. A look of disgust immediately crossed his face. He turned to the girl and scolded, "Aach! There is too much salt in this tea! This tastes horrible; how can we drink it?" The young nun apologized meekly and set about rectifying her error.

I felt sorry for the girl. Her childhood was flitting away in the gloomy recesses of her grandfather's home, as she cared for a man who became more cantankerous with the inevitable onslaught of infirmity. I also felt sympathy for my once formidable companion. Rigzen Dorje had difficulty coping with old age. In the past he was a force to be reckoned with. Not only had his religious services been in high demand, but he had acted as a powerful politician whose domineering conduct had often swayed fellow villagers to his cause. Now he could barely hear the words of others, and many among the younger generation chose to ignore his advice, though it was based on wisdom he had accumulated over an entire lifetime. One of the most poignant scenes of village life can be witnessed during village council meetings. Elderly men, former leaders in the community, strain to hear opposing arguments while attempting to raise their enfeebled voices above the din of debate. Once a man's life force diminishes beyond the point of no return, his advice is rarely solicited, and his opinions are no longer treated with respect. Perhaps this is one of the reasons Rigzen Dorje enjoyed my company so much. I was there to listen, and to learn.

I began to reflect on a story he had once related with pride, about the crowning achievement of his long life. In 1959 Rigzen Dorje and some companions set forth on an epic adventure that is still considered one of the most remarkable events in local history. In the prime of life, at a time when his robust constitution was matched by the dynamic personality of a true leader, he organized a rescue mission. One of Tibet's most sacred images, a wooden sculpture known as Jowo Rinpoche of Pagpawati Temple (The Precious Jowo of Sublime Wati), in neighboring Kyirong, was being threatened with destruction at the hands of marauding Chinese soldiers. Rigzen Dorje therefore vowed to save this object of veneration so that future generations could benefit from the blessings bestowed by Precious Jowo.

The statue has a well-known history in the myths and legends of Tibet. In the fourteenth century the scholar Sonam Gyaltsen wrote the following narrative about how the image came into existence:

> Songtsen Gampo [a Tibetan emperor who died around 650] then thought to himself, "At the present time in the southern land of Nepal, there is a hidden manifestation which will miraculously benefit sentient beings in the future." With these thoughts he supplicated his tutelary deity, and from the breast of the self-formed image there arose a ray of light that extended to Nepal. Looking in the direction of the light, he perceived in a great forest on the borders of India and Nepal the self-created images known as the "Four Divine Brothers" arising from a *hari*-sandalwood tree that also radiated light in all directions. The king then sent the manifestation-monk Akaramatishila to fetch them. When the monk reached the city of Mangyul [in Southern Tibet], he beheld many people dying from pestilence. He proceeded from Mangyul to the city known as Kathmandu, where he saw many dying from leprosy. Next he traveled from Kathmandu to the border between India and Nepal, where a malevolent demon was causing many deaths among the inhabitants.
>
> At this latter location, a herdsman was tending many buffalo in a forest. One of these beasts, endowed with karma and good fortune, entered the forest during the day and circumambulated the *hari*-sandalwood tree that stood there, whereupon milk flowed from her udders. That evening, the buffalo's owner said to the herdsman, "You have been milking my beast!" The herdsman denied the accusation, saying, "I have done no such thing. During the day the buffalo were wandering in the forest." The next day, the herdsman, accompanied by the owner, proceeded into the forest to investigate. There they beheld the buffalo circumambulating the *hari*-sandalwood tree that radiated light in all directions, the milk flowing from her udders, and the two were amazed.
>
> Knowing that the sandalwood image of the king's tutelary deity would arise from this tree, the manifestation-monk split it open with an axe,

whereupon voices resounded from each of the four pieces thus created. The voice from the uppermost piece declared, "Hue me carefully and place me in the city of Mangyul," and from this piece arose the image known as the Sublime Wati. . . . Through the blessing of these images each of the three locations was freed from the threefold fears of untimely death described above.[13]

During the 1800s the statue was occasionally moved during the frequent border conflicts with Nepal, yet it was always returned safely to its home in Pagpawati Temple. In the 1960s, however, a new threat in the form of an avowed antireligious regime from China had descended on Tibet. After the Dalai Lama fled to India in 1959, the wholesale destruction of the country's religious infrastructure commenced. Tibetans living in areas situated on the Nepali side of the border, such as Nubri, were fully aware of what was happening due to the continuous stream of refugees flooding their villages. Rigzen Dorje was determined to prevent any harm coming to the revered Jowo Rinpoche. Here is his story:

It was the Year of the Pig [1959], and I was about forty years old at the time. Many people say that this was a time of evil, but here on our side of the border things were not so bad. For Tibet, however, it was definitely an era of evil. The Chinese had come and were creating all sorts of trouble. People fleeing across the border kept telling us that the situation was getting worse and worse, and that war had broken out between the Khampas [people from Eastern Tibet] and the Chinese.[14] We even heard that His Holiness the Dalai Lama had fled from his home in Lhasa. Everybody was worried.

At that time I had a dream while sleeping at our gomba one night. It was a strange dream in which Lord Jowo spoke to me and said that if brought to safety he would remain among us for many years to come, but if left at Pagpawati he would not last more than another year or two. I knew then and there that the statue of Jowo Rinpoche was under threat. So in the morning I asked Lama Gyatso's father and another man to come to my home. I told them, "I want to bring Jowo Rinpoche back here to Nubri for safekeeping. I will pay all the expenses for such an expedition." They replied, "If you do this, please let the two of us come along. We want to go with you."

We agreed to wait a bit and make plans. Soon thereafter an old friend of mine died. While I was performing the death rites up at the monastery, my wife came and asked me to return to the house. A message had arrived from a Khampa lama. He instructed me to come up-valley and meet him at a place about an hour's walk from the village. So I went with a relative to greet this lama, who told me, "Go wherever you are instructed to go; there is no danger." He then handed me a letter.

The letter was from His Holiness the Dalai Lama. This is not the idle talk of an old man. Really, it is the truth. The letter said that Jowo Rinpoche should be brought to Nubri, and that this task should be done during the third month of the year. Oh yes, if His Holiness commands me to go get Jowo Rinpoche, then that is precisely what I should do. If he commands me to stay put, then that is precisely what I should do. I had a sacred duty to follow his instructions.

When I came back to the village my uncles were performing some rituals. They advised me not to undertake this expedition. They told me to stay in the village and recite prayers, and that I should not bring Jowo Rinpoche here. They suspected that this grand plan was only a means for me to gain merit for myself. Their practical objection was that if Jowo were to be brought to Sama, then a bunch of Khampas would come as well. People were afraid of the Khampas, for they were known to cause trouble. My uncles said that if they stayed here, all sorts of disputes would break out because the Khampas are arrogant. They also said I had no friends to go with. Regardless, I was determined to go. For one thing, Tibet is the land of religion, so this was to be a sacred endeavor. Furthermore, I had permission from the Dalai Lama himself for this undertaking. He had sent a letter asking that Jowo Rinpoche be saved. Those who fabricated objections were not only helping the Chinese, but they were mocking us as well. I urged people not to make trouble during this time, and assured everybody that I would pay all expenses. I was determined to go, no matter what.

I knew that I could not manage this task alone, so I sought people to help from each village in the valley. I carried money and white scarves to give to potential helpers. I told the people in neighboring villages of my plans, and asked each village to supply some men to help. I assured them that bringing Jowo here would benefit all, not just myself. I knew that we could count on the Khampa soldiers to help us, and that if many were around, the Chinese could not stop us. But I wanted people from Nubri to come along as well. In some of the villages men willingly agreed to join me; in other villages debates arose, with some in favor of the idea and others objecting. Decisions are sometimes difficult to make in this way, so I did not blame people when they were reluctant to help. It would not be right to command people to undertake this expedition.

Eventually I assembled enough men. Back in Sama we burned some juniper outside of the gomba and then left on the second day of the third month [April/May 1959]. We traveled via the Tsum Valley, en route crossing several streams and some high passes. After a few days we reached Pagpawati Temple. The last time I had been there, the caretaker of the temple was a one-legged man. Since then he had died, so it was his son who showed us into the temple where Jowo Rinpoche was housed. We were allowed to take the statue, which sat in a carved wooden box that was open in the front. Rumor had it that Chinese soldiers were not far away, so we had to hurry. But we had some Khampas with us for protection, so I was not worried.

When we were about to leave I met a lama. In the past he had acted as my sponsor while I stayed at Pagpawati Temple. He asked me to stay awhile and lit a fire to boil some tea. He then told us, "If you take the statue from here, go without having any second thoughts. It is very auspicious if you are able to accomplish this mission. Anyone who has doubts will only create diversions." I replied, "We have decided to fulfill this mission. Even if it takes several months, we are willing to face the hardships."

We then went north toward the town of Dzongga. The men who helped carry the statue and our supplies did not turn back. They said they would remain with us even if it took months. I could hear them discussing among themselves, saying, "If we turn back now before crossing the border, who knows what the future will bring? If that is the wrong decision, we will have to live in shame for the rest of our lives." On hearing this, I knew the men would be reliable for the rest of the journey.

After a few days we crossed the pass back into Nepal without a problem. Although the statue was safe, we still had to figure out what to do with it. I suggested that we take it to a place below Bi called Durdzong [Cemetery Fort]. Everybody liked the idea, so I sent the monks ahead to make preparations. When we arrived, we worked day and night to build a reliquary chamber for the statue. After all, this is a very sacred object and could not be housed just anywhere. The task was completed on the tenth day of the third month.

The statue remained there until the fifteenth day of the third month. Then we took Jowo Rinpoche on a tour through all the villages of Nubri. I sent messengers to each village informing the people that Jowo was on the way. My intent was to make sure that even those who initially had been stubborn about the expedition would not be embarrassed. My fear was that now they would be reluctant to come and greet the statue. It would be very unfortunate if, in their effort to save face, they did not receive blessings from Jowo. Having arrived at this realization, I sent messengers in advance to encourage all to come and greet this marvelous statue. And since we would be carrying the statue through the villages, the old, blind, and infirm would not have to be borne on people's backs to receive the blessing. We told them just to sit by their doors, that we would bring the statue to them. In that way we went from village to village in a grand procession. It was quite a sight!

We started the procession before the end of the third month, and eventually reached Sama on the ninth day of the fifth month [June/July 1959]. You see, I had set a deadline, since the tenth day of the month is a special day on which we always worship Padmasambhava, the saint who helped establish Buddhism in Tibet long, long ago. We wanted to perform a large offering ceremony on this day. When we arrived I took off all my clothes and had a good wash. I then offered some nice silk clothing to Jowo Rinpoche and placed the statue on a throne in the gomba. Then I invited those men who had helped bear the statue to my house for tea. Meanwhile my uncles were preparing butter lamps in front of Jowo.

Guess what happened? There was an earthquake! Many people began to panic, thinking that something bad was bound to happen now that we had brought Jowo Rinpoche to our village. They claimed that the earthquake was an inauspicious sign. But they did not understand that this was in fact a good omen. Since we lamas admired and expressed our faith in Jowo Rinpoche, we brought the statue all the way here. The journey was complete, so the earthquake must be interpreted as an extremely positive sign. Why is that so, you may wonder? When the reincarnation of a great lama is born, there is an earthquake. If a great lama passes away, there is an earthquake. In both instances an earthquake is considered to be an auspicious omen. I told the people that there was nothing to worry about. Harm would not come to the people here. The earthquake was a good sign.

After we performed our ceremonies on the tenth day of the month, we knew it was time to take the statue down to Kathmandu. We had heard that His Holiness had reached India safely, so we wanted to get the statue to him. Thirty Khampa soldiers were chosen to take the statue down to the lowlands. I wondered whether I should continue this wonderful pilgrimage with Jowo, or whether I should now remain in the village and tend to household affairs once again. It was a difficult decision to make, but in the end I decided to stay here in Sama. Before Jowo Rinpoche was taken away I wanted to have some souvenir to remind me of his presence. So I quickly made a new box to hold the statue and placed the old box from Pagpawati in my own chapel. It is still there. At one time it was blessed with the presence of Jowo Rinpoche, so I treasure that box like no other object in my possession.

The next morning the Khampa soldiers came to carry the statue down-valley. My family and I had all washed that morning and put on our finest clothing. My wife cut all the strings holding jewels around her neck and gave the precious stones to Jowo as an offering. I had a beautiful turquoise earring that changed color with the changing light; that, too, I gave as an offering to Jowo. When the soldiers left, my daughter and some other people went all the way to the next village with them. I, however, went only a short distance along the trail. It is our belief that to go too far with a departing friend signals the end of the relationship, that we will never see each other again. I certainly wanted to see Jowo in the future.

I still remember so clearly the day the statue was taken away from our village. I was sad to see the statue leave, but pleased to know that it was no longer in danger. When some months later news reached us that Pagpawati Temple had been destroyed, I was content to know that we had done the right thing. Otherwise, as Jowo had told me in the dream, the statue would no longer be with us. Today it resides in Dharamsala, in the personal residence of His Holiness the Dalai Lama. Who knows, one day it may return to its home in Pagpawati.

As he concluded his story, my elderly companion beamed with pride. The rescue mission of a sacred statue nearly forty years ago had been the crowning achievement of a distinguished career as a lama and a village leader. He then turned to me again and said, "By virtue of this deed I have received much merit. But I do not need fame. For me it is enough that everybody in the village, from young to old, has benefited from my actions." His sentiments expressed the selfless motivations that lie at the root of the Buddha's message, the very same Buddha whose sacred image passed through this humble village during those chaotic days.

. . .

The journeys described in this chapter were not the last these men would undertake. Pema Döndrup ventured forth to Tibet again and again; sometimes he went to study at the feet of great Tibetan masters, other times he went to circumambulate sacred mountains or to meditate in special places where yogis can attain spiritual insights. Lama Gyatso and Rigzen Dorje also continued their quests for merit and religious instruction. For them, the destinations of pilgrimage shifted from Tibet to Nepal and India owing to political events beyond their control. Although the geographic loci of pilgrimages have changed, the intent of the sacred endeavor remains the same. Each winter Rigzen Dorje still makes his way down the treacherous trails to the lowlands of Nepal. While the village of Sama sits beneath of thick blanket of snow, he spends his days circumambulating sacred sites in Kathmandu, generating merit for his next rebirth. He assures me that he will continue to do so until he is no longer able to walk.

CHAPTER 6

The Merits of Matrimony

Commencing the Householder Life

The father is the head of the family,
But the mother is its foundation.
                    Tibetan Proverb

Buddhist clergymen consider marriage to be an obstacle to enlightenment. Marriage entails a commitment to perpetuating worldly suffering through procreation, as evident in the proverb "What is needed is the practice of the holy Dharma [the teachings of the Buddha], what is not needed is a wife for one's *samsara* [worldly suffering]." Yet whereas lamas and monks often rely on spiritual advancement to gauge their success in life, for the vast majority of humble householders marriage and procreation are the key to social validation. To the laymen of Nubri, a more pertinent proverb reads: "A single wild ass doesn't get water, a single man doesn't live life fully." Conflicting attitudes prevail with respect to the relative merits of family life versus religious celibacy.

RULES OF ENGAGEMENT

Every society has its rules, whether implicit or explicit, for who can marry whom. The Tibetans of Sama have a preference for joining cross-cousins in matrimony. They refer to such an arrangement as an *ashang-ani* marriage, meaning maternal uncle–paternal aunt. Thus, a man's ideal marital partner would be his mother's brother's daughter, while a woman's would be her father's sister's son. To most Tibetans such a union is considered incestuous, as it involves first cousins and thereby violates the cultural prohibition against engaging in sexual intercourse with anyone not removed by at least seven generations on the patrilineal side and three on the matrilineal side.[1]

Violating the incest taboo invites village-wide retribution from local protective deities. I once asked some Tibetans from Kyirong about cross-cousin marriages. One commented that offspring of such unions are destined to be mentally disabled and will experience a truncated life span. Another, looking deeply disturbed, noted that this was a common practice among ethnic Tamangs who live just across the border in Nepal.[2] After commenting that cross-cousin marriage is a shameful custom, he said, "Animals do not know who is a relative, but we are humans—not bovines. We believe that cracks will develop on your forehead if you marry a relative. In the past, two cousins related through matrilineal descent married in our village. They were sown together in a leather bag and cast into the river." Indeed, Tibetans take the incest taboo very seriously.

The Tibetans of Sama have a more relaxed incest rule that relates predominantly to patrilineal descent. The primary rule prohibits two people from the same lineage, called a *gyupa* in the local vernacular, from marrying. Every child assumes the gyupa membership of his or her father. In fact, Sama's social hierarchy is stratified according to the relative prestige of its four lineages. Listed in order of diminishing prestige, these are Ngadag ("Possessing Power"), Pönzang ("Good Rulers"), Yorkung ("Irrigators"), and Chumin ("Low and Inferior").

As discussed previously, the Ngadag gyupa is made up of married lamas and their female kin who trace a direct line of descent from the medieval emperors who ruled Tibet. Penzang gyupa members, as their name implies, were the traditional political heads of the village. They also claim an imperial pedigree, although their claim is backed only by oral and not written evidence and hence is less convincing to other Tibetans. Pönzang lineage members trace their origin to Kyika Ratö, the disgraced illegitimate son of a Tibetan queen.[3] The majority of Sama's population is composed of Yorkung and Chumin gyupa members. Yorkung ancestors were, according to legend, the first to settle in Sama. They migrated from Tibet, established the community, and then later invited the Ngadag lamas to preside over the religious life of the village. Tashi Döndrup belongs to the Yorkung lineage. Chumin members also claim Tibetan origin; as their name implies, however, they are considered to be socially inferior to all other clans.

Nobody is allowed to marry within their gyupa, since that would violate the incest rule prohibiting sexual relations with people having common patrilineal descent. Beyond that, cross-cousin marriages involve only the matrilineal line of descent and so are not only permitted but encouraged, since the practice allows families to remain linked over the course of generations.

Giving a bride to another family is considered a great sacrifice, one that requires reciprocation. Families keep tallies of bridal debts spanning generations, and these social arrears figure prominently when marital partners are being sought for children, the goal being the erasure of any bridal debt during the next generation so that the net flow of women between households remains in balance. That is one of the incentives for cross-cousin marriages.

Other than the prohibition from marrying within one's own lineage, gyupa membership is not a barrier to marriage—with one notable exception. Male members of the Ngadag lineage are not supposed to betroth women of Chumin descent. According to one lama, the Chumin are so fundamentally inferior that marrying one would result in a loss of spiritual powers. Indeed, I did not encounter a single case where a Ngadag lama has wed a Chumin woman. Nevertheless, the situation is far from simple. Ngadag lamas have a penchant for initiating extra-marital affairs, and I did encounter several cases where the mother of a lama's illegitimate child was a member of the Chumin gyupa. As mentioned before, the father of a bastard, or *nyelu,* is under no obligation to provide for the child. Yet by virtue of patrilineal descent, any progeny of a Ngadag man is a member of the Ngadag lineage, regardless of the status of his mother or the dubious circumstances of his birth. A male nyelu who was sired by a Ngadag father thus finds himself in a socially ambiguous position. On the one hand, he can lay claim to the prestigious Ngadag affiliation; but on the other hand, he has no rights to his father's land, herds, home, or ritual implements. More important, he is excluded from acquiring the religious knowledge that has been transmitted from father to son over the course of generations. Several such marginal Ngadag members have ended up marrying women from the Chumin clan. As in every society, rules are dictated by circumstances as often as circumstances are dictated by rules.

GIVING AWAY THE BRIDE

For a young lady, marriage signals the transition from adolescence to womanhood. People marry at a relatively early age in Nubri, generally around age twenty-three for men and twenty for women. Marriages are arranged between parents, except in those cases when a couple falls in love and elopes before parental designs can be set in motion. But before formal marriage negotiations between families can commence, the parents must ensure that their children are astrologically compatible. The couple's natal horoscopes are compared by the village astrologer; if they are not in conflict, negotiations can move forward.

The wedding day begins with the groom and his party of male companions walking slowly in procession and singing boisterously all the way to the bride's home. As they enter the home, they are greeted by the bride's mother and father and by the bride herself, who sits with her family for the last time as a member of their household. After the groom's retinue is served refreshments, the bride is symbolically expelled from her natal household. At this moment she lets forth heart-wrenching cries and flings herself down before her relatives, clutching their knees and begging them to forgive her for abandoning them. Bear in mind that she may be moving only a few houses away or at most to a village within a few hours' walking distance, where she most certainly has relatives who can look after her. Regardless, leaving the house signifies a girl's transformation to a woman. She is physically dislocated from the lap of familial security to a household where she will have little power and where she must commence the extremely hazardous duty of bearing children. The emotional scene of the bride's grief brings tears to the eyes of older women as they recall the day they, too, were wrenched from the sheltered confines of home, and brings anxious expressions to the faces of those girls who have yet to be given away in matrimony.

Mountain imagery is evoked throughout the wedding ceremony. The following words, for example, are sung by the groomsmen when a bride departs her natal home for the last time and starts the journey to join her husband:

Ama layho!
The snow peak up there is the eldest,
The earthen mountain below it is younger.
Earthen mountain, please protect the snow mountain!

Ama layho!
The earthen mountain up there is older,
The rocky cliff below it is younger.
Earthen mountain, please protect the rocky cliff!

Ama layho,
The earthen mountain up there is older,
The grassy hillock below it is younger.
Earthen mountain, please protect the grassy hillock!

Vertical layers of mountain topography are used here as an allegory to highlight cultural ideals about social relations within the family. The Tibetans of Sama envision a mountain's structure to consist of four layers: snow peak, earthen mountain, rocky cliff, and grassy hillock. Each symbolizes one of the four generations in an extended family. The grandparents' generation, the snow peak, is the highest and most venerated. Although age commands respect, the elderly are often infirm and thus need to be sheltered by their middle-aged children, who are represented in the song as the solid earthen core of the mountain. Middle-aged householders are the nucleus of a multigenerational family. They still possess the strength of body to be economically productive; they have invaluable knowledge of farming and herding practices; and they have acquired social acumen and political savvy through years of practical experience. In the song they are called on to protect the other layers of the mountain—in other words, to support aging parents (the snow-covered peaks), to provide guidance for their own children who are coming of age (the rocky cliffs), and to nurture their own grandchildren who are just entering the world (the grassy hillocks). In an important sense, the song conveys the bride's hope that her new family will shelter her from harm.

When the wedding party approaches the groom's home, the men sing the following verses:

> In the song of the ladies,
> There is a mountain of *yang* [material prosperity].
> Because it is filled with yang,
> Animals flock to the mountain,
> Their fleeces become fuller,
> They all flock to the mountain of yang.

> In the song of the ladies,
> There is a mountain of victorious lotus flowers.
> A lotus tree is erected
> And is piled high with *khata* [ceremonial scarves],
> Filling the whole world with life.

> In the song of the ladies,
> The house of the man who sits at the head of the line
> Is a house built from piled stones of gold.
> To those who are lined up to the right and the left,
> We offer our apologies.

The first stanza reflects the groom's family's wish that the bride, here portrayed as a mountain of yang, will bring material prosperity into the household. The second stanza makes reference to the wedding feast:

The bride is likened to a lotus flower, which in Buddhism is a symbol of purity rising above the murk below. At the conclusion of the feast the bride and groom sit side by side and have khata, ceremonial scarves that represent blessings and good fortune, draped over their necks by every member of the village until they are literally buried under a pile of offerings. The third stanza honors the father of the bride, who sits at the head of the table at the wedding feast, the place of highest prestige. He and his family are paid homage for the sacrifice they have made in giving away a daughter. In contrast, the groom's family members are seated in less conspicuous places. At the wedding feast the status difference between bride-givers and bride-takers is symbolically displayed—a reminder, perhaps, of a debt that will one day need to be repaid.

Once the wedding ceremony concludes, the bride is officially a member of her husband's household. Marriage represents a transformation for a young woman to the tenuous status of daughter-in-law, now, as an outsider, at the mercy of her in-laws. Until a bride can prove her worth by bearing children—particularly male children—she will occupy a position of inferiority in the household. My neighbor Tubten once explained the relative merit of male and female offspring:

> If you need a servant to help with household chores, then it is better to have a girl. For this reason many people hope that their first-born child is a daughter, since she can help her mother raise all of the children who come afterward. But if you want somebody to take over the house and estate, it is better to have a boy. Sons are more beneficial, for they can engage in trade and so have a chance of becoming wealthy. Girls have no such opportunities. When a girl gets married, she is sent away to her husband's household, where she must remain to care for her own children.

In Sama, as in most Tibetan societies, a son is entitled to inherit a portion of his father's estate upon marriage. In reality, however, the division of assets does not occur until the new bride bears a child. A long-term household partitioning process thus commences when the eldest son in the family marries and brings his bride home to reside in an extended-family household. This living arrangement is only temporary, however. Once their first child is born, the young couple claims their share of family assets (which if there are two sons would be one-third of all land and cattle; one-third is reserved for the younger son when he marries, and one-third remains with the father until his death) and then moves into a separate home to commence life as independent householders. When the youngest son marries, he likewise brings his bride home to reside with her new in-laws. Once their first child is born, however, they do not have to move out and build or buy their own residence. Rather, it is the parents who must seek shelter elsewhere. Parents can linger for a while, but those who remain too long are derided for not allowing their sons to mature and become self-sufficient. Generally they move to a retirement home on the grounds of Pema Chöling Gomba.

TAX, RITUALS, AND SPIRITUAL SECURITY

Although the details vary from place to place, most Tibetan villages have devised some sort of tax system to make sure that public coffers are full enough to support the performance of communal rituals. In Sama, the tax system is directly related to marriage and the formation of new households.

For taxation purposes, each household in Sama is represented by a *kyimdag* (head of household), generally the senior male, although in some cases a woman can act as kyimdag. When a son first marries yet is still living with his parents, his father is considered the kyimdag. This changes when a child is born and the son moves with his family into a new, separate household. At that point, in addition to the assets they receive through inheritance, the young couple receives a "loan" *(bulön)* of seventy-five measures of corn and/or barley from Pema Chöling Monastery, which is administrated by the head lama of the village.[4] The household is then obligated to repay five measures of barley, five measures of corn, and four measures of rice to the monastery each year until the death of the kyimdag. The repayment is considered "interest" *(kyeka)* on the loan. By meeting the tax obligation each year, the household retains the right to access all communal resources around the village, most notably the pastures and forests.

Simple arithmetic tells us that a considerable surplus of grain is generated through the tax system, a surplus that is then used to fund four annual communal rituals. In this way, the tax system provides spiritual security for the entire village, since the primary purpose of the communal rites is to ward off potentially malevolent forces, thus ensuring peace, health, and prosperity for the coming year.

One of the highlights of the ritual cycle in Sama is the annual Kanjur Circumambulation Festival (Kanjur Khora). The Kanjur (translations of the words of the Buddha) is a collection of texts that forms the core of Tibetan canonical literature.[5] Most major Buddhist institutions in the Tibetan world have a collection of these works, each volume carefully wrapped in cloth and stored within specially constructed alcoves. As a physical manifestation of the Buddha's teachings, the Kanjur is laden with symbolic value that can be harnessed for the purpose of fulfilling mundane goals.

In Sama the Kanjur Circumambulation Festival commences in the middle of the second lunar month (early March) and coincides with the end of the winter retreat period. The timing brings the community together between the bleak winter months of seclusion and the abundant summer months of intensive economic activity. The first part of the festival is marked by the reading of all 108 volumes of the Kanjur. Participation in the reading is restricted to chöpa; lamas and high-ranking monks exclude themselves, whereas nuns are discouraged from participating. A record is kept of who shows up for how many days, so that the readers can be compensated for their efforts. Each individual receives a text and reads at his own pace. The most adept readers can complete a volume in a day, whereas novices may take as many as four days to work their way through one book.

After all the volumes have been read, a day is set aside for circumambulating all the fields of Sama. Men and adolescents (not necessarily those who participated in the reading) wrap one to three volumes of the Kanjur in a piece of cloth and then strap the bundle to their backs. Preceded by a retinue of men and boys blowing conches, carrying banners and a statue of the Buddha, and playing instruments, the book-bearers depart from Pema Chöling and descend the hill toward the village. Along the route, groups of elderly men, women, and children sit beside lit piles of juniper. As the books pass by, these villagers bow their heads in reverence and receive the blessings of being in such close proximity to the sacred words of the Buddha.

The goal of the circumambulation is to symbolically demarcate village boundaries. After completing each section of the route, the entourage stops and is served food and refreshments by a patron, usually the male head of a household that was especially successful during the previous year. The progression, alternating between circumambulation and feasting, continues throughout the day.

Lama Gyatso told me that the ritual is analogous to taking refuge in what Buddhists refer to as the three jewels: the Buddha, his teachings, and the community of devotees. At another level, Lama Gyatso clarifies that this ritual has specific benefits that are of particular concern to the worldly villagers. Bearing the Kanjur around the village and all the fields helps ward off insect infestations and crop diseases, ensures healthy and productive cattle, keeps the human residents of Sama free from ailments, and increases the overall prosperity of households. In an important sense, this is an agricultural rite. Everybody involved obtains a blessing through contact with the sacred teachings of Buddha; in addition, their fields and herds receive symbolic protection against the dangers of this often hostile environment.

At an important level, the combined tax and ritual system acts as a mechanism for redistribution. As spring arrives, food stocks are generally running low. At this critical time of year, Kanjur readers are fed three meals a day that are drawn from communal stockpiles, and circumambulation participants are permitted a day of feasting, sponsored by patrons who have been relatively fortunate and accumulated modest surpluses. All of this activity transpires shortly before the labor-intensive agricultural season commences. It should come as no surprise that the timing of the ritual is well coordinated with major economic activities and a time of nutritional insecurity.

INFERTILITY AND FIDELITY

In most cases a newlywed bride will eventually give birth to a child, an event that leads to the division of assets as a household begins to partition. More important, from the bride's perspective, childbirth enhances her status in the household by providing either a male heir or a daughter who can help solidify future social links through marriage. Tibetans have a saying: "However ferocious a warrior may be, a friend of valor he shall need. However pretty a wife may be, a son on her lap she will need."

Not all couples in Sama are successful when it comes to the art of procreation, however. Infertility is a prospect everyone dreads. The inability to conceive within marriage is almost always deemed the fault of the woman, and is considered fair justification for the husband to divorce her and seek another wife. After all, children represent both economic security and family continuity. Although nothing prevents a divorced woman from remarrying, who is likely to give her a second chance in a society where offspring are so highly valued? As in so many societies, pregnancy in Nubri validates a woman's status both within the household and throughout the community. Nevertheless, couples do occasionally remain together despite having no offspring. One couple in Sama provides a touching reminder that personal affection can and does make a difference, since they are still together long after the woman passed beyond her prime reproductive years without bearing a single child. They are the exception, however.

One day while measuring fields on the outskirts of Sama I was approached by Sonam, a man in waning middle age whose face is lined by the wrinkles of time and whose smile is marred by toothless gaps. Like so many of these hearty mountain folks, he still possesses a solid frame, taut muscles, and a chiseled jaw. When Sonam hailed me, I took a break and sat beside him on a large stone. Our conversation meandered for a while before coming back to the inevitable topic of family. "So," he inquired, "are you married?" I replied in the affirmative. "How long have you been married," he probed. "A bit over five years," I replied. "Ah, you must have several children by now. How many kids do you have?" "None yet," I told him, tactfully refraining from elaborating on the efficacy of modern contraceptives. To my surprise, he exclaimed, "Your wife is defective! Get rid of her!"

The topic of my spouse was a delicate matter. Communication difficulties had enlarged the physical distance that separated us for months on end. At the time of Sonam's terse directive, my yak-express postal system had blown a hoof, so to speak, since not a single letter had arrived from home. But a few days later a message arrived from Hritar, a young, well-traveled, and highly respected man from the neighboring village of Lho. Apparently a packet of my mail had wound up at his home.

It was early afternoon, so I hastily organized my backpack and hustled down the valley to Lho to pick up the letters. When I arrived breathlessly at sunset, Hritar handed me a tattered, weather-beaten parcel. "At long last," I sighed, ripping through the tape seal, eager to devour the envelopes of various sizes that I was sure would come spilling out. To my dismay, though, yet another foul-up had occurred: these were not the eagerly expected letters from home, but glossy newsletters announcing expatriate events in Kathmandu—tennis matches, furniture swaps, and pot-luck dinners! To me, Kathmandu was as distant and remote as America. It takes an arduous seven-day trek to reach the former; it takes that same trek plus a mere plane ride to reach the latter. Imagine Hritar's surprise when I perused the various documents, let out a roar of disgust, crumpled everything in my hands, and cast a large paper sphere into the blazing hearth! Hritar sprung forth to save the pages, but I restrained him. Junk mail is junk mail, wherever one happens to be.

The next day I awoke before dawn, had a farewell tea with Hritar's family, and commenced a somber trek back to Sama. En route I met another acquaintance from Lho who asked what I had been doing in his village. Once my litany of invectives had subsided and he was able to unravel the purpose of my mission, his eyes lit up. "Ayah!" he exclaimed. "Last month I brought some letters from Kathmandu for you, but I got drunk at a friend's house and left them there!" A broad smile broke across his face, thinking that I would greet the news with cheers of approval and a hearty slap on the back. I did not share this man's enthusiasm for what I considered to be a monumental blunder. It took an enormous effort to compose myself. I fixed him squarely in the eye and said, "Get those letters to me as soon as possible—please!"

In fairness to this man, the people of Nubri do not have a tradition of sending or receiving mail. Furthermore, time has a different dimension for them. The men of Nubri are used to spending weeks, months, and even years away from family members with no means to communicate. What difference could a few days make? This understanding allowed me to maintain a semblance of calm when informed that my precious letters were probably now stuffing chinks in the walls of a stranger's house.

That evening back in Sama my despondency was evident as thoughts flitted between the waylaid letters and Sonam's distasteful remarks concerning my "defective" wife. Tashi noticed my agitation as we passed the evening immersed in our own thoughts, listening to Tibetan music from Lhasa on our shortwave radio. My usual quips and mindless wisecracks, so much a part of our nightly attempt to stave off boredom, were not forthcoming. Tashi tossed a chunk of wood across the fireplace to get my attention, and then asked point blank, "What's bothering you?"

I reiterated the conversation with Sonam. To my surprise, Tashi became wracked by convulsions of laughter. Eventually the aftershocks of his outburst subsided and he said, "Do not be offended, my friend. The fool who in ignorance speaks of his knowledge reveals his own defects for others to see. Who is Sonam to talk about children? I remember when he was first married. No children, none at all for many years. Then he divorced his wife, thinking she was defective. Sonam remarried, and how many children does he have now? None! What about his ex-wife? She remarried and a year later gave birth to a son! So now we have a nickname for Sonam. We call him Dzo [the sterile male crossbreed between a yak and a cow]."

Tashi lifted my despondent mood with his keen sense of irony. In many ways I pitied Sonam, for he had failed to fulfill the most important task in a householder's life. Despite clear evidence to the contrary, he lived in denial by continuing to blame the lack of offspring on his wives.

THE SEXUAL LIVES OF SAVANTS

Tashi is a lifelong bachelor. I could not help but wonder whether he had ever had a relationship with a woman. One day I mustered the nerve to ask him. He broke into laughter and said, "You know, I was a good-looking guy in my prime. I was strong, handsome, and everybody liked me. So naturally I stole a wife or two!"

Stealing wives is the way men speak about adultery. As in most places, sexual banter is one way men assert their virility among peers.[6] I already mentioned that men often joked that Tashi and I, as "brothers," should consider taking a common wife. They often suggested one particular elderly spinster who lived in the neighborhood and, as I later learned, had once given birth to an illegitimate child that later died. Tashi lost his usual composure and became combative when this particular union was suggested. I could not help but wonder if she had been one of my companion's conquests of bygone days. He refused to elaborate.

To the common suggestion that Tashi and I should claim a wife, my usual response was, "Sorry, but according to your traditions one woman can have two husbands, but one man cannot have two wives. I am already married and do not want to cause a scandal here." My escape was not so easy, for one man explained how to get along in the absence of a wife. "Since your wife is not here, butter up your hand and see what happens next!" I accepted the ribbing in stride, knowing full well that being the butt of a vulgar joke implies a certain degree of acceptance.

Talk of sexuality and "wife stealing" is not restricted to the male domain. One day the boisterous Chimi came by to visit a house where I was drinking arak with a friend and his wife, a pretty woman in her early thirties who has an engaging smile. We could hear Chimi's guttural voice from outside, and the floorboards shook as he stooped and staggered to avoid banging his head on the lintel when entering. It was late afternoon and he had just started to imbibe, so his mood was jovial and not yet churlish. (Arak can lift one's spirits when consumed in moderation; in excess, it often leads to ugly encounters.)

Chimi plopped his stout frame down upon a threadbare carpet and grinned at our hostess as she poured him a cup of arak. He then leaned toward our host in a gesture of contrived confidence before calling out for all to hear, "We are like brothers, so lend me your wife for the night! It is my right as your brother!" While my host and the other men present laughed at this obvious mockery of the polyandrous marriage system, the object of Chimi's lustful intent shot a venomous glance in his direction and spat on the floor in feigned disgust. The effort she exerted in repressing a smile, however, revealed that she was probably not truly offended.

•   •   •

"Tashi," I asked one day, "I have heard a Tibetan saying: 'For a young wife, her old husband is more boring than a corpse.' Is this expression common in Sama?" While on the trail between Kutang and Sama, Tashi and I had been discussing the meanings behind certain proverbs. We had just stopped to catch our breath and wallow in the sun after a long, steep climb. Below us a tributary rumbled over boulders as it plummeted into the main river of this narrow valley. Above the valley was a wall of snow-clad peaks. We shared a smoke, reclining side by side on flat rocks with hats shielding our eyes from the intense sun. This was one of our favorite resting spots along the trail.

Tashi began to snicker. "You know, it is not always that way. Remember when we visited Hritar's father?"

I remembered the encounter well. We had met Hritar's father while on the trail to Trong, a gomba across the valley from Lho. The man's unblemished skin, glistening black hair, and nimble gait belied his true age. He had a retirement home at Trong, so we gratefully accepted his invitation for a cup of tea and some food. Tending the hearth of the single-story house was a young woman with an infant suckling at her breast.

Tashi continued, "Hritar's father is older than I am, so he must be at least seventy-five by now. Therefore he was over seventy when he fathered that little boy of his!" A few years before, Hritar's father had divorced the woman who was the mother of his many sons and daughters. He then established a separate residence at Trong, where he now lived with his young bride from Kutang, a woman more than forty years his junior. Not only had this event incited vicious gossip among the villagers, but it had been the cause of an intergenerational rift. As discussed before, each son inherits a portion of his father's land and herd when he marries; the father holds on to his share until death, at which time it is divided between the sons as their final allotment of inheritance. Hritar and his brothers were managing households of their own. With expanding families, they fully counted on receiving the last portion of their inheritance. The fact that one more son had arrived infuriated the brothers, especially since this child was a full generation younger and was born to a mother other than their own. They banded together and vowed to disallow any transfer of property to their half brother. When land is scarce, conflicts are inevitable, a theme that is reflected in yet another proverb: "Prosperity makes even enemies into friends. Poverty makes even relatives into enemies."

As we sat in the brilliant sunshine discussing the significance of these events, Tashi was reminded of a related adage. He said, "When fire burns in the mouth of the eighty-year-old man, ashes are poured into the mouths of his brothers."

"What does that mean?" I asked.

Tashi explained:

> I remember long ago there was a man named Natsung. He had no sons, so when he was eighty years old he thought, "Hmm, my brothers and nephews want to inherit my estate when I die. This is not good, for I do not have sons of my own who can inherit my property." You see, this is our custom here. If a man has no son, then his brothers and nephews will inherit everything.
>
> There was a young woman in the village who understood the situation quite well. She knew the man had a large estate but no sons, so she hatched a scheme. One day the old man went outside to urinate and she secretly followed him. When she spied the gentle frothing of his urine, the woman thought to herself, "I believe this old man still has a bit of vigor left in his ancient body." Afterward she began to pamper him and give him many gifts. To the elderly man's surprise, he was still capable of an erection. He then impregnated the young woman. She gave birth to a son. The brothers and nephews were enraged knowing that they no longer stood any chance to receive his property. That is why we say, "When fire burns in the mouth of the eighty-year-old man, ashes are poured into the mouths of his brothers." When an old man decides to have more children, the hopes of his kin turn to ashes.

• • •

The theme of feminine power exercised through sexuality is common among the people of Nubri. Sharp gender imbalances persist that are directly related to the control over productive resources such as land and animals and the political authority that such control entails. Landownership entitles men to participate in village councils. Women are shunted off to the background where they can listen, but they are not encouraged to voice any concerns of their own. This gender-based differential does not, however, mean that women lack any form of power whatsoever. Inside the home it is clear who is in charge: women manage domestic affairs and are responsible for such critical responsibilities as food budgeting and petty barter that keeps a family well fed. A woman who runs an efficient household wields much influence over her family and, by extension, her community.

Nevertheless, women's power is rarely, if ever, acknowledged by men, except in relation to sexuality. Men claim that women use their feminine charms to beguile and manipulate men. As such, women are perceived as forces to be reckoned with. Perhaps this is an oblique admission by men that subtle forms of power exist outside the publicly displayed and culturally validated edifices of authority. This theme is illustrated in a tale my neighbor Tubten told me one day.

> Once long ago a very beautiful girl was traveling by foot to her village. Along the way she met a man who was leading a horse. She was tired and so wanted to ride instead of walk. The man took one glance at her and was overcome by lust. He then began to plot how he could have her. But this girl was quite clever, and she asked the man whether she could borrow his horse to cross the river to her village. The man contemplated the request, thinking that this might be an opening for fulfilling his wanton desires. She, however, knew his type and could see through his transparent intentions. Before the man could speak, she said, "I am a girl who just wants to ride a horse, and you are a man who only wants my body." She then shocked him by chanting what seemed like a sacred mantra, "Om tetu retu tare soha!" [I pay reverence to your mount, and leave you with the fantasy of my genitals!]. The man was shocked into inaction on hearing such vulgar words in what sounded like a religious chant. When he recovered, he saw her on his horse disappearing on the other side of the river.

· · ·

The frivolity of youth gives way to the angst of maturity when the householders of Nubri make the transition, through marriage, from adolescence to adulthood. Marriage gives meaning to their lives, through the interfamilial connections that are thereby formed and through the social roles incumbent in procreation. Whereas clerics are expected to renounce reproduction, householders consider it a necessary and even desirable endeavor, one that involves the excitement of flirtation and the exploration of sexuality. Eventually the youthful vigor

of newlywed householders wanes, replaced by middle-aged compla-
cency, which is just a step away from old-age despondency. One's own
children will one day become the earthen mountain that protects and
nurtures the white-capped snow peaks above. In the meantime, the
struggle to survive is the most fundamental and ever-present task at
hand. Misfortune can strike at any time.

CHAPTER 7

High Peaks and Deep Valleys

The Imponderable Nature of Everyday Life

If you never experience both happiness and sorrow,
You will never know the difference between the two.

Tibetan Proverb

A WINTER STORM

Tashi awoke first and emerged from beneath his pile of bedding beside the hearth. His face was barely discernible in the faint morning light as he squinted toward the hole in the wall that served as a window. A frown crossed his face, followed by an audible groan. I immediately understood: it was still snowing. Grudgingly I sat up in my bed, which consisted of a thin foam mat resting on the wooden floorboards on the other side of the hearth from where Tashi slept. After brushing away some flakes of snow that had managed to seep through the porous walls, I peered through the small rectangular aperture into another gray and dreary day. The mountains across the river were completely obscured by the wind-driven snow. Once again we would be forced to spend interminable hours within the confines of this cold, drafty, unlit house. I echoed Tashi's grumble of dismay.

The snowstorm had been raging for several days. Houses in the village now looked like a jumble of boulders strewn across uneven ground and covered by a thick, undulating white blanket. Unlike other mornings when we awoke to the sounds of horses neighing, roosters crowing, and neighbors shouting greetings from house to house, today was completely silent. All but the most essential outdoor activities had ceased.

Tashi mumbled a brief prayer while rising. Without bothering to put on shirt or shoes, he stumbled out onto the porch to gather some firewood. I often marveled at these hardy people for whom the frigid temperature is a matter of small concern. Whereas Tashi walks outside in bare feet without complaint, my toes get frostbitten inside a down-filled sleeping bag. A lifetime of hardship has steeled his body.

Tashi reentered, dropped a load of wood on the floor, then knelt and blew into the hearth to revive some live embers. Eventually a few sparks emerged from the bed of ashes, on which he carefully laid some wood chips. The fire sprang to life, providing warmth, light, and a familiar crackling sound that signaled it was time to get up. In the past I had tried to rise before my friend, but he insisted that I stay tucked in until the fire was started. Tashi always seemed to make life more bearable in so many subtle ways.

"The wood supply is getting low," he mused. "I fear we may run out before the snow melts." It was late winter, a time when people begin to anticipate wood-gathering trips to the forest after long months of deep snow and howling winds. We could always ask a neighbor to lend us enough firewood to get us through the remainder of winter, but Tashi is a proud man. When the issue arose, he habitually told me, "I have never been a beggar. Why should I start now?" Begging contradicts his lifelong philosophy of earning everything that comes his way. As his body ages and his vigor wanes, Tashi is forced more and more often to rely on the generosity of his neighbors. It is unclear precisely where he will ultimately draw the line between independence and survival. For a man of principle, death is preferable to the humiliation of beggary.

As we passed the morning listening to avalanches rumbling in the distance, our mood degenerated from somberness to downright despondence. Eventually we heard footsteps ascending the ladder to our door, and a resounding male voice called out, "Anybody home?" Tashi replied with a note of cynicism, "Where else would we be in such weather?!" In walked our friend Chimi, covered with a fresh dusting of white powder. Chimi plunked his hulking frame beside the hearth, causing the whole house to shake. Like us, he was bored out of his wits and in search of companions with whom to pass the endless hours of this dreary day. Tashi offered him some tea, to which Chimi replied only with a roguish grin as he wrested a bottle of arak from the recesses of his woolen tunic. Tashi smiled for the first time that day.

Another visitor soon announced his presence at our door. It was Angjung, the neighbor with whom we share a common wall. Angjung's hearth was a mere three feet from our own, separated only by a permeable stone barrier. We could hear everything he and his wife, Dawa, said, and they could hear everything that passed between Tashi and me. Angjung and Dawa are good neighbors, as kind and generous as people can be. They knew they had a standing invitation to our house, just as we knew we could drop in on them at any time. Angjung must have heard Chimi's boisterous laughter and leapt at the opportunity to relieve his own boredom. He came laden with more arak. The mood in Tashi's house was discernibly improving on this, the fourth day of the storm.

Tashi passed filterless cigarettes around and began to warm the arak over the open fire. Meanwhile, our conversation focused on the potential hazards of this storm. "If it lasts much longer, we'll have to tunnel our way about the village," joked Chimi. He then became more serious and asked, "Has anybody been able to make it to Mimi today?" We all shook our heads, thinking about the cattle at Mimi, the winter grazing ground across the river, situated on a large, grassy slope with southern exposure. At high altitude the intense sunlight melts snow quickly on this slope, so cattle can graze most of the winter without requiring stall feeding.[1] Yet a deep snowfall prevents bovines from foraging, while also thwarting attempts by villagers to make the hour-long trek up to Mimi. Some yaks would certainly starve in this storm unless somebody was able to open the storage huts filled with fodder.

Angjung then expressed another fear. "Let's hope no avalanches wipe away any of our fields this year." Losing fields under a pile of debris left by snow-slides is a major concern in the village, where arable land is scarce and ground on which to create new fields does not exist. For this very reason the culling of trees on the slopes above most fields has long been prohibited by decree of the village council. Still, an especially large avalanche can cause irreparable harm to the agricultural component of the economy. Herds and fields, two pillars of the fragile economy, are threatened by winter storms.

Tashi added, "The way this blizzard is going, before you know it our only company will be the rats." The presence of rats requires villagers to store all food safely in the home. On most nights Tashi and I had nocturnal visitors who would scurry about the rafters, descend to the shelves where cooking implements are kept, and keep us awake by scratching away at the remains of our dinner encrusted on the skillet. As Buddhists, the villagers are supposed to tolerate the vermin. After all, every sentient being is entitled to compassion. Tashi, however, feels little remorse for liberating the occasional rat from its current incarnation in the animal realm. To accomplish this task he keeps a supply of poison on hand, which he mixes with some barley flour and butter and shapes into tasty morsels that are placed strategically about the house. I remember one night being awakened by a gentle thud beside my bed, then rising to find a large, dead rodent belly up by my side. Tashi rationalized this categorically non-Buddhist act by saying, "I am a poor man. The rats should take pity on me instead of the other way around!"

While my companions continued to contemplate worst-case scenarios, I rose and made my way to the other side of the room. The conversation had reminded me of a snowstorm that confined Pema Döndrup to his hermitage nearly three hundred years ago. After a few minutes rummaging through a chest filled with field notes, personal diaries, and stacks of photocopied Tibetan manuscripts, I located the biography of Pema Döndrup and brought it back to my seat by the fire. While Tashi filled our cups with another round of warm arak, I leafed through the pages in search of a particular passage. "What do you have there?" asked Chimi. "Hang on a second," I replied, "you're going to enjoy this." With my three companions looking on with rapt attention, I cleared my throat and began to read about Pema Döndrup's ordeal. The setting: a remote hermitage high in a side valley of Kutang sometime in the early 1700s.

Much snow fell during the eleventh month of the year [December/January]. All of the boulders, pine trees, and shrubs were buried and all of the large and small birds disappeared beneath the snow. The snow fell continuously for six days and six nights. There was no way to boil stew because I was cut off from any firewood supply. My tsampa supply was low, so I consumed it little by little. The door gradually sank in the snow; there was no way to go out. Recalling my elder and younger brothers [both of whom had recently died], tears flowed from my eyes.[2]

Oh, my lama, please have mercy on me! When I lived in the village I was covered by dust. Now that I live in the mountain retreat I am covered by snow. I, an unfortunate man, have no other place to seek refuge. Whether I live or die, am happy or sad, I leave everything in the hands of the Buddha, his teachings, and the community of followers.

When I looked at my clothing, it was torn everywhere. There was no firewood to burn in the hearth. There was no stew in the pot to be eaten. There was no way to tell when the snow would clear away. I could see no evidence of human activities. After I had endured these conditions for a while, the snow finally began to melt. I jammed open the door, pushed some snow aside, and went outside to look around. Not a single tree, boulder, or shrub was visible. Snow had fallen to the height of a person. The cloudless sky was clear blue. I sat upon a large boulder and noticed the

peace and quiet. Not a human's voice, a dog's bark, nor a bird's call could
be heard.

When I finished reading the story my companions nodded in sympathy, understanding Pema Döndrup's plight with the empathy that comes
from life in a hazardous environment. Tashi joked, "If that damn rat
keeps up his nightly raids, just like Pema Döndrup we'll also be without
food before this storm is over!" The tale from the past brought some
levity to our smoky, dimly lit hovel, but also evoked memories of storms
that had threatened the very existence of my friends. They began to
reminisce about blizzards that dumped so much snow on Sama that
people needed to break through deep drifts just to get from house to
house. They spoke of unseasonably late tempests that covered newly
sprouted barley with ice, dooming a good portion of the year's crop.
Chimi, the consummate trader, reminisced about the time he and some
friends were caught in a storm high on one of the passes leading to
Tibet. With unseen avalanches roaring down slopes in every direction,
they only just survived by sticking together and praying continuously.

Tashi Döndrup fell silent, an uncharacteristic state for my old friend,
who was so often the life of a party. We all noticed the change in his
mood. A somber spell fell across the room as he began to reminisce
about the tragic consequences of a storm and its aftermath more than
forty years before. The blizzard caused an avalanche that destroyed
Pungyen Monastery, the temple dedicated to the village's protective
deity, situated high in the summer pasture at the base of Mt. Pungyen.
There were human casualties as well. Tashi recalled:

> My sister and I have the same mother, but different fathers. Although much
> younger, like me she was a *nyelu*, an illegitimate child. Her father was a
> monk who broke his vows. It was my mother's decision to make her a nun.
> She was sent to Dagkar Taso Monastery for training. Lopön Zangpo
> donated some clothing and other items for her. After her ordination at
> Dagkar Taso, she usually lived with my mother and me in the village. But
> she had to go to Pungyen during the first month of the year. In the past
> people still went to Pungyen Monastery for a winter religious retreat.
> Nowadays they only go during the warmer seasons. Perhaps the monks and
> nuns are not as dedicated as in former times. Who knows, but at that time
> people went every winter for a religious retreat during the first month. The
> elder ones went to pray and meditate, while the younger ones went to learn
> reading and writing. When I was twenty-four, she was thirteen and was
> staying at Pungyen Monastery. Eleven people in all were there that winter
> [1953] when a snowstorm struck.

Among the eleven people staying at Pungyen Monastery, three nuns were killed by an avalanche. My sister was one of them. Of course, at the time we knew nothing, since the monastery is hidden behind that ridge over there. In the afternoon Dawa Tenzin and I were playing dice in the courtyard. A man came running into the village and called to me, "Your sister the nun, she is dead!" I was stunned, not ready to believe what he had said. My mother began to cry.

Several men and I grabbed digging tools and headed up to Pungyen Monastery. We climbed and climbed, anxious to see what had happened and what we could do. The trail is so high and so cold and so difficult to get through due to snow. But now we had to go—we had to see if we could save my sister.

When we got to the temple we found the buildings had been buried under huge chunks of ice. It was a disaster. We started digging furiously—I have no idea where my energy came from. Eventually we found the rubble of the temple, and we found the bodies. Three nuns were dead, including my only sister. That was the saddest day of my life. With heavy hearts we brought the bodies down to the village for a proper cremation. My mother and I sold everything we had in order to perform a merit-making ceremony on her behalf. We were poor, but we had to do this to honor our kin. Later some people managed to dig up most of the statues and other valuable items housed in the temple. The temple has since been rebuilt, but it will never be the same.

People wondered why such a tragedy struck our monastery. Some said that the protector of our village who lives on the mountain must have been angry with us, and even blamed the Japanese mountaineers who had tried to climb Mt. Pungyen during the past autumn, saying that the climbers must have defiled the sacred slopes of the mountain. I don't know if this was the reason. But when the climbers came back the next year for another attempt, we refused to let them go up.[3]

VERSES IN PRAISE OF THE PROTECTOR

Life in the harsh, unpredictable environment of Sama is too often punctuated by sudden tragedies. Despite the constant threats of natural disasters, crop failure, and disease, the people of this village strive on a daily basis to raise their families and live respectable lives. Meanwhile, the majestic Mt. Pungyen envelops the valley in its shadow each afternoon. High on the icy, crystalline peak dwells the deity called Lord Pungyen. Paintings in the village temple depict this protector wearing a white turban, brandishing a sword, and riding a white horse. When properly appeased, he battles enemies lurking in the spirit world. When angered, he can send avalanches tumbling down from the lofty heights on unsuspecting villagers.

Pungyen literally means "Ornamented Heap." According to Lama Gyatso, "This is because in one sense the mountain is just a heap of earth, rocks, and cliffs. That is the way it may appear to you. But to us it is an ornamented heap of religious teachings, an ornamented heap of riches, and an ornamented heap of mountain-dwelling animals. Just watch, tomorrow morning the radiant light of the sun will ornament that mountain. The mountain is the divine palace of Lord Pungyen, his consort, and son."

Mountain deities in the Tibetan world are imbued with many of the social characteristics of the human communities over whom they watch. Pungyen is no exception. According to Lama Gyatso's description, the protector Pungyen is a father; his son and wife live, respectively, on the summits of mountains to the west and east. The mountainous landscape is thereby animated with divinity cast in the image of a human family.

Pungyen, whether seen as the mass of ice and rock itself or the war-riorlike protector who dwells on the summit, is the object of veneration. The mountain inspires the inhabitants dwelling below to write verses of praise, such as this homage:

> I bow before the protector of our land,
> the awe-inspiring snow mountain Pungyen,
> situated most auspiciously at the border of Tibet and Nepal.
> According to prophecies made by Lord Buddha,
> there will one day emerge a mighty rock, the king of all mountains.
> On the outside the mountain resembles a chöten,
> made of light refracted through a white crystal.
> On the inside reside Lord Pungyen and his divine retinue,
> purely reflected as if from a mirror within.
> From the dwelling place of the deities above,
> the mountain descends to the ground like a chöten.
> From the netherworld palace of the serpents,
> the mountain rises high in the sky like a jewel.
> The protector, Lord Pungyen, lives like a king here in the middle realm.
> I bow with reverence before him who dwells on this magnificent mountain.

Scores of miraculous sites associated with the worship of Lord Pungyen are scattered across the flanks of his alpine residence. Tashi Döndrup once explained:

> There are one hundred and eight places where we make offerings to Pungyen. These sites are associated with miraculous powers. Let me tell you about two of them.
>   In the good old days there was a blacksmith. But he was not really a human. A lama from our village used to travel up and down the valley that

ascends the north flank of the mountain to the grazing grounds above. On his way he would pass by the place where the blacksmith worked. When going up he asked the blacksmith to put some nails in his boots. When he came back down the blacksmith customarily left the repaired boots there by the trail. The same routine took place when the lama requested the blacksmith to repair knives and other metal implements. The lama liked to chat awhile with the blacksmith, who was very fond of talking. Nobody ever saw the blacksmith work, but somehow his chores always got done. The place where he used to work is one of the miraculous sites where we make offerings to Pungyen.

Another site is located beyond the lake at the base of the glacier cascading down the side of Pungyen. There is a large boulder. In the good old days people did not have to seek hither and thither for grass for their cattle. They just extracted it from beneath that boulder. There are two narrow paths connecting the upland and lowland pastures. When both paths are obstructed, it is impossible to get to the pastures. So people go to the boulder, where they find heaps of grass. That is another miraculous site where we make offerings to Pungyen. If we make offerings with sincere devotion, and if we keep Pungyen pleased, then he keeps us safe. He is the protector of our village.

TO PLEASE IS TO APPEASE

Lord Pungyen is actively present in all spiritual, social, and economic aspects of village life.[4] Thrice yearly people make offerings to Pungyen at a cairn situated outside the village. On these special days devoted to the village's protective deity, a young man carries a small, uprooted birch tree from house to house. Each family attaches to the branches a wad of wool, a lump of butter, and a white scarf. Through these gifts they provide the protector with symbolic offerings of food, clothing, and wishes for good fortune. In addition, they proffer arak to the man whose duty it is to collect the gifts. Needless to say, by the end of his rounds to the ninety-odd households of Sama the poor fellow is inebriated to the point of being barely able to stand, let alone lug about the tree. Nevertheless, he stoically carries on, for his duty is not complete until the tree laden with offerings is erected on the cairn dedicated to Pungyen. Three men wait by the cairn, and when the tree arrives they offer arak to Pungyen and perform a *lhasol* (offering to the deities) ceremony. The men, who are known as *pajo*, represent yet another layer of religious complexity in Nubri, their main function being to appease deities such as Pungyen.[5]

Despite outward displays of levity, villagers observe the three annual offerings to Lord Pungyen with much reverence, realizing that they can ill afford to neglect the potential consequences of failing to please their protector. In Tibetan religious ceremonies deities are treated like honored guests. First, they are invited to take up temporary residence in *torma,* conical cakes made from tsampa that are placed on an altar. Once the deities have been enticed through prayers to embody themselves within the torma, they are feted with fine scents, tasty morsels of food, strong liquor, and kind words. Lord Pungyen is always offered a special torma, and separate ones are made for his consort and his son. The objective of treating Lord Pungyen like a venerated guest is to please him so that he consents to safeguard the lives of his devotees for another year.[6] Lapses in protocol can have dire repercussions. Once angered, the mountain-dwelling god is known to react with a vengeance.

In addition to the three special days dedicated to Pungyen, the villagers perform other rites to secure the deity's continuing protection. I once encountered Lama Gyatso painting what looked like a saddle design on the flanks of a small white yak. He explained:

> Each year we release an animal to the wilds. A white yak is one of the mounts of Pungyen, the vehicle on which he rides. We release a white yak to the wilds so that our protector will have a mount. That's right, we paint a saddle on his flanks, and then shoo him off into the mountains. No longer will he be beholden to the company of humans; henceforth he is the property of Pungyen. We do this for the benefit of all worldly householders in the village. In exchange, Pungyen removes all obstacles that prevent a happy and healthy life. The villagers prosper.

The ultimate rite of appeasement is accomplished by honoring Pungyen through play. The most anticipated event of Sama's ritual calendar occurs on the third day of the third lunar month (usually in April or May), when the villagers organize a horse race in honor of Lord Pungyen. Such a competition, according to local beliefs, provides him with a pleasing diversion. Excitement builds well in advance of the competition, as young men run practice races through the village to tune up both horses and riders. Although the race is a playful event, men take the contest quite seriously. Winning the horse race provides one with bragging rights during the coming year.

One year I was fortunate to be in Sama during this memorable event. Early in the morning the customary birch tree was circulated throughout the village, laden with offerings, and installed at the special place dedicated to the worship of Lord Pungyen. Meanwhile, those wealthy enough to own horses decorated their mounts by braiding the tails, tying colorful ribbons in the flowing manes, and placing finely woven traditional saddle rugs on their backs. The race participants donned their finest clothing: clean woolen tunics festooned with sashes from which long knives hung in silver sheaths; traditional felt boots rising to the knees, where they were tied off with black and red strips of wool woven on local looms; and floppy fur hats embellished with the finest silk. The men paraded through the village, seated proudly on their mounts, and then congregated at the home of the *jindag* (sponsor). A different man volunteers each year to fete the participants, and in so doing he obtains the favor of the deity, who looks on from above. At the sponsor's home the horses were tethered in the courtyard until the confined space overflowed with colorfully decorated beasts. Outside the low courtyard wall, gawking children jostled for the best vantage point to view the spectacle.

The sponsor's home was transformed into an exclusive club for jockeys, for only race participants were permitted inside, where they were honored with food and drink. Once the refreshments were consumed, a buzz filled the morning air, as if someone had uttered words akin to "Gentleman, start your engines." Men elbowed their way through the narrow doorway of the house, untethered their horses, and began to prance about the village on their edgy mounts. They then trotted in procession, followed by the entire village, to the broad meadow beyond the fields to the east of the settlement.

A makeshift altar was constructed within a small tent in the center of the meadow. Inside, the lamas burned incense and read aloud prayers from a ritual manual dedicated to Lord Pungyen. Lama Gyatso's great-grandfather had composed a verse in one of these texts, a verse that is followed by ritual specifications detailing how to honor Pungyen through offerings. The verse reads:

When compared to the supreme entity,
The attentive dharma body,
This mountain is like the waxing moon.
This most sacred of all holy locales,
This great mountain that resembles a flaming jewel
Is like a cloud set within a rainbow in the sky.
It is like a fine, misty drizzle,
Which has the radiance of a flower,
And from whose slopes fragrant scents diffuse.
It buzzes with the song of the bee,
And sends forth a myriad of melodic sounds.
Tumultuous streams cascade down its flanks,

Forming crystalline blue ponds below.
The call of the vulture carries far in its clear mountain air,
Causing the terrified mountain goats to flee in haste.
From this most holy place of wonder
The father Pungyen, accompanied by his consort, son, and retinue,
Sits upon the throne of the lotus, the sun, and the moon.

While the lamas chanted verses in praise of Pungyen, the jockeys sat in a circle around an assortment of containers, ranging from blue plastic jugs to cylindrical wooden vessels inlaid with copper, each brimming with arak. From within the recesses of their tunics they also pulled out cups, some carved by hand from the gnarled roots and burls of trees, some fired in the kilns of China and carried over the passes from Tibet. As the arak began to flow, the discussion of rules commenced. As with most public events in the village, lively quarrels broke out. Each year the same event is held, and each year it is prefaced by acrimonious verbal disputes concerning race protocol. The men of Sama actually revel in a good altercation, for it is an opportunity to assert one's dominance by displaying the power to persuade others through force of argument and oratorical skill.

Eventually the squabble died down and all cups were drained. The time had come to mount and proceed to the far end of the plain. The horses lined up behind a rope stretched across the ground, marking the starting point. When the starter gave the signal, all made a mad dash to the opposite end of the meadow.

As the horses spread out across the flat ground, several inadvertently thrust their hooves into marmot holes, sending riders plummeting to the ground. My neighbor Tubten, the odds-on favorite and winner of the three previous races, got off to a slow start but managed to negotiate his mount successfully through the pock-marked ground. After being bunched up in the rear of the pack, Tubten broke free and made a furious charge at the leaders. His stout golden mare seemed invigorated by the excitement. Tubten continued to gain ground until he appeared to edge ahead at the finish line.

The race was too close to call. Spirited arguments broke out over who should be declared the winner. Since Tubten had many friends in the village, he won by acclamation. His string of victories was preserved. In a rare moment of affection between man and beast, Tubten hugged his golden mare in celebration.

Afterward, those who did not own horses were permitted a chance to ride. This was more or less a comic event. The crowd of spectators roared with laughter as inexperienced riders fell to the ground, occasionally being dragged for some distance as they frantically tried to extract entangled feet from the stirrups—only to mount again with obstinacy spawned by inebriation. The hysterics finally ceased when Tsedrup, a seventy-five-year-old Tibetan refugee from a nomadic region to the north, sat astride a brown stallion and rode with a distinction ingrained in him from childhood. Nomads learn to ride practically before they are able to walk.[7] Despite being horseless in his forty years in the Nubri Valley, Tsedrup had never lost his knack as an equestrian. The lowly status of being a refugee prevented him from partaking in the formal race. But clearly, despite his advanced years, this proud nomad was superior in skill to all of Sama's farmers on any given day.

People began to make the slow trek back to the village. Clouds had hidden the summit of Mt. Pungyen since noon, but it made little difference, for the deity's omniscient vision can never be obscured. Everybody was in a jovial mood as they lined the main pathway through the village, awaiting the return of the riders. One by one the men trotted their mounts through the *kani,* a religious structure marking the entrance to Sama Village, which is decorated within by a painting of Lord Pungyen. The riders broke into a gallop to the cheers of the gathered assembly. This was one last chance to display their bravado and skill as horsemen. The men of the village sat high in their saddles, women beamed with pride, and young boys dreamed of the day when it would be their turn to bring pleasure to Pungyen by virtue of their equestrian skill. Sounds of revelry could be heard echoing throughout the village all night long. Eventually the clouds dispersed. Mt. Pungyen was clearly visible in the faint light of the new moon. The protector seemed to smile down on his charges from the lofty heights of his mountain abode.

EVADING MORAL MANDATES

Everybody in Sama must consider the presence of Lord Pungyen, even during the course of seemingly mundane activities. After all, the deity is both omnipresent and easily offended. For instance, all smoke that rises from the village is a potential offering to Lord Pungyen. That is why the Tibetans of Sama are so fond of throwing juniper branches on their hearths: the fragrant smoke is said to please the mountain-dwelling deity. In a similar frame of mind, villagers prefer to boil meat in a stew rather than roast it over an open fire. The latter method, they claim, is offensive to Pungyen, since it sends black, greasy fumes of singed flesh and gristle into the pristine alpine home of their protector. Many people cite a disastrous Korean mountaineering expedition in the 1970s as an example of consequences incurred from insulting Pungyen through the giving of such acrid offerings. Several local villagers who had taken work as porters were aghast when they witnessed the climbers roasting meat over an open fire on the very slopes of their protector's home. Shortly thereafter, a massive avalanche struck, killing several of the climbers. Sama residents had no doubt that Lord Pungyen had exacted retribution for the despoilment of his sacred abode.

Necessity often forces people in Sama to choose between acting in strict accordance with moral mandates and feeding their families. Because Lord Pungyen is a Buddhist protective deity, he frowns on transgressions such as the taking of life. Yet these days the food supply is a perpetual problem. Such was not always the case, for in the past the villagers acted as middlemen in the trans-Himalayan trade network that brought salt, sheep, and wool from the Tibetan Plateau to the middle hills of Nepal in exchange for rice and other lowland grains. Sama prospered then. The wealthiest traders took caravans of one hundred yaks or more over the passes into Tibet each summer. Most houses had more than enough food for their needs, and some even accumulated sizable surpluses to see them through lean years. But all that has changed now, to the point where trade has been reduced to an essential activity to supplement what cannot be produced locally. More than at any time in history, subsistence is now a problem in Sama.

The local economy is based mainly on farming and herding. The rocky fields surrounding Sama produce only a single harvest of barley, potatoes, and radishes each year due to the length of the cold, snowy winters. Herds of yaks and yak-cow hybrids are used in this high altitude for draft power to plow fields and as pack animals for conducting long-distance trade. In addition, they provide dung for fertilizer and fuel as well as food items such as dairy products and meat. Meat is an extremely important part of the diet, and in fact Tibetans everywhere are known for being voracious consumers of flesh. Yet Buddhists are prohibited from killing. So how can they convert living cattle into meals without violating their ethics or offending their protective deities?

One solution employed by many Tibetan communities is to permit a special caste of people, called *sheyba* (butchers), to reside on the outskirts of their villages. Butchers occupy the lowest rung of the social hierarchy. Yet because they are adequately compensated for their services with meat and other staples, butchers willingly assume the burden of sin that results from the killing of sentient beings for food. The consumers of the butchered animals, meanwhile, rationalize their behavior by claiming that if an animal has already been slaughtered by a butcher, eating that meat is not a moral transgression. Even the basic economic equation of supply and demand has its ethical dimensions, and moral ambiguity is unavoidable when these are skirted. In the end, though, every culture must grapple with contradictions such as this.

Sama has no butchers, a situation that causes a major dilemma, since people are very concerned about the ethical ramifications of killing. They are fully aware that, according to Buddhist teachings, killing an animal will bring negative consequences in this or the next lifetime. Karmic retribution is inevitable. Yet meat is an integral part of the diet and a vital source of protein in this pastoral community. Who, then, does the killing?

I often encountered men coming down from nearby pastures laden with bamboo baskets from which fresh blood seeped, staining their clothing. When I asked innocent questions about their loads, a consistent response was, "My yak fell off a cliff." In one case a man reached into his basket and extracted a large foreleg that was grotesquely twisted and had splinters of bone protruding at crazy angles. "The fall must have broken its leg," he explained. Indeed, even though yaks are known for agility and a nimbleness of foot that belies their massive bulk, they do have mishaps in this steep and rocky terrain. The winter is an especially dangerous time. Sometimes the treacherous footing on icy slopes sends an animal plunging off a cliff. More commonly, avalanches carry bovines to their demise. The people of Sama do not consider it sinful to consume the carcass of an animal that met its death through a mishap, or through natural causes. Yet I could not help but wonder, can yaks be so clumsy as to keep the villagers supplied with meat all year long?

Light was shed on this mystery one day while Tashi and I sat in our courtyard chatting. Angjung, our neighbor, came strolling by and sat down beside us. Something was clearly on his mind, for he remained silent for several moments. Perhaps as a way of inducing Angjung to speak, Tashi offered him a drag from the half-consumed cigarette that dangled from a corner of his mouth. As Angjung puffed away, he leaned forward and indicated a need to share something in confidence. In a barely audible whisper, he told us, "That mottled yak of mine is going to fall off a cliff tomorrow. Are you guys in for a quarter?"

Eureka! "Falling off a cliff," which on many occasions was an apt description for how a beast met its demise in this alpine environment, was also a euphemism for dispatching an animal through means that could in no way be described as accidental. Angjung needed meat for his family, yet none of his herd was willing to oblige by tumbling from a precipice. In addition, he stood to make a small profit by selling portions of the animal that his small family could not consume. In this village everybody is aware of everyone else's activities. Nevertheless, a subterfuge, even such a transparent one, is far preferable to a public admission of sin. Angjung's yak was still walking about in a state of ignorant bliss, not knowing that it was soon slated to "fall off a cliff." By consenting to buy a quarter of the carcass, Tashi and I made a direct contribution to the yak mortality rate of that particular year. When lots were drawn to see who would receive which portion of the animal, Tashi drew the right front quarter. For a welcome change, we were able to feast on meat for several weeks.

· · ·

A householder's life in Nubri is fraught with dangers that are a direct consequence of living in this harsh mountain environment. To make sense of their world, the local residents attribute the landscape with sacred features that mirror human society in many ways. Unpredictable events can be avoided, or at least mitigated, through worship of the mountain-dwelling deities. The protectors are, after all, similar in character to the humans they oversee. A vital objective for Nubri's villagers is to create harmony between the sacred and worldly realms. A pleased protector takes care of everybody in the village, from the most humble householder to the most highly esteemed lama.

Tashi Döndrup

First glimpse of Sama

Pema Chöling temple and retirement homes

Rigzen Dorje constructing an effigy in a ritual to keep illnesses from entering Sama

The villages of Bi (foreground) and Prok (background)

Pema Döndrup

Lama Tashi Dorje

Another winter squall approaches

Mt. Pungyen towering above
Sama's fields

Neighbor Angjung plowing his fields

Horses and riders at the annual race in honor of Lord Pungyen

Lama Gyatso and family

Paying respect to Lama Karma, the head lama of Sama

Chöten in Sama with the omniscient eyes of the Buddha

A nun with younger sibling in Sama

Offering libations to Buddha

CHAPTER 8

Anticipating the End of the Life Course

The Anxieties of Old Age

What destiny has decreed one cannot turn away.
The lines upon the forehead, though wiped, will stay.

Tibetan Proverb

The inexorable progression of time eventually forces all householders to come to terms with the dual frustrations of old age: recalling bygone days of status and authority that can never be recaptured, and becoming dependents of their own children. The cycle of suffering, driven by the desire to cling to those things that are impermanent, intensifies and becomes more self-evident as one experiences the unavoidable bodily degeneration that accompanies old age.[1]

AN INVALID'S PLIGHT

"Friend! Oh, my friend! Help me! Help me!" Old Dorje, who lived to the west of my makeshift office at Pema Chöling Monastery, was in distress. Usually, as soon as my typewriter's keys punctured the crisp morning calm with its staccato clatter, this elderly, brooding gentleman would beckon me with a calm voice to come over and relieve the tedium of his lonely existence. Today was different. His familiar voice contained more than a hint of desperation.

Most gomba residents merely strolled over to my courtyard when in the mood for a chat. Old Dorje, however, had no such option. He was an invalid. During the past several years he had gradually lost the use of one arm and both legs. Although Old Dorje's mind was still sharp, the ravages of a terminal affliction left him physically tormented and emotionally frustrated. Who could blame him, for in the past he was a successful trader, a proud man of initiative whose business ventures took him from the barren Tibetan Plateau to the teeming metropolises of India. Now his enfeebled body was no more than a shell of loose skin enclosing his worn-out bones. Like a helpless infant, he lacked the capacity to feed and clothe himself, or even to perform basic bodily functions, without assistance. But in sharp contrast to an infant whose entire life lies ahead, he had nothing to anticipate but further deterioration until death.

Old Dorje did not live alone, but shared a humble gomba house with his daughter, who was a nun. Each morning she hand-fed her father, perched him in the sunny courtyard, then departed to work in her brothers' fields or to tend their cattle in a nearby pasture. Around noon she would return to make tea for her father and, if the skies looked threatening, drag him back inside the dark, smoky interior of the home.

The caretaking nun was nowhere in sight on the morning that Old Dorje called out for help. I scurried to his courtyard, pushed open the double wooden door, and was immediately overwhelmed with pity. With legs still tucked under him in the cross-legged seating posture, Old Dorje lay helplessly on his side like an egg that had tipped and could not be righted. Pain and humiliation were etched on his contorted face, which was pressed against the cold paving stones of the courtyard. He gazed at me with imploring eyes, struggling to keep at bay the tears that would cost him any remaining vestige of self-respect.

I quickly remedied my companion's plight by grasping his shoulders and gently rocking his body until he was again seated upright. With no control over his extremities, he was in constant danger of tipping over again, so I maneuvered his cumbersome frame backward to a wall that could provide additional support and stability. Once resettled, he reached inside his cloak with his good hand, gnarled and arthritic though it was, and pulled out a snuff container. I took the small box and emptied an ample portion on the curved backside of his thumbnail, grown long specifically to serve as a snuff receptacle. He snorted the stimulating powder and sneezed. A tear trickled slowly down his craggy cheek, pausing among the gray strands of his uncut beard before dropping to the ground. Old Dorje sat hunched over, eyes downcast, quivering as he struggled to suppress sobs. He hissed, "Old age is infernal! The young ones do not want me around any longer. I am just waiting to die." His voice trailed away, and like a muffled echo he repeated, "I am just waiting to die."

This very sentiment was often expressed by the old folks of Sama, uttered sometimes in exasperation, sometimes in resignation. The plight of the elderly in this remote and impoverished setting is a somber reminder of the impermanence that we all face.

WHOSE BURDEN ARE YOU?

As rambunctious youths, my brother and I caused our mother incessant stress. Perhaps anticipating future retribution, she hung a sign in the kitchen that proclaimed, "Avenge yourself! Live long enough to be a burden to your children!" Only while living in Sama did I truly appreciate the irony of this message, for it underscored a strong contradiction in this particular Tibetan society: Whereas age entails deference and respect, it also breeds resentment when old folks become an encumbrance to their offspring.

According to the Tibetan conception of the life cycle, old age is a time ideally devoted to attaining merit in preparation for the next incarnation. The decline of physical aptitude is a reprieve in one sense, for it frees the elderly from many mundane responsibilities. Once retired from village life they are permitted, and even expected, to spend their waning days in prayer. On pleasant days the elderly of Sama gather in courtyards to chat and spin their ever-present prayer wheels, which are designed with each rotation to symbolically disperse the good tidings written within outward for the benefit of all sentient beings. In effect, the elderly represent a corps of devout individuals who continually produce merit both for themselves and for the community at large.

Attitudes toward all creatures great and small undergo a visible transformation as people in Sama approach old age. Men and women who previously never flinched when whipping a horse or kicking a yak become more apprehensive about the consequences of their each and every action. For example, one common activity is to sit in the sun and pick lice and fleas from one's own clothing or from the hair of a companion. Whereas young people tend to squash the critters between thumb and forefinger, the elderly gingerly expel pests from their midst on the theory that killing any sentient being is a sinful act that will have future consequences. Such concerns are far more immediate to those nearing the end of the life course.

Although the elderly in Sama are respected for wisdom accumulated through a lifetime of experience, caring for them can be a contentious issue. In a place without pensions or government safety nets, children are the primary caretakers for their aged parents. In this marginal economy the necessity of having to dole out food during lean years to people who have surpassed their ability to make substantial contributions to the household places the elderly in the unenviable position of competing with their grandchildren for scarce resources. The cultural ideal of reverence for the elderly is mitigated by the harsh pragmatism of economic reality.

The Tibetans have a proverb: "After crossing the river, don't forget the bridge. After gaining maturity, don't forget your parents." Tashi Döndrup embellished the proverb with his own thoughts and experiences. He said, "It is a disgrace to the entire community when children don't help their parents. We scold such individuals by saying, 'Your parents helped you when you were too young to piss or crap on your own. Now your parents need help, and you cannot even give them a bit of food? Have you no shame?'"

Siblings are also expected to help each other in times of need. Tashi elaborated further by citing the relationship between himself and his half brother, Balang (Ox), who is two decades younger. According to Tashi, who is alone in old age, with nobody to care for him:

> Balang's mother died when he was four, then our father died when he was eight. He received the entire inheritance. As you know, I was the illegitimate son, so no inheritance whatsoever came my way. We say that my half brother is a son of the summer, the season of abundance. If that is so, then I am a son of winter. Nevertheless, I felt sorry for the boy. I helped him all the time, fed him from our meager supplies, and acted like a true elder brother, or even a father. Yet how has he repaid such kindness?
>
> Since the death of his parents Balang has not accomplished a single virtuous deed. He squandered his entire inheritance; now there is nothing left. Not only that, but you should see the way he treats me! Remember the first months when you lived here? He used to come by all the time, sit there silently like the bovine he is, and act as if he were king. He ate all our food and treated me like his servant. He never cleaned the dishes or did anything helpful. He treats me like a lowly servant. I acted as his guardian when he was a child. But these days I no longer even speak to him. I have no use for a brother like that.

Despite Tashi's increasingly frail condition, Balang lacks the courtesy to assist his only close kin, despite the help he received as an orphaned child. Tashi's bitterness is understandable. Just imagine how parents must feel when it is their own children who deny them the basic necessities of life.

Given the chronic economic insecurity that plagues Sama, a long-term goal of all parents is to somehow obligate at least one child to assist them in making the transition from productive householder to dependent retiree. This leads to the question of which child is most able to care for his or her elderly parents.

Although sons often lend assistance to their aging parents, especially with such labor-intensive chores as cutting wood and plowing, they must fully commit themselves to raising their own emerging families. But what about sons who do not marry? Some men, like Tashi Döndrup, remain single because of unfavorable economic circumstances. In his case, as a bachelor with no children, he was in a good position to care for his aging mother until her death. Just as Tashi depended on her in his youth, so she depended on him when her energy gave out.

Tashi's case is rare, however. Men in Sama generally marry unless they become celibate monks. As mentioned before, these days most monks are dispatched to monasteries in Kathmandu. Although the cash they earn from performing rituals is often an important economic supplement for their aging parents, they are in no position to provide physical care. Doing so is indeed considered inappropriate for those whose lives are supposed to be dedicated to the quest for enlightenment. Regardless of whether they are monks or laymen, sons rarely become primary caretakers of the elderly.

A woman who marries is in no position to help her own parents either, since she is now beholden to her husband's household. According to another Tibetan proverb, "The hen eats at home and lays its eggs outside"—a reflection of the fact that the cost of raising a girl is borne by the parents, whereas the products of her womb, her offspring, become members of her marital household. After marriage a woman is certainly permitted to remain in close contact with her parents, yet it is highly inappropriate for her to divert scarce resources their way. Daughters who marry simply cannot be counted on as caretakers for the elderly.

The process of elimination leaves unmarried daughters. The decision to become a monk or nun in Sama is almost always made by parents when their child is young. The constellation of social and demographic factors described in chapter 4 has resulted in the evolution of a curious situation in Sama. Equal percentages (roughly one in five) of male and female children are designated to be monks and nuns by their parents. However, while monks are exported to Kathmandu, nuns are retained within the village. There is no convent in Sama.

I once asked Lama Gyatso why so many families designate a daughter to be a nun. He replied, "There are two reasons. The first is that parents will acquire much merit by making their daughter a nun. The second is that, by doing so, they will have somebody to care for them in old age."

The first reason conforms well to a widespread Tibetan cultural ideal, whereas the latter explanation seems to flout convention. After all, Buddhists emphasize that those in clerical positions should refrain from engaging in worldly activities. The gender-based contradiction is emphasized by the tendency to send monks away to distant monasteries while nuns are retained within the village—which brings to mind yet another Tibetan saying: "If you want to be a servant, make your son a monk. If you want a servant, make your daughter a nun."[2] For to be sure, designating a daughter to be a nun in Sama embodies a conscious strategy to ensure a more secure future for her elderly parents. A nun cannot be sent to another household in marriage. Her celibacy is guaranteed (in most cases at least) through religious sanctions against sexual involvements, so she will never be burdened with the rearing of children. Because parents need somebody to care for them in their twilight years, who better to do so than a daughter who is a nun?

Recall that parents are expected to retire from their village home once their youngest son marries and starts his own family. Pema Chöling Monastery is considered the perfect retirement setting given that, at this stage in the life cycle, the elderly should devote their time to praying and otherwise generating merit for their forthcoming rebirths. The connection between stages in the life cycle and conceptions of sacred and profane space are emphasized in the distinction between the gomba as the "Realm of Religious Practitioners" and the village as the "Realm of Worldly Suffering." When parents eventually make the move to a gomba retirement home, they are often accompanied by the daughter they earlier designated to be a nun. In return for caring for them, she eventually inherits the gomba home, consisting of a living quarter centered on a hearth and an attached den for prayer. This explains why Pema Chöling Monastery resembles a cross between a geriatric home and a convent.

Let's illustrate this long-term family management strategy with a concrete example. Old Dorje and his younger brother, Pemba, married Dolma sometime in the 1950s. Over the next twenty years the family expanded with the births of successive children. Two daughters and four sons survived and grew to maturity. The first child, a daughter, was designated to be a nun when she was eight years old. Her sister married a young man in the village and went to live at his home. Among the four brothers, the eldest and youngest married polyandrously, like their parents, and now occupy a house near to where their parents lived in the village. The third son was removed from the inheritance equation when he was sent to a monastery in Kathmandu. The second son was the last to marry, and he brought his wife home to his parents' house. True to cultural expectations, the birth of their first child signaled that it was time for the aging parents, together with any dependents, to move to a retirement home at Pema Chöling Monastery. Instead of all trying to squeeze into a single home (remember, gomba homes are very small), they occupied two adjacent houses. One was shared by Pemba and Dolma; the other was occupied by Old Dorje and their daughter, the nun.

Tibetan society is far from homogenous; no single cultural pattern can be used to describe Tibetan communities dispersed across a vast geographical area. Even in Nubri we find significant variations in the pattern of old-age care. The above description applies to elderly care in Sama. In Kutang, in contrast, parents rely on their married sons and daughter-in-laws for support. What happens, then, when a son decides to pursue a career as a celibate recluse and there are no siblings available to care for his parents? That is a situation that needed to be resolved by Pema Döndrup and his family three hundred years ago.

REJECTING FILIAL RESPONSIBILITIES

You will recall that Pema Döndrup's parents resisted his decision to become a celibate practitioner. At the very least they wanted him to become a married householder lama, which, by restricting his activities to the local temple, would have kept him in the village. The following narrative returns us to the tension between family responsibilities and individual aspirations. Pema Döndrup's parents had six children, three sons and three daughters. But mortality took its toll on the family, and by the time they approached old age the parents' support system had eroded. We rejoin the narrative as Pema Döndrup describes the death of his brothers in the late 1600s.

> My younger brother, Sonam Norbu, died at age twenty-five. Nyima Norbu, my elder brother, passed away shortly thereafter. He and my elder sister Yuga had been mired in the suffering of worldly existence since they did not dedicate their lives to spiritual pursuits. As for Mother and Father, their suffering was at its apex, like the fully waxed moon.

Nyima Norbu approached me with a final request: "Just as our youngest brother died, it is certain that I too will die. Little brother, practice religion diligently. After I die you must release my soul, prepare my corpse, and have monks perform prayers on my behalf for a week. After seven days have elapsed, do not remain in the village! Go to the mountain retreat! Do this regardless of what happens to our parents in the future. Do not turn your back on religion. Most important, if a need arises for you to regress on your vows, take my wife, your sister-in-law, as a spouse." Having said this, Nyima Norbu died.

I did everything according to my elder brother's instructions, and then went into retreat. After a large snowstorm struck, my mother and father approached me and implored, "We are old and can no longer walk far or support ourselves. If it is possible, please stay at Bi Gomba so that we two old folks can feel at ease. If it is not suitable to stay at Bi, then please stay at nearby Beypug."

Thinking that I would be more distracted if I stayed in Bi, I went to Beypug and lived there. Meanwhile, some hypocritical neighbors told my parents, "If you don't leave that house of yours, there will be illness and death within the family." So my old parents, my elder sister, my sister-in-law, and her two children abandoned the home and began living in the courtyard. Father's house was transformed into something like a bird's nest that had been set on fire.

When my two elderly parents next came to visit, they stood outside the cloth door and wept. "Son, come and look at us two old folks with bad karma!" A tear fell from my eye too. I said to my old parents, "Do not speak like this. Listen to me. Elderly parents, in the past you said this is our ancestor's house. These days the crumbling walls look like the desiccated corpse of a horse. As for me, your son, I have no wish but to practice religion. My aged parents, recite your prayers. In the past there was one whom I called brother. These days his corpse lingers without help, without protection. As for me, your son, I have no wish except to remain at the mountain retreat. My aged parents, recite your prayers. There is no true substance to whatever you perceive. Nor is there true substance in any thoughts. As for me, I have no wish but to seek perfection. Do not suffer, elderly ones; just recite your prayers. Even the house that one builds and the wealth that one accumulates are examples of impermanence. Through the passage of time we witness the deaths of those who were once friends and relatives. This is also the phenomenon of impermanence. Do not suffer, elderly ones; recite your prayers. All sentient beings are destined to die. Among those who are born there are none who shall escape death. Not only that, one will also have to face the suffering of damnation. Recite your prayers, my parents. In your past lives you neglected the practice of religion. But now, my parents, at the end of this life you must continuously recite your prayers each and every day. By doing so, memories of Thugje Chenpo, the merciful *bodhisattva*, will come to you when you enter the intermediate realm between death and rebirth. My parents, set your mind to the three jewels: the Buddha, his teachings, and the community of followers. Having listened carefully to my message, please leave now and you will suffer no longer. Please leave now, for I must resume my solitary retreat."

Father sobbed, "So this is your advice, my son. But even if we do not think about it suffering comes automatically." Mother added, "We two old folks have no one to seek help from in this life or the next life. Your elder brother and younger brother are both dead, and our house is abandoned. We are left in a state of lingering, and in a state of suffering. Oh, my son, please conclude your retreat soon."

Mother and Father left in tears. At this place of solitude, I understood the impermanent nature of everything. I contemplated long and hard on the suffering caused by our tendency to grasp for permanence.

Later, I heard my sister Nyisem outside the cloth that covered my entryway. She grieved, "We have no house, so we have no place to live. There is nobody from whom we can seek help. What shall we do? Please take care of us!" I consoled her by saying, "I am a man of religion who abstains from worldly activities. Be a servant for our elderly parents who have no means to care for themselves. You are their only hope. There is nobody other than you who can care for them. Crying will not help. Be a servant to Mother, Father, and me." I consoled her with some more advice before she departed.

Another time my sister-in-law [elder brother Nyima Norbu's widow] came and wept, "Look at the karma of your parents and siblings; look at the clothing that they wear. Loving children are left on the ground without care." I became saddened and embarrassed by their plight, so I thought of moving to another place. She left after I gave her some general advice.

I stayed in solitary retreat for an extended period of time. When that ended, my elderly parents came to me and said, "Son, if you are finished with your retreat, then you must come to the village one time to meet with us two elderly ones." This was the command of my parents, so I went and resided there for a while. By that time my sister-in-law's faith in religion was growing much stronger. Because she was the daughter of my mother's brother, she was like an elder sister to me. She expressed the opinion that I should not meander hither and thither, but should stay at home. But I am a religious person who wanders about in the solitary mountain retreats. It is not good for me to linger in the village for too long. So I went again to visit all of the isolated mountain retreats, forest retreats, and meadow retreats. I wandered for a few years among the various paths, bridges, abandoned houses, cemeteries, dilapidated properties, temples, and valleys.

Three years had elapsed since my elder brother died. One day my sister-in-law decided to abandon her two children, a boy and a girl, declaring, "I will seek religion." Cousin Möndar came to care for my elderly parents, who felt that fate had played a trick on them. He said to my father, "Your celibate son only goes for religious retreats, and now your daughter-in-law wants to lead a religious life as well. So who will look after the two of you, your grandson, and your granddaughter? That celibate son of yours needs to be converted into a groom."

Later my parents changed their minds. They summoned me, and Father said, "I can no longer go up and down the hills. Fire, water, and wood are not readily available. I can no longer work. When we need food and clothing, there isn't any. Our lives are not over, yet our standard of living pales in comparison to that of others."

What was my old father saying? I am not one who acts contrary to the teachings of our religion. Implying that I had corrupted her, Father told me once again that my sister-in-law was determined to lead a religious life. He argued that since I am unable to take care of anything, then I should at least take care of [marry] my sister-in-law. But I told him, "Whatever argument you offer is an empty wish. Oh, Father! Oh, Mother! How can you, who gave me this human form, tell me to turn my back on religion? There is no chance that I will live in any way that is not in accordance with my previous karma." Having uttered these words, I vowed to the three jewels that I would not live in the village.

Angry and upset, I returned to the gomba but could not sleep. I lay awake thinking that when all worldly deeds are examined, they have no substance. Since they have no substance, how can I engage in worldly activities and give up on my religious practice? Ayiiii!

The lama instilled within me the ability to meditate by setting his hand on the crown of my head, so how could I bring myself to place the strap of a basket there? How could I dare discard the religious garment that I wear to help overcome the lower realm of worldly existence in order to take a plow in hand? How could I dare cast aside the religious garment that covers the lower part of my body in order to fornicate? How could I dare uncross my legs that have been locked in the meditative sitting posture in order to scurry uphill and downhill for nothing? I have motivated myself to pursue a religious life. Thus I sang this song for my father:

Please listen, elderly parents, for you are indeed benevolent.
I, your son, know this for a fact.
To carry out your own commands would lead me on a journey of worldly
     suffering.
So to carry out the commands of my lama, I hasten to the solitary moun-
     tain retreat.
I abandon my father's village,
And hasten to the solitary mountain retreat.
I renounce my father's home,
And hasten to the cave in the rocky cliff.
I discard this very clothing,
And retain only a single piece of cotton.

I renounce all of you,
And leave behind this cattle enclosure together with its inhabitants.
I renounce my patrilineal kin,
And make friends with whomever I meet, with neither attachment nor
    desire.
Father's village is a prison of demons.
Parents are the teaching masters of the demons.
Matrilineal kin are warriors of the demons.
Women are the ones who drag people down to the demons.
Material wealth is the rope of the demons.
The tendency to grasp for permanence is the guide of the demons.
I am unable to follow the commands of you, my parents.
I will go to pursue the oral instructions of the lama.
I pray that I see you again, my parents, before I die.

After saying this, they rose, prostrated, and wept while saying, "My son, most excellent practitioner of religion, don't go to Tibet. Please stay, please stay." Cousin Möndar, who had been taking care of my parents, added, "Your elderly parents are without spiritual defect. I confess my wrong deed [of instigating the parents to recall their son to the householder's life]."

I went to the gomba where I stayed for a long time. Several years later I decided to go on pilgrimage to the sacred mountain of Tsari in Tibet.[3] Both of my elderly parents were still alive, so I gave each of them some new clothing and said, "Please do not worry. Even if I stay here in the village I cannot help you as a servant. I will go to offer prayers at those untainted sacred places. I will request the lamas to say special prayers on your behalf."

Because the three of us had remained on good terms, my parents began to cry. They turned away from me, one to the right and one to the left. I was struck by the thought that perhaps this was the last time I would ever see them. Tears began to flow from my eyes. My father stood up and said, "The two of us, father and son, will never meet again. Practice your religion well! It is certain that we will never meet again, so make sure that you pray with diligence at the sacred places, and pray with diligence at the feet of the lamas."

I replied, "Do not worry about me. If you do, then people will disgrace me. I will offer prayers to the holy places, and will request the great lamas to bless you." I then departed. At some of the most sacred sites in all of Tibet I requested that prayers be made for the purpose of transferring merit to my parents. They died before I returned.[4]

Pema Döndrup's heartrending narrative illustrates the dilemma embodied in his desire to lead a reclusive, spiritual life. His ambitions clashed with the precarious position his parents found themselves in after their other sons died. Although Pema Döndrup wavered, he did not break his resolve, instead remaining true to his calling in life and refusing to renounce his hard-won vows. Pema Döndrup tried to console his mother and father by stressing the basic lesson that life is impermanent, pointing out how human suffering is only increased by ignorance of the Buddha's teachings. In verse he even went so far as to repudiate the very foundations of family life. But his parents were incapable of grasping the message, or maybe they could find no solace when their carefully laid plans for family succession and retirement were shattered by events beyond their control. In the end Pema Döndrup chose to forsake the very people who brought him into the world and then nurtured him through the perilous years of infancy and adolescence. The mendicant's life is never without consequences.

FROM A NUN WHO NURTURES TO A NUN IN NEED

In the autumn of 2000 I went once again to Sama. After arriving and settling in with Tashi I strolled up to Pema Chöling Monastery for a wistful look at my old office, the small gomba house that was now vacant awaiting a future inhabitant. Near the door to the courtyard I noticed my elderly neighbor, the nun Ani Kunsang. She sat tranquilly on the dry earth, leaning back against a wall of loosely piled stones. The only detectable motion was a well-rehearsed gyration of her right hand, which clutched a prayer wheel. When I approached, she did not glance up at me, but a smile crossed her face as she whispered, nearly inaudibly, "It is you. I remember the sound of your walk. I wondered if we would meet again."

I crouched beside her and placed a hand on her shoulder, a humble gesture indeed, but one meant to convey through simple contact that it was good to meet again. Her forehead was shrouded by a cloth that was wrapped around her head, protruding like a visor to shade her face from the intense rays of the sun. Her head never lifted to seek out visual confirmation of what she already knew. "I would like to offer you some tea, but I would probably end up pouring it all over the ground," she muttered with a frail smile. At that moment I realized that Ani Kunsang could no longer see. Old age had robbed her of vision.

The seasons change, the years creep by, and the elderly grow ever more infirm. Ani Kunsang had been a good neighbor who always respected my desire to be left alone while working in the makeshift office. Our courtyards were separated by a low wall stacked to chest level with gnarled branches of dead trees, sprigs of juniper, and odd twigs that she squirreled away in preparation for winter. We often chatted over this improvised barrier, exchanging greetings but rarely any information of importance. I realized now that she knew little about me, and I knew nearly nothing about her. Regrets began to impose themselves on the nostalgia that I felt for this place. What stories could she have told? What insights on the life of a nun could she have related?

We sat side by side in silence for a while, and then she said, "My time is near. There is nothing left for me in this lifetime. I am blind now, and there is nobody to care for me." I tried to comfort her, citing her life devoted to religion and to the care of others—words that somehow seemed trivial given the gravity of her condition. But Ani Kunsang needed no comforting; she had accepted her destiny.

Ani Kunsang's words of resignation echoed in my head when I rose to leave. Her vacant gaze was still directed at the trammeled dirt on the path before us as she said, "I guess we will never see each other again." "Perhaps you are right," was the only reply I could muster. As I walked slowly away, she said, "Go in peace."

Ani Kunsang's life of sacrifice had included caring for her younger siblings and aging parents. Ironically, in her final season of need, brought on by infirmity and blindness, she now found herself alone and virtually helpless. There was no one even to comfort her. Such is the fate of the nun who nurtures.

CHAPTER 9

Parting Breaths

Death Is But a Transition

It is far better to go to hell blessed with goodness
Than to live in the human realm burdened with ill repute.

Tibetan Proverb

In Buddhist belief, death merely marks the transition point from one bodily form to the next. Death should not be feared, since it is not the ultimate cessation of life. Rather, it marks the commencement of one's next existence. Upon death one's consciousness principle enters the hazardous intermediary realm, called *bardo*. For forty-nine days, the time that one spends in bardo, lamas read from a special text called Bardo Tödel (popularly known as the Tibetan Book of the Dead) that helps guide the person to their next incarnation. Reemergence from the intermediate realm occurs at the instant when a sperm and egg meet in a womb that is designated, by virtue of the accumulated karma of all those involved, to be the next birthplace. Life, death, and rebirth are all part of a long continuum.[1]

VIOLENT DEATH IN A CULTURE OF NONVIOLENCE

Was it an act of self-defense? Or a cold, calculated murder? That question still reverberates in my head. News had arrived that my good friend Hritar, the one who collected my mail in the neighboring village of Lho, was dead. A bright and energetic man with sound ideas on how to improve the lives of his fellow villagers, Hritar had nevertheless made many enemies in the valley during his rise to political power. Although the precise circumstances of his death remain murky, one fact is perfectly clear: he was skewered through the midriff with a rusty old bayonet by Kunsang, another man from Lho who also happened to be my close associate. One friend is dead, another lingers in jail.

A religiously sanctioned philosophy of nonviolence has never been sufficient to prevent Tibetans from occasionally engaging in homicide and other acts of aggression. Tibetan history, similar to the history of any people, is rife with conflict: fights over grazing land, political assassinations, and intermonastic warfare. Even the Fifth Dalai Lama, considered to be an incarnation of the compassionate and fully awakened being Chenrezik, espoused the use of force to protect his political interests. When confronted with a rebellion in 1660, the Fifth Dalai Lama issued the following instructions to his Mongol allies on how to dispose of the Tibetan insurgents:

> [Of those in] the band of enemies who have despoiled the duties entrusted
>   to them:
> Make the male lines like trees that have had their roots cut;
> Make the female lines like brooks that have dried up in winter;
> Make the children and grandchildren like eggs smashed against rocks;
> Make the servants and followers like heaps of grass consumed by fire;
> Make their dominion like a lamp whose oil has been exhausted;
> In short, annihilate any traces of them, even their names.[2]

Perhaps interest in questions of Buddhist philosophy, such as the intriguing issue of what happens to a person after death, has grown so large as to eclipse other important questions pertaining to the living. The raw intensity of everyday life in the villages of Nubri, however, has taught me to ask: What happens to those who are left behind? How will Hritar's widow cope with raising their children without the help of her husband? Two of them were residing at an expensive boarding school in Kathmandu. Prior to Hritar's death his children could look forward to a future of promise. Now their status had been flung into limbo by the premature demise of the family's breadwinner. What will happen to Kunsang's wife? She is from a neighboring valley, without close kin in Lho and therefore reliant on her husband for protection. Kunsang's homicidal act left his spouse in an extremely vulnerable position. Now she is truly alone, living in the same village as Hritar's relatives, who will certainly treat her with contempt. Death in a small village affects everybody. The dead move on to a new existence; the living are left behind to deal with the consequences.

· · ·

One of the downsides of working in a place like Sama is that death is always present. During the initial stages of my fieldwork death was little more than an abstract concept, since it takes time to cultivate bonds with people. Those who died were unknown faces in the crowd. That all changed the day Pemba passed away. A rambunctious old man with a wry smile and twinkle in his eye, Pemba had been more than willing to spend quiet afternoons with me discussing topics ranging from yak herding to local politics. One afternoon we chatted for hours. The next morning his death was announced by the wailing of female kin. Pemba was old and often mentioned to me the possibility that he could die any day. How right he was.

Reaching the age of seventy is no negligible feat in Sama. Only those endowed with a hearty constitution and a generous helping of good fortune manage to attain that ripe age. When an old person dies, therefore, people accept that the karma of the deceased has rightfully run its full course. When a person dies in the prime of life, however, friends and relatives wonder how the imponderable workings of karma can be so cruel.

When Pemba died my thoughts turned back to those first few days in Sama when everything was new and confusing and everybody was a stranger. I recalled my first encounter with death.

BRING OUT YOUR DEAD

A horn sounded below while I sat on the porch of the lama's residence. All morning people had been gathering in the courtyard of the deceased, awaiting the corpse's final departure from home. Smoke billowed from a fire of juniper branches, an offering of incense to the deities above. The wailing of the women started slowly, almost as a low moan, and gradually built to a high-pitched crescendo as the body emerged from within, wrapped in white cotton and borne on a palanquin by male relatives. The piercing cries of women splintered the still air with a plaintive call to the dead, as if imploring the body to regain its life force. The procession, led by a lama, wound its way through the muddy paths of the village to a cremation ground at the monastery above. It was my second morning in the village. I had just arrived, and yet was already encountering death.

Who was this person? I hardly knew a soul in the village. My guide Karma had brought me here, hurriedly introduced me to some people, and dashed off the next morning, leaving me to fend for myself. The first few days in Sama turned into an advanced seminar on how to manage intense feelings of loneliness. I was a novice anthropologist, and the time had come to make the transition from classroom scholar to solo fieldworker. This was a professional rite of passage. Nevertheless, I could not help repeating what became a mantra during those first days of uncertainty: "What the hell am I doing here?" As I looked down at the palanquin-borne corpse on that dreary day, I reflected on the irony that this deceased person and I had something in common: we were both undergoing transitions. Mine happened to be the more desirable of the two. Far worse occurrences can disrupt the life course than being isolated in a place far from home.

A few weeks after the funeral I discovered the identity of the dead person. I was talking with some people who were cutting grass for winter fodder, when a haggard, middle-aged man staggered into our midst. Wangchuk's long hair was not braided in the typical fashion but hung loose about his gaunt, sallow face. His sunken eyes gave him the look of one haunted by ill fortune. The stench of alcohol exuded from every pore and befouled his breath. Many men in Nubri take to drinking heavily for weeks, even months or a lifetime, after losing a close family member. He was neither the first nor the last man I would encounter in a condition of postmortuary intemperance.

Wangchuk had been on a binge for several weeks by then, staggering aimlessly through the streets, shamelessly demanding arak at the doors of his neighbors, who hurriedly concealed bottles, hoping he would go away. Most everyone treated him politely with understanding and pity, though a few would click their tongues in disapproval. The day we met in the fields Wangchuk had a young daughter in tow, whose morose expression revealed a weight of misfortune far too heavy for her tender years. Wangchuk began sobbing about the death of his wife—it was her funeral procession I had witnessed on that second day in town. He and his younger brother had married as a team and managed their humble estate with a woman everybody regarded as both a competent spouse and a caring mother. Now she was gone. Wangchuk and his brother were now confronted with the prospect of raising several young children on their own without the help of a wife. At least there were two of them, two able-bodied men who owned land and who would no doubt cope with the household burdens if and when sobriety was restored.

• • •

When somebody in Sama dies, family members must immediately summon a lama to cut the hair from the crown of the corpse's head. Doing so allows the soul to escape and commence the transmigratory process to a new body. Timing is critical, for if the body is disturbed in any way following death, the soul may be prematurely ejected and begin wandering about in a confused manner, unable to locate the path to its next body. I have witnessed bereaved family members maintain enough composure to dispatch a runner to the nearest lama's home moments after a person has died in order to assure that the protocol is properly followed.

Once the hair has been cut, the lama chants prayers in an attempt to send the soul directly to Dewachen, a heavenly paradise presided over by a Buddha. Rebirth in Dewachen is the goal of many laypeople. Indeed, some people offer prayers or erect sacred monuments to assist their loved ones in reaching this paradise. Those reborn in Dewachen can more easily attain an awakened state of mind, and thereby release themselves from the cycle of suffering characterized by endless births, deaths, and rebirths. Generating merit for the benefit of the deceased is a solemn undertaking of the living. Just as model citizens act with compassion toward all living beings, so too are they expected to alleviate the plight of the deceased in whatever way possible.

With the assistance of the lamas, family members must then dispose of the body, which is now just an empty vessel, a depressing reminder of mortality. It is wrapped in a white funerary shroud and arranged in a seated position in the house. Friends and relatives visit, bearing gifts of white scarves and arak and offering words of condolence. "Do not be sad, for this was his karma" is an especially common sentiment on this occasion. On the day following death, lamas and their assistants read from the Bardo Tödel and perform rituals intended to assist the dead person through a labyrinth of dangers lurking in the intermediate realm between death and rebirth.

On the second day following death, young male relatives gather at the home of the deceased and drink arak until they can barely see or walk a straight line. They then don horrific masks and grab destructive implements, such as long-bladed knives and blunt axes. At predetermined intervals during the rituals performed by lamas in the courtyard, they are sent out into the village to create mayhem. These fearsome characters, called *shidur,* symbolize the messengers of death who have come to violently disrupt the lives of the living. Crazed with drink, they induce panic-stricken cattle to crash through and topple courtyard walls. They horrify small children who flee, shrieking in terror. They forcibly enter houses where they fling pots from the shelves and scatter household belongings across the floor and out the door. With mock blood smeared on their faces and wild looks in their eyes, these messengers of death leave a path of destruction in the orderly lives of the villagers.

The following day is the day of cremation. The body makes its final exit from the homestead, borne on a palanquin to the monastery grounds where a suitable site is chosen to build the funeral pyre. Only a lama and his assistant remain there to tend the fire and to recite the scriptures that assist the deceased on the journey to a new incarnation.[3]

SILENCE ON THE OTHER SIDE OF THE WALL

In 1998 I returned to Nubri following an absence of more than a year. After walking for days, ascending and descending the rocky trail as it wound its way up the Buri River, I eventually crested the final ridge overlooking the fields and village of Sama. Stretching before me was a familiar scene: a verdant pasture flanked by evergreens ascending the steep slopes to a row of cliffs, breached in several places by the white streaks of cascading streams, above which was a thick forest of birch trees displaying golden autumn hues. Nestled in the middle of the pasture was a large white chöten, the place where I had met my first Sama residents several years before. I hurriedly crossed the plain, which gave way to patchwork fields of leafy potato plants and golden stalks of barley swaying gently in the breeze. As always, I paused while passing through the kani, the structure marking the symbolic boundary between the ritually secured confines of the village and the dangerous world outside. Lord Pungyen is depicted on one of the wooden panels inside, gazing down from the seat of his white horse while holding aloft the weapons he uses to dispatch malevolent forces that threaten the people of Sama. Reassured that the protector still looked with benevolence after the fortunes of my friends, I turned and walked along the path descending into the village. Children spotted me and vaulted over stone walls separating courtyards to run and inform Tashi Döndrup that his brother from America had returned. "He's back!" cried Tsogyal from the loom where she sat weaving. "Tashi, Geoff's here!" she called out again.

Tashi Döndrup emerged from his doorway looking older and more stooped than ever. Without speaking, he took hold of my arm in a vicelike grip, grinned from ear to ear, and then pulled me inside the house. He immediately poured some local distillates into a kettle placed on the iron grate above the fire. Such is the custom when welcoming a friend or relative.

Word of my return spread rapidly, and friends began to trickle by, feeling their way into the darkened room toward the fire and then jostling each other in the confined space before settling in to the customary cross-legged sitting posture. Several women entered, pausing by the doorway until their eyes adjusted to the light, before making their way to Tashi's side of the hearth bearing flasks of arak. My eyes roamed about the room, taking in well-known sights: the flickering light from the fire dancing on Tashi's weathered face, the smoke wafting upward through strips of meat suspended from bamboo sticks, and the fading white sacred emblems that had been etched on the soot-encrusted rafters. The slightly bitter taste of arak chased by pungent butter tea was well known to my palate. My nostrils recognized the distinct aroma of my companions, and the ever-present odor of smoke emanating from burning logs of pine and birch. The familiar sounds of laughter abounded, punctuated by the unique greeting in the Nubri dialect, "Kam sangbo!" (How are you!) every time a person entered. Everything seemed as it had been before, yet something was subtly and distressingly amiss. I withdrew mentally from the revelries for a moment, foraging through the recesses of my memory in search of the missing element in this prosaic scene. And then it struck me. Where were our neighbors? The lyrical voice of Dawa singing to her child and the soothing baritone of Angjung reciting from a sacred text were absent.

You met Angjung and Dawa in a previous chapter. He is the man whose yak managed to fall off a cliff the day after Tashi and I agreed to buy a quarter of the animal. Angjung and Dawa were not a typical couple in this village, where personal compatibility between marriage partners is secondary to social and economic prerogatives. Marriages are arranged, and in many cases spouses simply do not get along. Such was not the case with Angjung and Dawa. They sang to each other at night, and during the day they often made public displays of affection—truly a rare sight in this village where modesty prevails. They shared in the duties of caring for their son, and most revealing of all, they never fought.

Houses in Sama are constructed in a row so that neighbors share a common wall through which sounds penetrate nearly unhindered. Angjung and Dawa's hearth sat no more than a few feet from our own. Each dawn we were awakened by their young son, whose morning tantrums were more effective than the crowing of roosters in forcing us from slumber. Each evening we were soothed to sleep by the melodic tones of Dawa's lullabies. So porous was the wall that we could carry on a conversation without needing to step into each other's homes. Tashi would crane his neck toward the wall and contribute odd quips when Angjung and Dawa's topic of discussion was more interesting than what I had to offer. When Tashi and I argued at night, the whole village knew it by the next morning. Gossip spreads rapidly through the inter-wall communication network.

Angjung and Dawa were the best neighbors one could ever hope for. When Tashi and I returned from long trips down-valley, Dawa would immediately come by to kindle the fire and pour us hot tea from her own kettle. On sunny days when I worked in Tashi's courtyard, Angjung would amble by with his child strapped to his back in a coarse woolen blanket. Angjung's curly locks enlivened a young and intelligent face that was always blessed with a smile. He was the strong, silent type. While I worked, he watched with fascination as strange symbols appeared on the paper as I struck the keys of my typewriter. Tashi, finishing his chores elsewhere, would then sit with us in the courtyard, signaling break time. The three of us would pass a smoke back and forth and dabble in the pleasant, often frivolous chatter that characterizes so much of human interactions. When one becomes accustomed to the daily sights and sounds of a community, deviations from the norm are very conspicuous. On this day when I returned to the village there was silence on the other side of the wall.

"Tashi," I inquired, "where are Angjung and Dawa?"

Tashi's jubilant mood sobered in an instant. Even in the dim light I could feel his eyes meet mine through the soft wisps of smoke rising from the hearth. "Angjung is dead," he informed me tenderly. "A few months ago he began coughing up blood and then died in great agony."

How could a man who was so young, so vibrant, and so full of love for his family die at such an early age? Angjung was gone, leaving behind Dawa, who is far too young to be a widow, a son who was his pride and joy, and an infant daughter whom he never knew, for she was still tucked in her mother's womb when Angjung died. Perhaps the little girl was lucky. She would not have to wear the pained expression of loss that her brother wears to this day. Death had struck once again, this time far too close to home.

Dawa now lives with her elderly mother and father together with one capable sister who is a nun and another sister, also a nun, who is deaf and mute. When we met the next day, the topic of Angjung was too painful to broach. Dawa knew how I felt about him, a friend lost forever. But how could I ever imagine the loss she was feeling? It was bad enough to have a loving husband wrenched from her just as their family was beginning to blossom. Now she had to face life as a widow, a status that women dread for good reason, since most land is owned by husbands and their brothers. A young woman without property is hard-pressed to raise a family. If only she had lost her husband in old age, when her grown children would be in a position to protect and support her. Dawa is still young. But the soft, supple skin of her cheeks and forehead is now creased with lines of worry. Her smile, once so spontaneous and radiant, is now forced and tinged with anguish.

A TRAIL OF TEARS

I was dismayed to learn that Angjung was not my only friend who had died since my last visit to Sama. Tsipa Ongyal, the village astrologer (the man who composed the natal horoscopes in chapter 3), had passed away as well. He used to show me with pride his collection of astrological treatises, each manuscript hand-copied years ago from a prototype held by his teacher and then used so heavily that some passages had become nearly illegible. His death was not entirely unexpected, for he had attained the ripe age of seventy and had been chronically ill for some time. With his passing, however, I wondered who would write the natal horoscopes for newborns. Prior to his death he often expressed a fear that none of the young people in the village had enough interest, or competence, to carry on with this ancient tradition. He may be right.

Ongde and Namgyal had also perished. Unlike Tsipa Ongyal, they did not go quietly in their sleep. The winter had been especially brutal, with unusually heavy snowfall. Nearly seventy animals were swept to their deaths in one avalanche at Mimi, the winter pasture across the river from Sama. Afterward men picked their way across the jumbled debris below the cliffs, excavated the bovine carcasses, carved them up on the spot, and hauled the meat back to the village. Carrion could not go to waste. For the time being there was much meat in the village, although this was no cause for celebration. It takes years to build up a healthy and productive herd; it takes but seconds to erase the hard-earned fruits of diligent planning and industrious labor.

Ongde and Namgyal, father and son, had climbed to the cliffs above Mimi to find one of their missing yaks. The footing was treacherous. Suddenly the father slipped and began to slide perilously close to the rocks marking the edge of the precipice. Namgyal desperately grasped his father's outstretched hand, but lost his own foothold in doing so.

The two were last seen clinging together in a grisly embrace as they plummeted to their deaths on the debris of rock and ice beneath which so many cattle lay buried. Winters are treacherous for man as well as beast.

Tales of premature and tragic death did not end in Sama during this trip. In the winter of 1997 I had come to know Khamsum, a man from Tonje Village in Gyasumdo, a region to the west of Nubri on the other side of Larkye Pass.[4] Short, stocky, and bald, he had an engaging smile that radiated vigor. Khamsum and his wife, Dorje, were the proprietors of a successful hotel for foreigners along the popular Annapurna trekking circuit. He often came to Sama to purchase yaks for his business ventures. We met for the first time during a communal festival in Pema Chöling Temple. We were seated side by side when, at the climax of the ceremony, the lamas circulated to bestow blessings on the congregation. Such a circumstance is considered by Tibetans to be a most auspicious commencement to a friendship. Khamsum then invited us to visit his trekking lodge in Tonje.

Tashi and I enjoyed the prospect of visiting Tonje at the conclusion of a long period of fieldwork. Much lower in altitude, the village would provide welcome relief from the frigid winds that always blew in Sama. Not only that, but the lodge had a telephone with international calling capability, meaning that after a long separation I could finally talk with my family. That June of 1997, then, Tashi and I packed our bags and left Sama. Three days later, after ascending to the upper reaches of Nubri and crossing the Larkye Pass in a late-season squall, we were approaching our destination. As we wound our way down through villages nestled in terraced fields, I excused myself and literally sprinted the last couple of hours down to Tonje. True to form, the telephone line was down. Nothing ever seems to work in Nepal when you need it. Yet my inconvenience paled in comparison to an unfolding tragedy that could have been averted had the telephone been operational.

Tashi soon arrived, and we began to paint the town red. Cold beer was a welcome break from the fiery arak of Nubri. A hot shower, a luxury unheard of in Sama, cleansed the encrusted filth from my unwashed body. Western-style foods fulfilled the culinary fantasies that had occupied my mind for months. In between showering and gorging Tashi and I lazed about outside, wallowing in the sun and chatting with the Tibetan residents of Tonje, whom Tashi knew well. After a few days of placid debauchery it came time for us to leave. I wanted to repay Khamsum and Dorje's hospitality, so I offered to take a family photograph that I would deliver at my next visit. Everybody began to scurry about and put on their finest clothing—for in Nepal, a photograph is a formal rather than a casual affair. The parents posed proudly in front of the lodge with their son and two daughters. The elder daughter was dressed in white, and her hands rested on her abdomen, which protruded visibly with Khamsum and Dorje's first grandchild. This family photo turned out to be a touching reminder of better times.

More than a year later, in 1998, Tashi and I again crossed Larkye Pass and made our way down to Tonje. We were in high spirits, ready to take full advantage of all the town has to offer. Khamsum was not at home when we arrived, but Dorje was. She disappeared into the kitchen, and shortly after sent one of the lodge workers out with tea and a hot meal.

After eating and resting for a spell we entered the kitchen, where Dorje sat coddling a small child in her lap. Dorje did not seem as buoyant as usual, so we asked about her family. She replied in a voice choked with emotion, "Our daughter died just after you left last year. She died giving birth to this child."

We sat together in silence for a few moments, remembering the radiant, congenial young lady dressed in white whose future seemed so bright. Now the family had only this grandchild as a tender memory of their daughter's smiles and laughter. One life had been exchanged for another. Meanwhile, an especially painful reminder lingered in my backpack. During the past weeks I had been looking forward to giving the family portrait to Khamsum and Dorje as a way of expressing my gratitude for their hospitality and friendship. Now the simple gift would only evoke pain and sorrow.

As the afternoon wore on, international trekkers entered the rectangular, wood-paneled room crowded with rows of tables and benches and adorned with posters of Indian movie stars. Tashi and I occupied one corner, inconspicuous among the growing throng of weary travelers. He was drinking Dorje's homemade arak, while I nursed my customary post-fieldwork beer. Our moods were less than celebratory.

The clanging of bells dangling from the necks of ponies together with the shouts and whistles of horsemen announced Khamsum's return. He had gone up-valley with a dozen ponies to purchase potatoes to feed the tourists. Dorje handed the child to a servant and made her way to the door. Tashi and I followed her outside and helped unload the cumbersome sacks of potatoes, stacking them in the storehouse. Khamsum was all smiles. He was happy to return home after a long day on the trail and equally happy to greet his friends from the other side of the pass. Once the potatoes were stashed, he directed a servant to corral the ponies and then beckoned for us to enter the lodge.

The three of us sat apart from the tourists to exchange news. Dorje joined us and poured a round of arak. It seemed as good a time as any to give the special gift, so I reached into my backpack for the long cardboard tube and extracted the carefully rolled photograph. Extending it in both hands toward Khamsum, I bowed my head slightly and said, "I made this last year and wanted to give it to you as a token of our friendship. Dorje told me about your daughter, so now I am afraid that my gift will only bring sorrow." He grasped the picture with trembling hands and gently unrolled it. On seeing the image of their intact family, both parents broke down in tears, lamenting once again the loss of their departed daughter. Tourists looked on in bewilderment, unaware of the tragedy that Khamsum and Dorje had endured. Sometimes ignorance truly is bliss.

Khamsum grasped my hand as tears trickled down both cheeks. "We are not like other families. Many people only want sons and think that daughters are of no use." His words rang true, and reminded me of something my neighbor Tubten had told me back in Sama: "When a son is born people ask, 'How is the child?' When a daughter is born people ask, 'How is the mother?'"

Khamsum continued, "We love our sons and daughters equally. To us there is no difference; each of them is our child. A week after you left last year our daughter suffered intense abdominal pains. She was going into labor, but something was drastically wrong. The child was not coming out. She struggled and struggled to give birth, and finally a baby girl emerged. But my daughter was bleeding—we could not stop the flow of blood. I wanted to call Kathmandu and have a helicopter sent up here so that we could take her to a hospital. But that damn telephone line was still down! If only the telephone had been working, she would still be with us today." He started sobbing at this point, unable to say another word. The granddaughter, attracted by the commotion, toddled out from the kitchen. One day the little girl will come to know the tragic circumstances of her arrival in this world. Until then she will continue to call her grandparents Mother and Father.

COMING FOR TO CARRY ME HOME

The string of tragedies continued to unfold. Tashi and I left Tonje and trekked down through the steamy lowlands to a road where we caught a bus to Kathmandu. When we arrived I was looking forward to seeing Kalsang, a young, well-educated Tibetan man who was an emerging scholar. We had been working together for some time, transcribing recorded interviews into written Tibetan, which I would then translate into English. That is how many of the stories in this book were transformed from the Nubri vernacular into written English. Our partnership was fruitful, fun, and intellectually stimulating.

Kalsang and I had a long history. As a college student in 1984, I had been posted at his uncle Kunga's home in Kathmandu for a home stay. Kunga is a refugee from Tibet who fled to Nepal in 1959 and has since become a prosperous carpet merchant. Two days before I arrived, Kalsang's elder brother, Yönden, had run away from home, sneaked across the border into Nepal, and sought refuge at his uncle's home. Yönden and I, two youths without a common language, forged brotherly bonds by wrestling in the backyard and teaching each other scatological terms in our respective tongues. By the time I had become familiar with the Tibetan language, Yönden had returned home. As the eldest son in the family, he was desperately needed on the farm. Shortly thereafter I visited his village in Tibet and had the opportunity to meet his exceptionally gifted younger brother, a boy whose natural inquisitiveness suggested great promise. This was Kalsang.

Kalsang followed Yönden's lead by fleeing to Nepal, for he craved the freedom to pursue that which was denied him in his land of birth: an education in traditional Tibetan culture. We met again at Kunga's house more than a decade after our initial encounter in his home village. At the time I was seeking a research assistant, and he was seeking employment as a scholar. It was an ideal match.[5]

Kalsang, however, had a hidden executioner lurking in his body—tuberculosis. Growing thinner day by day, he made innumerable trips to doctors, practitioners of both Western and Tibetan medicine, yet his efforts proved ineffective because the disease was already well advanced. At one point Kalsang headed for the fresh air of the hills to recuperate. He rented a room at a border town, where a lonely bridge connected Nepal with Tibet, and through informal communication channels was able to get word about his circumstances to Yönden. One day word came that Yönden had arrived on the other side of the border. The bridge, only a few hundred feet long, spanned a deep gorge filled with a furiously roaring river. Yönden could not cross, for he was a Tibetan citizen; Kalsang could not cross, for he was an illegal alien living in Nepal. The cacophony of the river below prevented the two brothers from doing anything but wave to each other across the narrow chasm. Kalsang told me that Yönden had wept, as had he.

On many occasions Kalsang and I spoke face to face, as brother to brother, about his condition. He told me quite bluntly, "You know, Geoff, I will probably die soon." He was several years my junior, so this grim prognosis seemed unthinkable. Despite so many experiences with death in Nubri, I refused to believe that Kalsang would succumb to his incurable illness. Before I left the capital for Nubri in 1998, he wished me well and promised to finish the tasks that were in progress.

Upon returning to Kathmandu I immediately called Kalsang to touch base and to schedule the recommencement of our collaborative efforts. When Uncle Kunga answered the phone, his voice was melancholic. Kunga is a man whose feelings are rarely if ever revealed to the world; he is generally rock solid, a pillar of emotional stability. I should have known immediately that something was amiss. When I asked for Kalsang, his reply was muffled and incoherent. Thinking that we had a bad connection, I told Kunga I would drop by that afternoon. Kunga became agitated and said, emphasizing each word: "Geoff, listen to me! Kalsang is dead!" There was a pause, and I could hear gentle sobbing on the other end of the telephone line. The death of his nephew two days earlier had shaken the otherwise stoic Uncle Kunga to the core.

I returned the phone to its cradle, feeling empty, not yet comprehending the full magnitude of the news. Somehow I began going about my business. The first appointment of the morning was with the principal of the Tibetan boarding school where Dawa Norbu, an energetic eight-year-old boy from Sama, was living. Tashi Döndrup had recognized Dawa Norbu to be a bright and exceptional child, a good prospect deserving a chance for education, so I had arranged a sponsorship for him. A Nepali watchman, dressed in drab green clothing, greeted me at the iron gateway to the school. He touched his right hand to his forehead, smiled, and moved aside to let me pass. I entered the school compound, my head numb and whirling from a combination of the tragic tidings and the city's choking smog of petrol fumes emptied from exhaust pipes directly into the open windows of my taxi.

Scores of children were gathered in the brick-paved courtyard rehearsing for the school's annual performance. Dawa Norbu broke free from the crowd and strode over to greet me. He stuck out his hand in a confident gesture, showing off to his mates that he had mastered the foreigners' handshake. I enfolded his small hand between both of mine, squatted down to meet him at eye level, and gave him a big hug. He is a special child, in many ways the future of his village. For a moment my thoughts were taken away from Kalsang. Here in this frail child was life, hope, and unlimited potential.

Our moment together was broken when the teachers clapped and barked out instructions to the students. Dawa Norbu snapped to attention and hustled back to a group of children who were forming into ranks. The principal motioned for me to take a seat and enjoy the performance. When the music started, I was transported to another dimension as the children's falsetto voices began to sing words that at the time seemed utterly surreal:

> I looked over Jordan and what did I see,
> Coming for to carry me home,
> A band of angels coming after me,
> Coming for to carry me home.
> Swing low, sweet chariot, coming for to carry me home,
> Swing low, sweet chariot, coming for to carry me home.
> If you get there before I do,
> Coming for to carry me home,
> Tell all my brothers I'm coming there too,
> Coming for to carry me home.

Never again will I listen to that song and not think of my departed companion. Children represent hope for the future; the mournful song evokes bittersweet memories. Life was juxtaposed to death; youthful innocence was projected against a backdrop of innocence lost. I shed silent tears for Kalsang. This was to be his memorial service.

· · ·

Life begets death: that is a universal constant. Whether one believes in reincarnation, an afterlife, or neither, a human's physical existence is shadowed by the inexorable march toward decay and dissolution. Allowing oneself to become emotionally bound to something as flawed and impermanent as the human form can only lead to sorrow and misery. To Buddhists, everything has the inherent quality of being devoid of longevity. Recognizing impermanence allows one to take the first faltering step toward becoming a fully awakened being. When Buddhists speak of emptiness, they do not mean that nothing exists, but that nothing endures through time. Life is no exception.

CHAPTER 10

Transcending Death

Rising Corpses and Reincarnations

Just when you think you are poised to be reborn as a human,
you get a dog's form instead.
Just when you think you are poised to go to hell, you get a
lord's form instead.

Tibetan Proverb

Sincere devotion to the Buddha's teachings and a life dedicated to virtu-
ous deeds of compassion toward all living things can lead to rebirth
as a human as opposed to a dog, or worse. Despite the many inherent
flaws, attaining the human form is the penultimate goal. In the Buddhist
worldview humans alone among all sentient beings are endowed with
the intellectual capacity and temperament required to pursue enlightenment. To awaken one's mind is to release oneself from the cycle of
rebirth and perpetual suffering. But very few are able to attain such a
grand objective; as a result, most people in the Tibetan world die and
are subsequently reborn. Following death their bodies are recycled back
into the soil, either through cremation on the funeral pyre or by means
of the grisly practice of cutting the flesh from the bones and feeding it to
vultures. Meanwhile, their souls commence the transmigratory journey
that culminates with conception within the womb of a human, if one is
fortunate, or another type of being for those less fortunate. However,
rebirth is not the only option. Sometimes the body and the soul that
once inhabited it deviate from the script.

WHEN CORPSES RISE

"A few days after we arrived in Manang," begins a macabre tale, "a
lama told the three of us to go to the cemetery and fetch a skull that

could be used in a certain ritual.[1] So that very night we entered Cool Grove, the great cemetery of Manang. We found some head rests in a mausoleum and lay down to sleep." The events described in this story, as related by Pema Lhundrup, another yogi from Kutang, a disciple of Pema Döndrup and a contemporary of Pema Wangdu, transpired during the first half of the eighteenth century. Unlike Pema Döndrup, who preferred relatively innocuous mountain retreats for his spiritual endeavors, Pema Lhundrup had a penchant for frequenting cemeteries. He literally moved from charnel ground to charnel ground in search of the perfect setting to inspire his meditation and to compose his verses of spiritual insight. For many Tibetan yogis, direct confrontation with death is the best way to truly understand the impermanence of life. By overcoming one's fear of physical decay, one can better grasp the true nature of existence. Yet there are risks involved.

Pema Lhundrup's story continues:

Just past midnight we left that mausoleum and went in search of a skull. My friend found pieces of a woman's skull in one of the mausoleums while I was searching in another one. Suddenly I heard a shout that sounded like "Haaaang!" I thought to myself, "What kind of animal makes such a noise?"

The noise was coming from within a mausoleum. I thought that this must be some sort of magical occurrence, so I sat cross-legged, holding fast on top of the mausoleum, and sang this short song that emerged from my state of meditation:

> What is happening now is merely a magical creation.
> When looking upon appearance and emptiness,
> Without the obstructions of conceptual thoughts,
> I will not be deceived.
> Oh, assembly of spirits,
> Let the magic of the *rolang* [rising corpse] appear!

Then the mausoleum burst into flames and began to quake. The very stones were shouting, "Rog! Rog!" and my body began to quiver! Even though I recited prayers and did rituals of propitiation, the force that was causing this disturbance could not be pacified.

Suddenly, as I rummaged about the various arms and legs within the mausoleum, I was seized by the meaty hand of a cadaver. He drew himself up with one mighty effort, appearing right before my face, and emitted a cry. As soon as this happened I grabbed the rolang's two arms and dragged him outside.

It was the corpse of an old man with white hair who had been dead for about one month. His body and face, which had not decomposed, were a bronze hue. I performed a brief ritual to release the rolang from its suffering [i.e., de-animate the corpse]. After that, my friend came and we extracted the thigh bone from the corpse and took it with us back to the village.

I related this harrowing tale to the lama. He told us that, indeed, we had encountered a real rolang, a magical creation of the spirits. He then announced to the villagers that I had vanquished a rolang![2]

. . .

For Tibetans, the interlude between death and the disposal of bodily remains is an especially perilous stretch of time. When ritual protocol is not adhered to, corpses have been known to arise from the dead. These rolangs are a source of dread throughout Tibet and the Himalayas. Small wonder, for who would want to encounter an animated cadaver under any circumstances?

I often heard the people of Sama make references to rolangs, and decided it was time to learn more about this curious phenomenon.[3] So one blustery night I wandered over to Lama Gyatso's home after dinner. A frigid winter wind howled with a fury. Inside his house drafts forced their way through chinks in the stone wall, causing the fire to leap and crackle. The dancing light shed an eerie glow on the lama's face: shadows flickered across the crevasses of his weathered skin, and yellow teeth, elongated with age, protruded from his mouth as he greeted me with a mischievous grin. Lama Gyatso is always a font of information on most topics, spiritual or otherwise. The topic of rising corpses was particularly appropriate on a night such as this.

"Long, long ago, a family was staying at Hinan Gomba," Lama Gyatso began as we huddled beside his warm hearth. "You know Hinan; you went there with Tashi Döndrup." Indeed, I knew the place. Tashi and I had visited there several weeks earlier. Hinan is a spectacular site. The gomba is situated on the pinnacle of a rocky outcrop in a narrow, forested valley. The surrounding land had been cleared centuries ago and now accommodates a scattering of small houses that are used primarily as summer grazing huts. Beyond the clearing, towering pine trees gradually climb to the base of precipitous rock faces that stretch upward to snow-capped mountains. In the winter Hinan is deserted, with the exception of one lama who resides there permanently and a few nuns who attend to his material needs. During the summer, however, the valley springs to life as people from villages lower down herd their cattle to the lush, high-altitude pastures. Depending on the time of year, Hinan can either be a place of solitude or a full-fledged community bustling with activity.

Lama Gyatso continued:

One particular family stayed on at Hinan during the fall after most other people had gone down-valley. They were alone. One day the husband decided to return to their home in the lower village, so he left his wife and child on their own. That evening the mother placed her toddler in a cradle and went outside to milk the herd. Suddenly she heard the little one crying out in desperation, "Mama! Mama!" The mother quickly returned to the house, and upon entering let out a scream. Her child was perched on the lap of a huge, shaggy man with a flowing mane of hair. The boy struggled to get free, but the grotesque figure held him tightly. The mother thought, "This person looks like a monkey." She then remembered stories of such a man who came to steal children, so she quickly grabbed her son and sat him on her own lap. She rekindled the fire and began to smear butter all over the naked body of her child.

Lama Gyatso paused for a moment and explained, "This is what we do with our children, you know, to keep their skin soft and to protect them from the cold. All mothers in the village do this." He then continued the tale:

The monkey-man was intrigued and asked her to smear butter on him as well. Before doing so she threw some more wood on the fire and stoked it into a large blaze. Next she reached inside a container and took a large lump of butter into her hand and began to rub it all over his body. The woman beckoned him closer to the fire. As she slathered him with the thick layer of butter she beckoned him to move even closer. Gradually the woman enticed him so near to the fire that sparks leapt out and set his entire body ablaze. The monkey-man sprung to his feet and began to run about engulfed in the flames of his own burning hair. Then he died.

Lama Gyatso took a long sip from his tea cup and cast a glance in my direction, perhaps to judge my reaction. He went on:

But that was not the end of the story. You see, the next day the husband returned to Hinan. That night the monkey-man's corpse rose from the dead and killed the husband. The monkey-man had become a rolang, a rising corpse! It then went to live at a cemetery high up in the valley.

My uncle knew about that cemetery. He took me there one time and taught me a sacred rite that he promised would prove beneficial at a future time. It involves a mantra that I wrote down on a piece of paper. If a rolang appears, a certain ritual must be performed while chanting this mantra. My uncle also demonstrated the method of kicking the corpse with the sole of one's foot in order to vanquish it! These were his instructions:

If you want to subdue a rolang,
Concentrate emphatically on the precious teacher,

> Burn incense and white mustard,
> Then seize and vanquish the rolang!

You see, rolangs are very dangerous to the living. If a rolang breathes upon you, you will turn into a walking corpse as well. We lamas have to know how to take care of these things in order to protect our families and everybody in the community.

I asked Lama Gyatso whether he or anyone he knew had ever encountered a rolang. "No, no, no," he chuckled, "none have been sighted for a long time. The story I just told you is from way back in time, from the days of my ancestors."

Despite the long interval since the last rolang sighting, the people of Nubri still take preventive measures to protect themselves against rising corpses. "Do you know why our doorways are so short?" Lama Gyatso asked me. I shrugged, and he answered, "Because the rolang cannot bend his body. The inside of the home is always a safe place, since the rolang is unable to enter." This made sense, since the human cadaver stiffens due to rigor mortis. His explanation also gave me a different perspective on this architectural innovation. Being rather lanky and having somewhat inflexible joints, I swore that the doorways were built low as a way of keeping foreigners like me in our proper place. Each time I entered Lama Gyatso's home, I inadvertently smacked my head against the lintel above the doorway. His family would sing out in unison, "Geoff's here!" whenever they heard a thud at the door followed by a string of indecipherable profanities. Knowing that the diminutive entrances were designed to thwart the entrance of rolangs provided some relief from the throbbing lumps on my forehead.

THE LAMA, THOUGH ENLIGHTENED, TAKES THE FORM OF A MAN

Rising corpses represent an anomaly in the usual sequence of birth, death, and rebirth. Normally the process is smoother. Laypeople who do not devote sufficient attention to spiritual advancement can hardly hope for a human rebirth. Adept lamas, in contrast, expect to return repeatedly in human form because, as individuals well on their way to spiritual perfection, these masters of the Buddha's teachings have agreed to continue being reborn among humans in order to assist all others on the path to salvation.

The Tibetan world is filled with reincarnated lamas, known as *tulku* (literally, "emanation bodies"), the most famous of whom is the Dalai

Lama. The current incarnation of the Dalai Lama lineage is the four-teenth bodily manifestation of a famous teacher who lived nearly six hundred years ago. The Dalai Lama is widely considered to be the highest-ranking tulku, but he is by no means the only one.

Over the years tulku lineages have proliferated throughout the Tibetan world, representing spiritual continuity and the cumulative wisdom attained through lifetimes of spiritual study and practice. Once a tulku passes away, the search for his successor begins. Infants born around his time of death are scrutinized for any physiological or psychological traits that can be interpreted as evidence of continuity from one bodily form to another. Tulkus are thought to manifest special characteristics nearly from birth, such as the ability to walk and talk early, to chant sacred mantras instead of babbling incoherently as most babies do, or to recognize ritual implements used by their predecessor. A baby tulku is, in essence, the same person as his deceased predecessor. The only difference is his external form, the body.[4]

Sama has its share of tulkus. People often told me about Tsering Gyaltsen, a rambunctious married lama born around 1900 who had a penchant for stirring up trouble everywhere he went. Not only did this lama make repeated attempts to usurp gomba property for himself and his sons, but he apparently also used his spiritual authority to coerce and intimidate villagers from Tibet to Kutang. Eventually his penchant for provoking others brought about dire consequences. When religion and politics become entangled, things can get ugly.

One day in the early 1940s Tsering Gyaltsen and a couple of com-panions were walking through a forest in the lower part of Nubri when they were ambushed by enemies. The assassins had concealed themselves on a large rock overhanging the trail, and when their targets came in range they rolled boulders down on them. Those who survived the ini-tial onslaught were quickly dispatched with knives. Reprisals were swift. Everybody from the assassins' village was either killed or sent into exile. Tashi Döndrup told me this story while we took a break, seated on a log beneath that very same rock overhanging the site of the murder. I could not help but look up with a certain amount of trepidation.

Shortly after the murders, rumors began to circulate that Tsering Gyaltsen had been reborn. Generally only those lamas who excel in spiritual matters return as tulkus. By all accounts, Tsering Gyaltsen was more adept at politics than religion, which made recognition of his rein-carnation somewhat of a surprise. The irony of the situation is that

Tsering Gyaltsen was as contentious in death as in life. The naming of his tulku became a matter of dispute when two children manifested signs of being his successor.

Tashi Dorje, who is a nephew of the slain Tsering Gyaltsen, told me that the determination of the true incarnation was resolved only with the aid of higher authorities:

> Not everybody in Nubri goes to Tibet after somebody in the family dies. However, the men of our Ngadag lineage go on pilgrimage after a death in the family. One purpose is to make offerings on behalf of the deceased. We left for Tibet in the Sheep Year [1943], shortly after my uncle [Tsering Gyaltsen] passed away, and returned during the Monkey Year [1944]. When my uncle died we went to Tsurpu Monastery and asked the Lord Karmapa, one of the lamas whom we respect most highly, where to find his reincarnation. He helped us find the boy, who is now a monk in Kathmandu.

One day I had the good fortune of meeting this tulku. Tashi Dön-drup and I were hiking up the trail to the monastery near Kathmandu where our elderly friend Tashi Dorje resides. On the way we met a woman who immediately seized Tashi Döndrup by the arm and dragged him to a nearby home. Tashi turned to me with a smile and said, "She is like a sister. You must meet her husband. He is known as Tulku Dorje. You have heard of Tsering Gyaltsen? Well, this man is his reincarnation." Knowing the history of his predecessor, I figured this could be interesting.

The woman led us to a single-story brick house situated on a grassy meadow just below the monastery. Strung between trees, colorful prayer flags fluttered gently in the wind. The courtyard surrounding the house was guarded by a large and ornery mastiff, and enclosed by a low brick wall with shards of broken bottles cemented across the top—as if the mastiff was insufficient deterrent against nocturnal visitors. Our hostess signaled us to enter the house. We removed our shoes—a city custom that causes much embarrassment to rural people from Nubri, since many own only a single pair of socks that are rarely washed—and were led into a small room with an altar dominating one wall and a low couch propped against the opposite wall.

A garland of name tags dangled from a hook on one wall. As at academic conferences in the West, Tibetan exiles employ a name tag system for their major religious events. Each tag on this particular string was inscribed with Tibetan and English letters, identifying the name of the bearer and the ritual he was attending. The word *Tulku* was emblazoned boldly across the center of each. Being a tulku has its perks. Reincarnate lamas are allotted special seats close to the podium during teachings given by the Dalai Lama and other contemporary masters.

Tulku Dorje eventually returned from a temple where he had been leading a prayer ceremony. The curtain at the doorway parted as a shaven head poked through, followed by a portly body clothed in red robes. The middle-aged monk's alert eyes danced behind thick glasses, and his white teeth shone forth brilliantly with frequent smiles as he greeted Tashi Döndrup and me.

Having heard so many stories about the volatile Tsering Gyaltsen, I was expecting a similarly rambunctious character to appear. Yet Tulku Dorje displays none of the turbulent characteristics of his predecessor. In fact, he turned out to be one of the nicest, most congenial men I have ever met. He is admired by all as a devoted family man, and as a soft-spoken monk who prefers to serve the spiritual needs of the community rather than dabble in political intrigue. I felt immediately at ease in his company, and so, after the requisite social overtures, I asked him about his personal history.

"Well," he began,

> I was born into a very poor family in the village of Rue. This village is not in Nubri, but lies just across the border in Tibet. When I was young, people talked about my being the reincarnation of Tsering Gyaltsen. My parents were excited, but they also were convinced that official recognition of my status would be denied. You see, there was a very influential Ngadag family in Sama who claimed that *their* son was Tsering Gyaltsen's tulku. I was too young to understand anything that was going on, but I do remember the tension and excitement.
>
> As always in such disputed cases, a letter was taken to Lord Karmapa in Tibet. He was asked to determine the true tulku. The decision came down in my favor! What a surprise for my parents, for usually it is the powerful families who get their way. How many tulkus do you find from dirt-poor families such as my own? Not many!

At this he burst into laughter.

"Anyway," he continued,

> at a young age I was sent to study under the Ngadag lamas in Sama, one of whom was the father of the competing candidate. My main teacher was very strict. He would terrorize me anytime I made a mistake, which was frequently, by the way. There I was, far from home and under the guidance of a man of whom I was in constant fear. So what did I do? I ran away, of course! But once I arrived home my father flew into a rage and sent me back to the lama. I did not have a very happy childhood.

When I reached the age of sixteen I went to the neighboring valley, Gyasumdo. My intent was to work in the fields of others, or do anything to get away from my current life. I met a man on the trail who asked my name. Thinking that I was somewhat incognito here, I replied, "My name is Dorje." The man said, "This is very auspicious, for my name is also Dorje." Henceforth I became known simply as Dorje, until the people of Gyasumdo found out that I was a reincarnate lama. Then they started calling me Tulku Dorje.

We sat and drank tea for a while, discussing the story he had just told; then all of a sudden he jumped up and said, "Ayiii, I have something you may want to see!" He went to a small metal box beside the altar, opened it, and began rummaging through its contents. He extracted a piece of brown paper, which he carefully unfolded, revealing a few lines of cursive script. This was the very same confirmation letter that Tashi Dorje had requested from Lord Karmapa back in the 1940s. It read:

> You [the lamas of Sama] have requested that we perform a visualization meditation in order to determine who is the reincarnation of a certain lama from Nubri, the two candidates being the son of Lama Tinley Gyatso and the son of an impoverished man of an inferior lineage. Based on the visualization meditation hereby performed, the result is as follows: The true incarnation of the lama is the boy who lives a day's walk from Nubri, the boy who is the son of a beggar of an inferior lineage. Accept this result as a great omen that will benefit the religion and all sentient beings. Henceforth, we will pray and perform rituals in order to increase merit and remove all hindrances pertaining to this situation.

The commandment was clear: Tulku Dorje had been officially recognized as Tsering Gyaltsen's reincarnation by none other than Lord Karmapa, one of the most preeminent religious authorities in all of Tibet. Upward mobility is difficult to achieve in any stratified society. In this case the tulku institution was a means by which a child of humble origin could be elevated to a position of honor and prestige. One can only wonder where Tulku Dorje would be today if not for the fateful decision in his favor.

PARTING THOUGHTS AND THOUGHTS OF PARTING

We have now come full circle. Birth is not only the commencement of life; it is also the start of a journey toward death—a journey that may be interrupted prematurely (or so it would seen), as when an infant or a young person in good health is claimed by disease or by a tragic accident.

Between birth and death, the two events that demarcate a life, the individual must navigate through a perilous world filled with malevolent forces, both spiritual and mundane. In the meantime, each person strives to affix meaning to every transition within the life course. Success in life, and beyond life, depends as much on personal initiative and resolve as it does on the circumstances of one's birth.

Knowing and fully believing the Buddhist view that death cannot extinguish one's existence can provide comfort, especially to those who are old and forced to confront the reality of their own impending mortality. Nevertheless, for all but the most spiritually advanced Tibetans, death is approached with a certain amount of fear and loathing. No tenet, however ingrained in the cultural matrix of a society, can overcome the apprehension that this transition entails. Tashi Döndrup occasionally spoke of his own encroaching death. He knows that he is destined to be left alone and helpless when the time comes for him to slip off into a final slumber. My old companion's concerns are legitimate. He has no wife, no son, no daughter who is a nun; not even Balang, his half brother and closest kin, can be relied on for support. There will be nobody at all to care for him through the inevitable encroachment of infirmity.

In 1998 Tashi and I spent a few weeks together in Kathmandu after finishing fieldwork in Nubri. The evening before my departure for the United States we sat on the rooftop garden of a friend's house sharing a glass of whisky and enjoying each other's company. We reminisced about how we had first met, and about our numerous misadventures while trekking throughout Nubri and surrounding regions. Tashi expressed pride in the work we had accomplished as a team. We both appreciated that his illiteracy and lack of formal education were no hindrance whatsoever to the contributions he had made to this academic project. And we both appreciated that without his constant guidance through a veritable minefield of fieldwork hazards—everything from poisoned food to political rivalries—the project would never have been possible. Now the villagers of Nubri are abuzz with talk about the new school and health post that resulted from our work together. These are to be Tashi's legacy.

His end is near. That evening in Kathmandu Tashi told me, "I will die soon. Maybe I'll last one more year, maybe two, but certainly no more than three years." His attitude was stoic and rather matter-of-fact, although the tone of his voice indicated that he was ill at ease with the inevitable transition. So I asked a very simple, very straightforward question that each of us has to deal with at some point in life. "Tashi, are you afraid of death?"

He leaned forward, shook a cigarette from the packet on the table, lit it, drew the smoke deep into his lungs, and then slowly exhaled. Several minutes passed as he sat back in his chair, locked in contemplation. The ash on his cigarette grew longer and longer until it appeared poised to break free and scatter in the gentle breeze. Finally he looked me square in the eye and said in a hushed tone, "Everybody is afraid of death. I am no exception. It is ridiculous for anybody to think he will not die soon. As an old man, I must think about death constantly, for my time is certainly drawing near. Nobody can hold off against death."

I nodded in sympathy, admiring Tashi's ability to speak about something that had occupied his mind more than ever the past few months. This was a year in which many of his friends in Nubri had died. A few weeks earlier we had learned of the tragic death of Khamsum's daughter, followed shortly by the news of Kalsang's passing. Death seemed to be omnipresent. Of more immediate concern, both of us had fallen ill on the trip down-valley. Being younger and stronger, my recovery was rapid and complete. For Tashi, the ailment lingered in his aged body, sapping his strength and making him wonder if death had indeed come knocking. Tashi has been impoverished his entire life and therefore was reluctant to go to a doctor, despite my insistence. We argued, and finally he agreed to seek medical help. I realized when we arrived at the sparkling, newly constructed hospital that part of his hesitancy stemmed from the intimidation villagers feel when entering modern settings. Well-scrubbed urban dwellers often treat their rural compatriots with disdain, even turning their noses upward in disgust. The rural-urban chasm is so deep in Nepal that those with the least access to medical care feel the greatest reluctance to seek help when ill. We eventually managed to find an understanding young intern whose prognosis and prescriptions set Tashi on the road to recovery. He was still too weak to make the return journey to Nubri, so we arranged for him to stay at Tashi Dorje's monastery above the city. There, Tashi Döndrup would have numerous monks and nuns from Nubri to attend to his needs and see that he remained well fed, in good health, and in familiar company.

I continued to probe Tashi Döndrup's feelings about death. As on so many occasions, we turned to the biography of Pema Döndrup for inspiration. The well-worn pages of the photocopied manuscript were always close at hand. I began reading a passage in which this lama of bygone days had expressed his thoughts on death. Sometime in the early

1700s Pema Döndrup had become seriously ill during a solitary retreat, and was forced to exist solely on boiled water. He wrote,

> If illness is the reminder of impermanence, then it is also the reminder of virtuous effort. Illness teaches one to overcome ignorance. At the time of your death, if you lack the religious inclination that will benefit yourself, then even scores of caretakers will be unable to prevent the infectious spread of the disease. But just because you do not have caretakers doesn't necessarily mean that the illness will develop. If it is not your time to die, then you will not die, even if you have no caretakers at all. If it is my time to die, so be it as the life force is gone. If it is not my time to die, then I will remain here since my life force is not at an end. Fear of illness and fear of death represent the suffering induced by our tendency to grasp at that which is impermanent. If one is not liberated from this grasping tendency, how is one to achieve Buddhahood? If one does not seek Buddhahood, what is the point of practicing religion?[5]

Pema Döndrup was able to gain insight into the fleeting nature of existence from his brush with death. His is a typical Buddhist approach to life: one should continually examine circumstances in order to increase awareness, thereby perhaps moving a step closer to becoming fully awakened. I wondered whether a similar philosophy had been internalized by Tashi Döndrup. Because of his circumstances of birth, which required a constant struggle for the most fundamental necessities of subsistence, Tashi had never had the luxury of leading a contemplative life.

Tashi continued speaking about death:

> We grow old, and meanwhile our time in life expires day by day, month by month. When you are twenty you can look forward to being thirty, and when you are thirty you can look forward to being forty. But when you reach seventy there is no longer anything to look forward to. At this point in life I have to wonder what will happen if I become ill again. Who will cook for me? Who will get food for me? Who will light my fire? And what will happen if I go blind? My eyesight is getting worse and worse these days. I am alone. With nobody to care for me, I will die quickly if I go blind. This is my greatest fear—being blind and incapable of taking care of myself. If things get too bad, I will stop eating and just fade away. That would be far better than clinging to the last breath of life and having to endure the indignity of suffering like a helpless child.

· · ·

To know life is to know death. To know Tashi Döndrup is to know how to accept one's mortality with dignity. Tashi lives today; I know this for a fact. People from Nubri occasionally venture down to Kathmandu

bearing news of births and deaths, news that reaches me almost instan-
taneously through telephone calls and e-mails. Although it is said that
his strength deteriorates, Tashi still walks about in the shadow of Mt.
Pungyen, the Ornamented Heap, home of the deity who protects the villagers of Sama. One day a message will arrive informing me that Tashi
has commenced the transmigratory journey to a new bodily form. He
often told me that we were brothers in a past life, and will be so in the
future as well. Until his dying breath Tashi has promised to pray each
day for the welfare of myself, my family, and my children, who are destined to grow up hearing stories about their special uncle from a distant
land. When I think of this humble man, alone and silent in his solitary
abode, sitting beside the fire that provides meager light and comfort, I
think also of the empty place across the hearth, where his younger
brother, a man from another culture, used to sit and keep him company
through the long evenings. Tashi rotates his prayer wheel in a slow,
deliberate motion, sending good tidings through the porous walls of the
house and out into the cool mountain air.

The man who knows humility, even in poverty,
Is liked and helped by all.

Place Names

PLACE NAME	TIBETAN SPELLING	LOCATION AND NOTES
Bi	Bi'	A village in Kutang, home of Pema Döndrup and Pema Wangdu.
Dagkar Taso	Brag-dkar rTa-so	A monastery in Southern Tibet between Kyirong and Dzongga, founded on a site where Milarepa meditated in the eleventh century.
Dewachen	bDe-ba-chen	A Buddhist paradise where many people hope to be reborn.
Dorjedrag	rDo-rje-brag	Located in Central Tibet near the banks of the Tsangpo River, Dorjedrag is the monastic center of the Changter subsect of the Nyingmapas.
Drongdö	Grong-stod	"Upper Village": one of Sama's neighborhoods.
Dzongga	rDzong-dga'	A town in Southern Tibet, formerly the center of the Gungtang Kingdom.
Gangbala	sGang-ba-la	"Filled [with People]" or "[Situated] On the Spur of a Ridge": one of Sama's neighborhoods.

Godun	sGo-bdun	"Seven Doors": one of Sama's neighborhoods.
Gungtang	Gung-thang	A region in Southern Tibet, and the name of the kingdom that once existed there.
Gyayul	rGya-yul	One of the principal villages of Kutang.
Gyasumdo	rGya-gsum-mdo	A region of Nepal just west of Nubri that is inhabited by Tibetans and Gurungs.
Hinan	He-nang	A monastery in Nubri.
Kaniwa	Ka-ni 'Og-la	"Below the Kani": one of Sama's neighborhoods.
Kok	lKog	One of the principal villages of Kutang, and the place where Pema Döndrup's uncle Tsetan lived.
Kutang	Ku-tang	The lower section of the Nubri Valley.
Kyirong	sKyid-grong	A town and formerly a district in Southern Tibet bordering Nepal.
Labrang	Bla-brang	"Lama's Palace": the name of the house where Sama's head lama resides.
Lhasa	Lha-sa	The spiritual center of the Tibetan world, and formerly the administrative capital as well.
Lho	Blod	One of the principal villages in Nubri.
Manang	Ma-nang	A region in Nepal just northwest of Nubri, also known as Nyi-shang.
Nangzar	Nang-'dzar	A small village just across the border from Nubri in Tibet.
Ngari	mNga'-ris	Western Tibet.
Nubri	Nub-ri	"Western Ridge": the setting for the stories in this book.
Pagpawati	Phags-pa Wa-ti	The temple in Kyirong where the Jowo statue used to be housed.
Pema Chöling	Padma Chos-gling	The name of Sama's monastery.

Prok	Phrog	One of the principal villages of Kutang.
Pungyen	dPung-rgyan	"Ornamented Heap": the local (Tibetan) name for Mt. Manaslu (so called in Nepali); also the name of the deity who resides on the summit.
Rue	Rud	A village in Tibet just across the border from Nubri; birthplace of Tulku Dorje.
Sama	Sa-dmar	Known as Rö (Ros) in the local vernacular, and as Sama to most outsiders; the birthplace and home of many of the characters of this book.
Samye	bSam-yas	Tibet's first monastery, situated on the northern bank of the Tsangpo River in Central Tibet.
Tradumtse	sPra-dun-rtse	A monastery in Tibet; Sama's Ngadag lineage of lamas migrated to Nubri from here.
Trong	Krong	A monastery and retirement settlement near Lho.
Tsurpu	Tshur-phu	The monastic center of Tibet's Karmapa subsect of the Kargyupas.
Yarlung	Yar-klung	The first stronghold of Tibet's medieval emperors; many of their tombs are situated in this valley.
Yurdrung	Yur-drung	"Beside the Water Conduit": one of Sama's neighborhoods.

Notes

PROLOGUE

1. Ramble 1990, 185–86. In recent years the popular perception of Tibet as a "Shangri-la" has been deconstructed in several publications, most notably by P. Bishop (1989, 1993) and Lopez (1998), and in a collection of essays edited by Dodin and Räther (2001). See also Huber 1997 and Sperling 2000.

2. The objective of connecting this study with the ethnographic literature on Tibetan and Himalayan societies can begin here. Access to Tibet was problematic until relatively recently. Prior to the 1950s systematic first-hand accounts of Tibetan societies were written mainly by missionaries and British diplomats. See Filippi 1995 for an eighteenth-century Jesuit's account; for a twentieth-century account from Eastern Tibet, see Duncan 1964; for the perspective of a Tibetan Christian, see Combe 1989; for the observations of British diplomats, see Teichman 1922, S. Turner 1991, and Bell 1992. Following the 1950s, when Westerners were ousted from Tibet by China and a flood of Tibetan refugees crossed into Nepal and India, ethnographic accounts of Tibetan society were constructed from personal recollections (Ekvall 1964, 1968) or through retrospective interviews (Aziz 1978; Dargyay 1982). Two other descriptions of Tibetan culture deserving note are those of Thubten Jigme Norbu and Turnbull (1968) and Stein (1972).

Nepal became accessible to foreign researchers in the 1950s, making that country a primary destination for scholars who wanted to study Tibetan societies in situ. Fürer-Haimendorf (1964) led the charge to study the Sherpas, a people of Tibetan origin who had already caught the world's imagination due to their mountaineering exploits. Despite doing pioneering work, Fürer-Haimendorf was criticized by one scholar on the grounds that he was illiterate in Tibetan and thereby utterly failed to connect local cultural manifestations with broader Tibetan cultural themes (Snellgrove 1966). The issues brought up by Snellgrove remain with us today, though to a far lesser extent. Several ethnographic monographs on the Sherpas followed, for example Oppitz 1968; Ortner 1978, 1989; Fisher 1990; and Adams 1996. A sampling of works on Tibetan societies elsewhere in Nepal includes Jest 1975; Schuler 1987; Levine 1988; Mumford 1989; N. Bishop 1998; and especially Ramble 2004. As a side note, Tibetan enclaves in northern India such as Ladakh, Zanskar, Lahoul, and Sikkim have a long history as places where Tibetan culture is studied. The literature on these areas is far too vast to cite here, although some studies will be referred to in subsequent footnotes. Now that Tibet has opened up, we are starting to see more ethnographic accounts of life on the plateau, for example Goldstein and Beall 1990; Clarke 1998; Goldstein and Kapstein 1998; and Epstein 2002. Dunham, Baker, and Kelly (2001) present a popular account of the Tibetan life cycle that is richly illustrated by photographs. Although technically not falling within the category of anthropological literature, a short work by Namkai Norbu (1997) and a collection of essays by Karmay (1998) deserve special mention owing to their considerable ethnographic merit.

Also deserving mention are some outstanding studies of ethnic groups in Nepal that are linguistically related to Tibetans and have been heavily influenced by Tibetan culture, for example Holmberg 1989; Watkins 1996; and March 2002. In addition, several collections of essays that include anthropological and other disciplinary perspectives are valuable sources of information, the most notable being Fürer-Haimendorf 1974b, 1981; Fisher 1978; Macdonald 1983a; Rustomji and Ramble 1990; Ramble and Brauen 1993; and Allen 1994. Other collections of essays pertaining to specific topics will be mentioned in subsequent footnotes.

3. The theoretical thrust of my academic work falls within the general framework of ecological anthropology (see Moran 2000 for a cogent introduction to this subdiscipline) and, more specifically, anthropological demography. A sampling of the seminal works in this interdisciplinary enterprise include Howell 1979; Netting 1981; Wood 1994; Greenhalgh 1995; Kertzer and Fricke 1997; and Basu and Aaby 1998. I inhabit a niche between anthropology and demography, drawing inspiration from both disciplines. I rely on demographic analysis to provide quantitative insights into the dynamics of population processes, and turn to anthropological analysis to unveil the cultural significance behind important events in the life course. Demography tells us what is happening with a population; ethnography informs us about what it all means in the eyes of the actors; see Childs 2001b, c.

In Nepal, the academic research most similar to my own was undertaken by Macfarlane (1976) and Fricke (1994). Other notable demographic descriptions of societies in the highlands of Nepal and India include Weitz et al. 1978; Goldstein 1976; Ross 1984; Levine 1987, 1988; Attenborough 1994; Wiley 1997, 1998; and Haddix 2001. On the historical demography of Tibet, see Petech 1980a; Goldstein 1981; Schuh 1988; and Childs 2003. For divergent perspectives on population issues in contemporary Tibet, see Sun and Li 1996 and

Kikhang 1997. For a case study of reproduction in contemporary Tibet, see Goldstein, Jiao, and Beall 2002.

4. The classic statements on rites of passage were made by Arnold van Gennep (1960) and Victor Turner (1969). Descriptions of rites of passage and life cycles in other cultures can be found in most basic ethnographic texts. In recent years much of the life course literature has centered on studies of aging (see, for example, Lamb 2000).

5. Such stories form the core of this book; therefore, a note on methodology is in order. Driven by a wide assortment of fieldwork objectives, I drew on a range of methodologies for gathering data in Nubri. These include the customary ethnographic technique of participant observation, more formal procedures associated with microdemographic research that involve both quantitative and qualitative approaches (see Caldwell, Hill, and Hull 1988; and Axinn, Fricke, and Thornton 1991), and formal interviewing methods centering on life history and oral history (see Brettell 1998 for a succinct discussion of these methods). I used the life history approach to elicit details of several individuals' life course trajectories, with an emphasis on subjective experiences rather than objective facts (see Atkinson 1998 for methodological notes on using such a method). As for oral history, a field pioneered by Vansina (1985), I relied on this method to gather data that both fill in the blanks left by an incomplete written historical record and flesh out cultural themes that emerge from the telling of history. Key interviews were recorded and in some cases transcribed into written Tibetan by Tsering Dorje and the late Kalsang Tsering. Translations of both oral and written materials are by me unless otherwise noted.

CHAPTER I

1. The proverbs that serve as epigraphs to each chapter, as well as some that appear in the text, are taken from Lhamo Pemba's 1996 compilation of Tibetan oral verses. In one case (chapter 2) I changed *Tibet* to *Nubri* to give the proverb a more localized essence.

2. I was not the first scholar to visit Nubri. Those who preceded me on brief visits that were later described in academic accounts include an Indian pundit working as a spy in 1861 for the British in India (Montgomerie 1868); a team of Japanese ethnographers led by Jiro Kawakita in 1952–53 (Kawakita 1957); the British scholar David Snellgrove, who passed through the area in 1956 (Snellgrove 1989); the French scholars J. F. Dobremez and Corneille Jest, who made a brief visit in 1971 (Dobremez and Jest 1976); and the eminent British scholar Michael Aris, who recorded many remarkable details about the area after a mere eight-day visit in 1973 (Aris 1975). In addition, German scholars Franz-Karl Ehrhard and Klaus-Dieter Mathes spent time in the region during the 1990s while photographing manuscripts as part of the Nepal-German Manuscript preservation project. Although relatively unknown, Nubri was not ethnographic terra incognita prior to my arrival.

3. See Kapstein 1997.

4. *Gyemi* (outsider, foreigner) is a term applied to Westerners by people of Nubri. Because the term is similar in sound and perhaps in etymology to the

Tibetan *Gyemi (rgya-mi)*, meaning "Chinese," some foreigners have mistakenly thought they were being called Chinese by the inhabitants of Nubri (e.g., Snellgrove 1989). For a while I was known simply as Gyemi to the locals. These days they usually call me "Jeb" (since Tibetan does not have the *f* sound).

5. See Ramble 1993a and 1997 regarding the term *bhotay* and some of its social ramifications. On ethnicity among Tibetan highlanders of Nepal, see Tsering Shakya 1993; Ramble 1993b, 1997; and Mumford 1998.

6. The sacred biographies *(namtar)* were uncovered by Michael Aris in 1973 (see Aris 1975 for a description of how he located them). In 1979 Aris published a reproduction of the originals under the title *Autobiographies of Three Spiritual Masters of Kutang*. The three biographies in that collection that I have used for this book are listed in the bibliography under Pema Döndrup 1979, Pema Wangdu 1979, and Pema Lhundrup 1979.

Tibetans have a long tradition of writing spiritual biographies of great Buddhist masters, many of which are now translated into English. Some of the better translations into English include the autobiography of Shabkar (Ricard 1994) and the biographies of four lamas from Dolpo, Nepal (Snellgrove 1992); these represent just a sampling of the numerous biographies that now exist in translation. For a more academic study of two remarkable individuals' lives, see Aris 1988, on Pemalingpa and the Sixth Dalai Lama. For a description of "secret autobiographies," see Gyatso 1999.

7. Dagkar Taso (White Cliff Horse's Tooth) is situated just north of the current border of Nepal, between the towns of Kyirong and Dzongga. The site was originally a meditation cave used by the famous eleventh-century Tibetan yogi Milarepa. Dagkar Taso later became an important monastery for transmitting Buddhism into the highlands of Nepal.

See Lhalungpa's 1997 translation of Milarepa's biography for a description of the yogi's time spent at Dagkar Taso; see Chang 1977 and Lama Kunga Rinpoche and Cutillo 1995 for translations of spiritual verses composed by Milarepa while at Dagkar Taso.

CHAPTER 2

1. Rigzen Gödem 1983, 5a–9a. On Tibetan sacred geography, see Dowman 1997 and especially Huber 1999a, a seminal work on Tsari; as well as collected essays in Blondeau and Steinkellner 1996; Huber 1997; and Macdonald 1997.

2. The population of Nepal is composed of dozens of distinct ethnic groups (see Bista 1967 for general descriptions). For ethnographic accounts of Gurungs, of whom the Ghales are a sub-branch, see Messerschmidt 1976b and Pignède 1993.

3. See the essays in Toffin 1991 for details of housing styles in different ethnic communities of Nepal.

4. Havnevik 1999, 2:242–243.

5. Detailed descriptions of herding strategies and indigenous pasture management practices in Himalayan settings can be found in Brower 1991; Stevens 1993; and N. Bishop 1998.

6. See Robinson and Johnson 1997 for an introduction to the history and basic tenets of Buddhism. Other good sources of information include Rahula 1974; Williams and Tribe 2000; and Harvey 2000.

7. For a very accessible overview of the history, doctrines, and schools of Tibetan Buddhism, see Powers 1995; or for a more technical account of the Indian antecedents of Tibetan Buddhism, see Snellgrove 1987. For a more anthropological perspective on religion in Tibetan societies, see Samuel 1993. Several histories of Tibet that were written by Tibetan authors and that include indigenous insights on religious history have been translated into English; see, for example, Obermiller 1986; Roerich 1988; Ahmad 1995; and Sørensen 1994 (or Taylor and Yuthok 1996 for a nontechnical rendering of the same text). See Martin 1997 for an exceptional reference work covering Tibetan historical literature, and van der Kuijp 1996 for a concise introduction to Tibetan historiography.

8. A definitive overview of the history and teachings of the Nyingmapa sect was written by Dudjom Rinpoche in 1991. Other useful works include Dargyay 1979 and Tulku Thondup 1986. See Tulku Thondup 1996 for a discussion of lineal transmissions within the Nyingmapa sect, as well as details of the particular transmission lineage that the lamas of Sama adhere to.

9. On the life story and legends of Padmasambhava, see Dowman 1973 and Yeshe Tsogyal 1993. On his teachings, see Guenther 1996.

10. Tibetan art has been the focus of considerable academic attention in recent years. The best source on the history of Tibetan art is Jackson 1996. Other studies of note include Rhie and Thurman 1996; Heller 2000; and the collection of essays in Klimburg-Salter and Allinger 2002. On thanka painting, see Jackson and Jackson 1999; on medical thankas, see Baker and Shrestha 1997; for an analytical study of Tibetan mandalas, see Brauen 1998. See Dagyab Rinpoche 1995 and Beer 1999 for explanations of the symbols and motifs that are commonly found in Tibetan art.

See White 1990 for a basic introduction to Tibetan architecture, and Larsen and Sinding-Larsen 2001 on traditional architecture in Lhasa. A Tibetan perspective that includes details on where to site a temple and the rituals associated with building is found in Thubten Legshay Gyatsho 1979. Studies of temple architecture in the Tibetan highlands of Nepal include Sestini and Somigli 1978 and Jest 1981. For an analysis of a temple interior from the viewpoint of psychological anthropology, see Paul 1976.

11. For a more thorough examination of Nubri history, including details on primary source materials, see Childs 2000, 2001a. Other studies on the history of ethnically Tibetan enclaves in Nepal include Oppitz 1968; Clarke 1980a; Jackson 1984; and Ortner 1989. For introductions to the history of Nepal, see D. R. Regmi 1961a, b; Rose 1971; Stiller 1975; M. Regmi 1978; Sever 1996; and Pandey 1997. For general introductions to the history of Tibet, see Snellgrove and Richardson 1980 and Shakabpa 1988. The best source on Tibet's imperial past is Beckwith 1987; see also some of the contributions by Uray (e.g. 1960, 1980). On the history of Western Tibet, including areas in the vicinity of Nubri, see Tucci 1956; Petech 1977, 1980b; and Vitali 1996.

12. Tsewang Norbu 1990, 90–93, 108.

13. Milarepa 1985, 67b–68a.
14. Rigzen Gödem 1983, 2a.
15. A study of Nepal's historical social order is found in Höfer 1979.
16. Ethnographic and historical analyses of trans-Himalayan trade can be found in Fürer-Haimendorf 1974a, 1975; Fisher 1986; and van Spengen 2000.

CHAPTER 3

1. Cultural details about conception, pregnancy, birth, and childrearing practices in the Tibetan tradition have been collected by Norbu Chophel (1983) and Thubten Sangay (1984b). See Khangkar 1986 for a perspective from the Tibetan medical tradition, and Maiden and Farwell 1997 for an account of parenting among Tibetan exiles.

2. The most extensive catalogue of such beings is found in Nebesky-Wojkowitz 1956.

3. In an interesting and provocative study of the Nyinba, an ethnically Tibetan group of people living in Western Nepal, Nancy Levine (1987) demonstrates that differential child care is associated with higher infant mortality among less desired children, a category that includes girls as well as illegitimate children. Although I have observed a gender-based difference in Nubri in the way that parents treat their children, with sons receiving preferential treatment, the demographic evidence does not show a pattern of higher infant mortality among females. It remains to be seen whether Levine's findings apply to other Tibetan communities.

4. Polyandry, a rare form of plural marriage, has been the focus of much anthropological scrutiny. Some of the better sources on fraternal polyandry among Tibetans include Goldstein 1971a, 1976; Schuler 1987; Levine 1988; Crook and Crook 1994; Levine and Silk 1997; and Haddix 2001. See Childs 2003 for a quantitative analysis of the impact that polyandry and nonmarriage had on population growth in a historical Tibetan society.

5. For an inspiring ethnographic description of healing rituals in another highland area of Nepal, see Desjarlais 1992. An interesting collection of essays relating to spirit possession and healing in Nepal can be found in Hitchcock and Jones 1976. See Pigg 1997 for an insightful analysis of such healing traditions in the context of the modernization and development discourse.

6. For a full translation and analysis of three natal horoscopes from Sama, see Childs and Walter 2000. For a general description of Tibetan astrology, see Cornu 1997.

7. As mentioned before, to most Tibetan speakers the term Gyemi means "Chinese," whereas in Nubri it implies more generally "outsider" or "foreigner." Today people interpret the clan name Gyemi to mean simply that the founders of the lineage migrated from outside the area, from Tibet. The clan is reputedly descended from the minister Gar. The Gar family provided the Tibetan emperors with many important administrators and generals until they were perceived as a threat to the royal dynasty during the eighth century. Henceforth, they were either eliminated or driven into exile. Could they have ended up in Kutang? This is an intriguing question, given the uncertainties of

Tibetan historical migrations. See Beckwith 1987 and Richardson 1998d for information on the Gar family. The Kyung clan also figures prominently in the ancient history of Tibet. According to Tibetan tales of ethnogenesis, the first humans derived from the mating of a rock ogress and the bodhisattva Chenrezik, who had taken the form of a monkey. The offspring were born with tails and eventually displayed human traits such as avarice and a propensity to quarrel. From these first semihumans came the Tibetan protoclans, and later the Kyung (see Stein 1959, 1972). Based in Western Tibet not far from Nubri, the Kyung clan was associated with an independent kingdom called Zhangzhung that was eventually subsumed within the nascent Tibetan empire around 640. Kyung is widely considered to be one of the most ancient clans of Tibet.

8. In the past, Bhutanese lamas extended their religious influence into parts of northern Nepal. From this passage we can infer that they maintained early contacts with the kings of Gorkha who had yet to complete their conquest of Kathmandu and other territories that would subsequently form the borders of Nepal. Unfortunately, very little is known about the connections between Bhutan and Gorkha at this critical juncture of Nepali history. See Aris 1979, 1994; and the essays in Schicklgruber and Pommaret 1997, regarding the history and culture of Bhutan.

9. Pema Wangdu 1979, 8a–9b.

CHAPTER 4

1. The reference to sheep demonstrates that economic strategies vary over time in Nubri. Sheep are no longer herded in Kutang.

2. Pema Döndrup 1979, 2a–11a.

3. The threat to the continuity of the Ngadag family lineage has a long history in Sama. Tashi Dorje told me the story of his ancestor, Senge Namgyal, who was the head lama of the village nearly two centuries ago. Senge Namgyal died without begetting an heir, so the people of Sama requested that his cousin be sent from Tibet as the new head lama. At the time, the cousin's family resided at Tradumtse, a temple to the north of the Himalayas from where Sama's Ngadag ancestors had migrated in the mid-1600s. The cousin was a younger son in his family, and therefore by right of primogeniture he was not the incumbent of Tradumtse. In this case succession in Sama proceeded not from father to son, but from uncle to nephew.

4. The events leading to the flight of the Dalai Lama from Tibet and the establishment of a government in exile are described in the Dalai Lama's autobiography (Tenzin Gyatso 1990) and in Avedon 1986. For a nobleman's viewpoint of events prior to 1959, see Tsarong 2000; and for differing perspectives on the early days of life in exile, contrast Taklha 2001 and Taring 1986 with Goldstein, Siebenschuh, and Tsering 1997. Ethnographic descriptions of Tibetan society in exile can be found in Novak 1984; Forbes 1989; Fürer-Haimendorf 1989; Kleiger 1992; Diehl 2002; and the collections of essays in Korom 1997 and Kleiger 2002.

Lately the topic of Buddhism's encounter with the West has received considerable attention. See, for example, Fields 1992; Batchelor 1994; Lopez 1998;

Prebish and Tanaka 1998; Seager 1999; and Prebish and Baumann 2002. I am indebted to Lisa Frankel for these references. In addition, there is at least one study of the encounter between Westerners and Buddhism in Bodhnath, Nepal, where many of the exile monasteries are clustered (P. Moran 1998). For a revealing look at how Buddhist sacred paintings are marketed to Western tourists, see Bentor 1993.

5. The demographic situation among Tibetan exiles is summarized in Planning Council 2000. An analysis of birth rates in Nubri can be found in Childs 2001b. On the rise of the carpet industry in Nepal, which resulted in the accumulation of considerable wealth by Tibetan refugees, see McGuckin 1997.

6. Elsewhere I have described the tax system and economic stratification in Sama in more detail (Childs 2001d, 2004). For details on monastic and government taxation systems in traditional Tibetan settings, see Surkhang 1966, 1986; and Goldstein 1971b, 1989. Other sources on the government of Tibet prior to the 1950s include Carrasco 1959; Cassinelli and Ekvall 1969; and Petech 1973.

7. It is worth quoting anthropologist Charles Ramble here, who has weighed in with his own observations on external perceptions of Buddhist communities and their ramifications: "And now there is the Third Diffusion [of Buddhism], originating in the exile community. . . . The burgeoning international interest in the Tibetan cause has less to do with a sporting sympathy for the underdog than with a real appreciation of the universal relevance of Tibetan Buddhism. But the Third Spread is not limited to the first-world public undergoing a spiritual crisis. It is also reaching the Tibetan-speaking people of the Himalayan rimland. How?

"The common enough scenario is that a businessman from, say, Japan, United States or Taiwan becomes impassioned by the Tibetan cause and goes trekking in the Himalaya. Because he has Tibet on his mind, what he sees is a Tibetan culture apparently fallen into decline: a struggling language, illiterate monks, dilapidated temples, and a degenerate Lamaist tradition. With the blessing of his lama (who probably has never been to this place), he elects to help the area by building a monastery. No objection, naturally, from the locals, who have not to examine the gift horse too closely. To the outsider, at least, the generous act looks like the commendable resuscitation of a failing Buddhist heritage" (Ramble 1993b, 25).

8. Pema Döndrup 1979, 55b–56a.

9. Pema Wangdu 1979, 132b–133a. On animal sacrifice in Buddhist communities, see Holmberg 1989; Mumford 1989; Ramble 1990; and Childs 1997.

CHAPTER 5

1. Descriptions of hidden valleys *(beyul)* and translations of hidden valley literature can be found in Reinhard 1978; Aris 1979; Bernbaum 1980; Orofino 1991; Diemberger 1993, 1997; Ehrhard 1997, 1999; and Childs 1999.

2. The two most commonly cited translations of Tibetan texts describing places of historical importance are Ferrari 1958 and Wylie 1962. See Wylie 1970 for a fascinating nineteenth-century Tibetan perspective on global geography;

see Aziz 1975 and Huber 1992 for examples of indigenous Tibetan maps. The best study of Tibetan pilgrimage is Huber 1999a. See also the collection of essays in McKay 1998, as well as Jest 1993 for a lively account of a pilgrimage in Dolpo, Nepal. On pilgrimage in contemporary Tibet, see Kapstein 1998.

3. Tibetan is classified by some linguists as belonging to the Tibeto-Burman language family, and by others to the Sino-Tibetan language family. For linguistic overviews of the Tibetan language, see Benedict 1972; Hale 1982; Róna-Tas 1985; and Beckwith 2002.

4. The Northern Treasure (Changter) sub-sect of the Nyingmapas was established by Rigzen Gödem. For bibliographic outlines of the life of this remarkable figure, see Dargyay 1979; Dudjom Rinpoche 1991; and Boord 1993. Rigzen Gödem was a key figure in the hidden valley tradition alluded to above. The main center of the Changter School was at Dorjedrag Monastery near the confluence of the Kyichu and Tsangpo Rivers in Central Tibet. Changter adherents somehow incurred the wrath of the Mongols, who executed their abbot and destroyed Dorjedrag in the early 1700s; see Petech 1988.

5. Lhasa was the spiritual and administrative center of Tibet, especially during the imperial period (c. 640–842) and after the political consolidation accomplished by the Fifth Dalai Lama in the 1640s. For descriptions of the historical city, including sacred sites, see Alexander 1998 and Pommaret-Imaeda 2002. The Potala Palace, the most recognizable symbol of Tibet, was built by the Fifth Dalai Lama and the regent who ruled after his death in 1682. The massive structure became an important administrative center as well as the winter residence of all Dalai Lamas. Their bodies are entombed within. See P. Bishop 1999 for a fascinating account of how the Potala has figured in Western perceptions of Tibet. The Jokhang Temple in Lhasa was originally built by a Nepali princess during the reign of the emperor Songtsen Gampo (d. 649/650), and is considered to be the most holy site in the land. The legend on the establishing of the Jokhang can be found in Snellgrove and Richardson 1980. See Richardson 1998b for a description of the Jokhang, and Vitali 1990 for photographs and artistic details of the building's interior.

6. Samye, situated on the bank of the Tsangpo River in Central Tibet, is Tibet's first monastery. According to legend it was established in the eighth century by Padmasambhava; see Snellgrove and Richardson 1980.

7. Pema Döndrup 1979, 11a–19a. The Yarlung Valley was an early center of Tibetan imperial power, and the place where the ruined tombs of the medieval emperors can still be seen to this day. For descriptions, see Tucci 1950 and Richardson 1998a.

8. Shekar, a monastery and former administrative center in Southern Tibet, is the subject of a study by Pasang Wangdu and Diemberger 1996. Narthang was an important monastery in Central Tibet where religious texts were produced from block prints.

9. See Tsepak Rigzen 1993 for a brief description of Lhasa's New Year festivities.

10. Tsurpu is the monastic residence of the Karmapas, one of the principal branches of the Kargyupa sect. See Richardson 1998c for a personal recollection of Tsurpu from the 1940s, and Karma Thinley 2001 for a brief history of

all the Karmapa incarnations. Although predominantly Nyingmapa, the lamas of Nubri have maintained a long-standing affiliation with the Karmapas.

11. The document was first uncovered, photographed, and partially translated by Aris (1975). On the establishment of border-taming temples during the reign of the emperor Songtsen Gampo, see Aris 1979.

12. See Goldstein 1989 for a history of Tibet during the first half of the twentieth century. See Grunfeld 1996, Goldstein 1997, and Tsering Shakya 1999 for details on Tibetan history after 1950. Dawa Norbu's 1997 reminiscences on the early days of China's occupation provide a fascinating first-hand account from a villager's perspective. Schwartz 1994, as well as the collections of essays found in Barnett 1994 and Harris and Jones 2000, provides insights into the political situation since the 1980s. The recent biography of Tashi Tsering (Goldstein, Siebenschuh, and Tashi Tsering 1997) is a rare first-hand account of what it was like to be a Tibetan during and after the tumultuous Cultural Revolution. Of related interest are two collections of essays pertaining to the issue of Tibetan independence, one written by Tibetan exiles (Lazar 1994) and the other by Chinese dissidents (Cao and Seymour 1998).

13. The passage is from Taylor and Lama Choedak Yuthok's translation (1996, 115–16) of the fourteenth-century Tibetan chronicle rGyal-rabs gSal-ba'i Me-long. See Sørensen 1994 for an adroit, fully annotated treatment of this same text.

14. See Peissel 1972 and Jamyang Norbu 1987 for accounts of Khampa guerilla actions against China. See Knaus 1999 and Conboy and Morrison 2002 for details of the CIA involvement in equipping and training this resistance movement prior to Nixon's détente with China. One group of Khampa guerillas ended up in Nubri, where they launched actions against Chinese forces across the border in Tibet. Aris encountered some of these men shortly after the resistance movement had been abandoned (Aris 1975).

CHAPTER 6

1. Marriage and incest rules in other ethnic Tibetan settings have been described elsewhere, for example Bell 1992; Fürer-Haimendorf 1964; Levine 1981; Dargyay 1982; and Schicklgruber 1993. Curiously, in Nepal cross-cousin marriage in indigenous communities of ethnic Tibetans is quite common, despite the fact that in Tibet such a marital arrangement is considered unequivocally incestuous. It is important to bear in mind that cultural ideals, such as cross-cousin marriage, do not necessarily translate into statistical realities. In small communities such as Sama chances are great that a young man or woman will not have a cross-cousin who is of the correct age or gender to marry. Only about one in three marriages turn out to be between cross-cousins, even though most people state unequivocally that "this is what we do."

2. Tamangs, distant linguistic relatives of Tibetans, have a long history of cultural and economic exchanges with their neighbors to the north. They also practice cross-cousin marriage. For ethnographic details on Tamangs, see Frank 1974; Macdonald 1983b; Clarke 1980b; Toffin et al. 1986; Steinmann 1987; Holmberg 1989; Fricke 1994; and March 2002.

3. For legends about this mythical figure, see Aris 1979. Curiously, reputed descendants of Kyika Ratö appear in several places in Bhutan and Nepal. In the case of Sama's Pönzang lineage, the oral history states that they came from Barpak, an ethnically Ghale village to the south of Nubri where Kyika Ratö is supposed to have settled. Barpak and Sama have a long history of trade relations, and since Ghales and Tibetans share cultural and linguistic similarities, it would not be unusual for people of Ghale origin to assimilate to Tibetan society once settled in Sama.

4. On Tibetan weights and measures, see Surkhang 1966 and Osmaston and Rabgyas 1994.

5. On the history of the Kanjur, see Eimer 1992; Harrison 1996; and Germano and Eimer 2002. For an interesting commentary on some of the motivations behind Kanjur research, see Harrison 1992.

6. Tibetans are fond of jokes and stories that have sexual overtones. One need look no further than the stories of the trickster Uncle Tompa to understand this lesson (see Rinjing Dorje 1997). For a Tibetan view on sexuality derived from Indian sources and the personal experiences of Tibet's most controversial twentieth-century intellectual, see Gedün Chöpel 1992. Of related interest, see Hopkins 2000.

CHAPTER 7

1. Tibetans are known to intentionally deforest southern-facing slopes to make the landscape more amenable for herding. Doing so creates reliable winter pastures for their cattle, since the intense, high-altitude radiation melts the snow rapidly from the exposed ground. See Winkler 1998 for more on this topic. For ecological perspectives and the politics of ecology in the Himalayas, see Rhoades and Thompson 1975; Messerschmidt 1976a; Guillet 1983; Orlove and Guillet 1985; Thompson and Warburton 1985; Dobremez 1986; Ives 1987; Ives and Messerli 1989; and Fox 1993.

2. Pema Döndrup 1979, 24b–25b.

3. Snellgrove arrived some time after this incident and mentions the animosity by Sama villagers toward the Japanese climbers that stemmed from the avalanche. However, he erroneously reports that eighteen people died in the tragedy (Snellgrove 1989). See Takagi 1954 and Maki and Imanishi 1957 for accounts of the early Japanese mountaineering attempts on Mt. Pungyen (Manaslu).

4. See, for example, Karmay 1994; Schicklgruber 1997; Bellezza 1997; and Huber 1999a, as well as the collection of essays in Blondeau and Steinkellner 1996 and Huber 1999b for descriptions of mountain deities and associated ritual practices in other Tibetan societies.

5. The pajo tradition is fading away in Sama, an opinion expressed by one of the men who hold this position currently. By his own admission, he knows very few of the prayers in comparison to his predecessors, and is unsure if anybody else will take over his duties in the future. From what I could gather, each descent lineage in Sama, with the exception of the Ngadag lama lineage, has its own pajo. Sama's pajo tradition is perhaps a local manifestation of practitioners

that are found in other Tibetan cultural settings in the Himalayan borderlands such as *lhaven* (lha-bon), *bonbo* (bon-po), or *aya* (a-ya). See, for example, Höfer 1981; Holmberg 1989; Mumford 1989; and Diemberger 1991, 1996.

6. Ortner (1975, 1978) interprets such rituals in light of expectations in social behavior between hosts and guests in Sherpa culture. Descriptions of other rites, including translations of ritual texts, are found in Lopez 1997.

7. For descriptions of nomadic societies in Tibet, see Ekvall 1968, 1976; and Goldstein and Beall 1990. See Vitali 1997 for historical notes on the Tibetan nomadic regions to the north of Nubri.

CHAPTER 8

1. See Beall and Goldstein 1982; Goldstein and Beall 1997; and Childs 2001c for studies on aging in Tibetan societies. See also Mullin 1998 for Tibetan perspectives on impending death.

2. From Lopez 1998, 211. For discussions about gendered dimensions in Buddhism and Tibetan society, see Klein 1995; Campbell 1996; and the collection of essays in Willis 1987. Misogynist perceptions of nuns in Tibetan society are described by Havnevik 1989. Additional studies of nuns, other female religious practitioners, and gendered dimensions of religious practice in Tibetan societies include Diemberger 1991; Huber 1994; and Gutschow 1997, 2001. For an interesting perspective on nuns and the contemporary political context in Tibet, see Havnevik 1994.

3. Tsari, a major pilgrimage complex centering on a mountain in southeastern Tibet, is described in detail by Huber (1999a).

4. Pema Döndrup 1979, 24a–31a, 45b–46b.

CHAPTER 9

1. On the Tibetan Book of the Dead, see, for example, Fremantle and Chogyam Trungpa 1987; Thurman 1994; and Hodge and Boord 2000. See Cuevas 2003 for a history of this text, including how it became popular in the West. Sogyal Rinpoche (1994) provides a lucid perspective on death and dying in the Tibetan tradition. Interesting translations of writings about death from various Tibetan perspectives can be found in Lopez 1997 and Mullin 1998. See Germano 1997 on some of the ways that Tibetans prognosticate impending death.

2. Letter written by the Fifth Dalai Lama in 1660, translated by Elliot Sperling (2001). Some accounts of conflict and violence in Tibetan society are found in Ekvall 1964; Richardson 1998e; and Goldstein 1990; see also any basic history of Tibet for accounts of sectarian rivalries (e.g., Snellgrove and Richardson 1980; Shakabpa 1988). See Sperling 2001 for a provocative discussion on the difficulty of reconciling historical violence with contemporary perceptions of Tibet as a peaceful society; Lhasang Tsering 1993 for an interesting Tibetan perspective on the use of violence for self-defense; and Jamyang Norbu 2001 for a viewpoint on how the peaceful image of Tibetans has transformed a struggle for independence into an amorphous agenda centering on spiritual and pacifistic concerns.

3. On Tibetan mortuary rites, see Skorupski 1982 and Thubten Sangay 1984a. Wood is scarce on the Tibetan Plateau, so Tibetans generally dispose of the dead through a "sky burial," a ritual whereby the corpse is cut up and fed to vultures. See Martin 1996 for a historical and ecological perspective on this tradition. In Tibetan communities of the Himalayas such as Nubri, wood is abundant, so the dead are disposed of through cremation. See Downs 1980 for a sensitive photo essay on one such ritual in Solu-Khumbu.

4. Gyasumdo lies along the Marsyangdi River below Manang. The area is inhabited by Gurungs and (since the middle of the nineteenth century) Tibetans who migrated there to take advantage of the local trade routes. A description of religious practices and other ethnographic details of the area can be found in Mumford 1989.

5. Kalsang had already demonstrated his exceptional abilities through collaboration with another foreign researcher. Their publication (Bolsokhoyeva and Kalsang Tsering 1995), together with the stories in this book, is unfortunately the only scholarly legacy that Kalsang was able to leave behind in his short lifetime.

CHAPTER 10

1. Manang, known as Nyishang in the local vernacular, is situated to the west of Nubri in the upper stretches of the Marsyandi River. See Gurung 1976; Watkins 1996; and van Spengen 2000 for ethnographic and economic descriptions of this area.

2. Pema Lhundrup 1979, 51b–53b.

3. On the topic of rolang, see Wylie 1964. For near death experiences, see Epstein 1982 and 1990.

4. See Ngawang Zangpo 1997 for a Tibetan perspective on reincarnation and the recognition of tulkus. On the convergence of reincarnation and political institutions, see Goldstein 1973 and Michael 1982.

5. Pema Döndrup, 1979, 55a–55b.

Glossary

TERM[1]	TIBETAN SPELLING[2]	TRANSLATION
ajo	a-jo	"Elder brother."
ama	a-ma	"Mother."
ani	a-ni	"Nun"; also "paternal aunt" (father's sister).
arak	a-rag	Alcohol distilled locally from corn or barley.
ashang	a-zhang	"Maternal uncle" (mother's brother).
balang	ba-glang	"Ox"; nickname for Tashi Döndrup's half brother.
bardo	bar-do	The intermediate realm between death and rebirth. Bardo Tödel is the Tibetan Book of the Dead, which lamas read to assist the deceased through the bardo realm.

1. Nepali and Sanskrit terms are indicated parenthetically.
2. Tibetan spellings follow the Wylie system of transliteration.

beyul	sbas-yul	A hidden valley.
bhotay (Nep.)		A term applied to anybody of Tibetan extraction in Nepal.
Bodhisattva (Skt.)		An enlightened being who forsakes release from the cycle of continual existence in order to assist others along the path to enlightenment.
butsab	bu-tshab	"Substitute son": a son who is adopted into a family lacking male heirs.
chang	chang	Beverage fermented from corn or barley, either used as an offering to deities or distilled into arak.
Changter	Byang-gter	The "Northern Treasure" subsect of the Nyingmapas.
chöpa	mchod-pa	A male householder with rudimentary liturgical training who can act as a low-level ritual participant.
chöpey yul	mchod-pa'i yul	The realm of religious practitioners; cf. *jigtenpey yul*.
chöten	mchod-rten	Known more commonly in the West by the Sanskrit term *stupa,* a chorten is a reliquary, a multivalent symbol representing the structure of the universe as well as the body of the Buddha.
Chumin	Chung-dman	"Low and Inferior": the least prestigious descent lineage of Sama.
dharma (Skt.)		Teachings of the Buddha.
Dokdok	rDog-rdog	"Globular": a common nickname for chubby kids in Nubri.
dri	'bri	A female yak.
dzo	mdzo	The sterile male hybrid of a yak and cow; used as a nickname for an impotent man.

Gelugpa	dGe-lugs-pa	The reformed sect of Buddhism in Tibet that is headed by the Dalai Lama.
gomba	dgon-pa	"Solitary place" for religious practice; "monastery."
gyemi	rgya-mi	Term used in Nubri for "foreigner."
gyupa	rgyud-pa	A descent group traced through patrilineage.
jigtenpey yul	'jig-rten-pa'i yul	The realm of worldly suffering; cf. *chöpey yul.*
jindag	sbyin-bdag	A patron or sponsor (as of a ritual).
kam sangbo	khams bzang-po	"How are you?": a greeting unique to Nubri.
kani	ka-ni	A religious structure that one walks through marking the symbolic boundary between the ritually secured space of the village and the dangerous world outside.
Kargyupa	dKar-brgyud-pa	One of the four main sects of Tibetan Buddhism.
Karmapa	Karma-pa	A subsect of the Kargyupa sect of Tibetan Buddhism, headed by the Karmapa lamas based at Tsurpu Monastery.
khata	kha-btags	Ceremonial scarf signifying blessings and good fortune.
kukay	ku-skad	A term for the Kutang dialect; it is a double entendre, meaning "the language of Kutang" and "stolen language," in reference to the plethora of nonindigenous terms that have made their way into this dialect.
kuma	rkun-ma	"Thief."
kyekar	skyes-skar	A natal horoscope, composed by the village astrologer shortly after the birth of a child.

kyimse	khyim-mtshes	"Neighbors": a term often reserved for those neighbors one can count on in difficult times or who are generally helpful.
lhakhang	lha-khang	"House of the deities": a temple.
lhasol	lha-gsol	A ritual offering made to local deities.
mantra (Skt.)		Buddhist sacred verses that are chanted.
matsab	ma-tshab	"Substitute mother": a step-mother or wet-nurse.
mirig	mi-rigs	Race, nationality, or ethnic group.
miser	mi-ser	Subject of a lord; citizen of a country.
namshey	rnam-shes	Consciousness principle.
namtar	rnam-thar	Religious biography in the Tibetan tradition.
Ngadag	mNga'-bdag	"Possessing Power": the name of the prestigious lama lineage in Sama that traces descent to the medieval Tibetan emperors.
ngagpa	sngags-pa	A married, householder lama.
nuwo	nu-bo	"Younger brother."
nyeldang	nyer-ldang	Term for a person with whom one has a special connection by virtue of being born in the same year
nyelu	nyal-bu	An illegitimate child.
Nyingmapa	rNying-ma-pa	One of the four sects of Tibetan Buddhism, and the sect most commonly adhered to in Nubri.
pajo	dpa'-jo	A ritual specialist of Sama whose main duty is to perform rites of appeasement to the local deities.

Pönzang	dPon-bzang	"Good Rulers": the second highest ranking descent lineage in Sama.
Rinpoche	rin-po-che	"Precious One": an honorific title for a Buddhist teacher of high repute.
rolang	ro-langs	"Rising corpse."
rongba	rong-pa	"Valley dweller": term applied to lowlanders.
ru	rus	"Bone"; also refers to patrilineal descent lineage.
Sakyapa	Sa-skya-pa	One of the four sects of Tibetan Buddhism.
samsara (Skt.)		Worldly suffering characterized by cyclical existence.
sheyba	bshas-pa	"Butcher": an outcast in Tibetan society due to a profession that requires the taking of animal lives.
shidur	shi-dur	Messenger of death.
subbha (Nep.)		Local representative of the Nepali government, a legacy of indirect rule.
tobyig	thob-yig	A written record of the religious initiations or teachings one has received.
tsampa	tsam-pa	Roasted barley flour, the staple of most Tibetan agrarian communities.
tsewang	tshe-dbang	"Life empowerment": refers to a ceremony meant to give longevity to the recipient.
tsipa	rtsis-pa	An astrologer, responsible for composing natal horoscopes, determining the astrological compatibility of potential spouses, and setting auspicious dates for weddings and funerals.
tulku	sprul-sku	"Emanation body": a reincarnate lama.

ulag	'u-lag	Compulsory labor of all householders for the benefit of the head lama of Sama, or of monks and nuns for the benefit of the lama who initiated them.
yak	gyag	The preeminent bovine of the Himalayas and Tibetan Plateau.
yang	g.yang	Material prosperity.
Yorkung	Yur-khong	"Irrigators": one of the lower-ranking descent lineages in Sama, reputedly represented by the first migrants to the village.

References

Adams, Vincanne. 1996. *Tigers of the Snow and Other Virtual Sherpas*. Princeton: Princeton University Press.

Ahmad, Zahiruddin, trans. 1995. *A History of Tibet by the Fifth Dalai Lama of Tibet*. Bloomington, Ind.: Research Institute for Inner Asian Studies.

Alexander, Andre. 1998. *The Old City of Lhasa: Report from a Conservation Project*. Berlin: Tibet Heritage Fund.

Allan, Michael, ed. 1994. *Anthropology of Nepal: Peoples, Problems, and Processes*. Kathmandu: Mandala Book Point.

Aris, Michael. 1975. Report on the University of California Expedition to Kutang and Nubri in Northern Nepal in Autumn 1973. *Contributions to Nepalese Studies* 2 (2): 45–87.

———. 1979. *Bhutan: The Early History of a Himalayan Kingdom*. Warminster, Eng.: Aris and Phillips.

———. 1988. *Hidden Treasures and Secret Lives: A Study of Pemalingpa (1450–1521) and the Sixth Dalai Lama (1683–1706)*. Shimla: Indian Institute of Advanced Study.

———. 1994. *The Raven Crown: The Origins of Buddhist Monarchy in Bhutan*. London: Serindia Publications.

Atkinson, Robert. 1998. *The Life Story Interview*. Thousand Oaks, Calif.: Sage.

Attenborough, R. 1994. The Population of sTongde, Zangskar. In *Himayalan Buddhist Villages,* ed. J. Crook and H. Osmaston, 295–330. Bristol: University of Bristol Press.

Avedon, John F. 1986. *In Exile from the Land of Snows*. New York: Vintage Books.

Axinn, William G., Thomas E. Fricke, and Arland Thornton. 1991. The Microdemographic Community Study Approach. *Sociological Methods and Research* 20 (2): 187–217.

Aziz, Barbara. 1975. Tibetan Manuscript Maps of the Dingri Valley. *Canadian Cartographer* 12: 341–364.

———. 1978. *Tibetan Frontier Families*. New Delhi: Vikas.

Baker, Ian A., and Romio Shrestha. 1997. *The Tibetan Art of Healing*. San Francisco: Chronicle Books.

Barnett, Robert, ed. 1994. *Resistance and Reform in Tibet*. London: C. Hurst.

Basu, Alaka Malwade, and Peter Aaby, eds. 1998. *The Methods and Uses of Anthropological Demography*. Oxford: Clarendon Press.

Batchelor, Stephen. 1994. *The Awakening of the West: The Encounter of Buddhism and Western Culture*. Berkeley: Parallax Press.

Beall, Cynthia M., and Melvyn C. Goldstein. 1982. Work, Aging, and Dependency in a Sherpa Population in Nepal. *Social Science and Medicine* 16 (2): 141–148.

Beckwith, Christopher I. 1987. *The Tibetan Empire in Central Asia*. Princeton: Princeton University Press.

———, ed. 2002. *Medieval Tibeto-Burman Languages*. Leiden: E. J. Brill.

Beer, Robert. 1999. *The Encyclopedia of Tibetan Symbols and Motifs*. Boston: Shambhala.

Bell, Charles. 1992 [1928]. *The People of Tibet*. Delhi: Motilal Banarsidass.

Bellezza, John V. 1997. *Divine Dyads: Ancient Civilization in Tibet*. Dharamsala: Library of Tibetan Works and Archives.

Benedict, Paul K. 1972. *Sino-Tibetan, a Conspectus*. Cambridge: Cambridge University Press.

Bentor, Yael. 1993. Tibetan Tourist Thankas in the Kathmandu Valley. *Annals of Tourism Research* 20: 107–137.

Bernbaum, E. 1980. *The Way to Shambhala*. New York: Anchor Press.

Bishop, Naomi H. 1998. *Himalayan Herders*. Fort Worth, Tex.: Harcourt Brace.

Bishop, Peter D. 1989. *The Myth of Shangri-La : Tibet, Travel Writing, and the Western Creation of Sacred Landscape*. London: Athlone Press.

———. 1993. *Dreams of Power: Tibetan Buddhism, Western Imagination*. Rutherford, N.J. : Fairleigh Dickinson University Press.

———. 1999. Reading the Potala. In *Sacred Spaces and Powerful Places in Tibetan Culture,* ed. T. Huber, 367–385. Dharamsala: Library of Tibetan Works and Archives.

Bista, Dor Bahadur. 1967. *People of Nepal*. Kathmandu: Ratna Pustak Bhandar.

Blondeau, Anne-Marie, and Ernst Steinkellner, eds. 1996. *Reflections of the Mountain: Essays on the History and Social Meaning of the Mountain Cult in Tibet and the Himalaya*. Vienna: Verlag der Österreichischen Akademie der Wissenschaften.

Bolsokhoyeva, Natalia D., and Kalsang Tsering. 1995. *Tibetan Songs from Dingri*. Rikon, Switz.: Tibet-Institut.

Boord, M. 1993. *The Cult of the Deity Vajrakila*. Tring, Eng.: Institute of Buddhist Studies.

Brauen, Martin. 1998. *The Mandala: Sacred Circle in Tibetan Buddhism.* Boston: Shambhala.

Brettell, Caroline B. 1998. Fieldwork in the Archives: Methods and Sources in Historical Anthropology. In *Handbook of Methods in Cultural Anthropology,* ed. H. R. Bernard, 513–546. Walnut Creek, Calif.: Alta Mira Press.

Brower, Barbara. 1991. *Sherpa of Khumbu.* Delhi: Oxford University Press.

Caldwell, John C., Allan G. Hill, and Valerie J. Hull, eds. 1988. *Micro-Approaches to Demographic Research.* London: Kegan Paul.

Campbell, June. 1996. *Traveler in Space: In Search of Female Identity in Tibetan Buddhism.* New York: George Braziller.

Cao, Changching, and James D. Seymour, eds. 1998. *Tibet through Dissident Chinese Eyes.* Armonk, N.Y.: M. E. Sharpe.

Carrasco, Pedro. 1959. *Land and Polity in Tibet.* Seattle: University of Washington Press.

Cassinelli, C. W., and Robert B. Ekvall. 1969. *A Tibetan Principality: The Political System of Sa-skya.* Ithaca: Cornell University Press.

Chang, Garma C. C., trans. 1977. *The Hundred Thousand Songs of Milarepa.* Boulder, Colo.: Shambhala.

Childs, Geoff. 1997. Householder Lamas and the Persistence of Tradition: Animal Sacrifice in Himalayan Buddhist Communities. In *Tibetan Studies,* ed. Helmut Krasser, 141–155. Vienna: Verlag der Österreichischen Akademie der Wissenschaften.

———. 1999. Refuge and Revitalization: Hidden Himalayan Sanctuaries *(sbas-yul)* and the Preservation of Tibet's Imperial Lineage. *Acta Orientalia* 60: 126–158.

———. 2000. Claiming the Frontier: A Note on the Incorporation of Nubri within the Borders of Nepal. *Studies in Nepali History and Society* 5 (2): 217–226.

———. 2001a. A Brief History of Nubri: Ethnic Interface, Sacred Geography, and Historical Migrations in a Himalayan Locality. *Zentralasiatische Studien* 31: 7–29.

———. 2001b. Demographic Dimensions of an Inter-Village Land Dispute in Nubri, Nepal. *American Anthropologist* 103 (4): 1096–1113.

———. 2001c. Old-Age Security, Religious Celibacy, and Aggregate Fertility in a Tibetan Population. *Journal of Population Research* 18 (1): 52–66.

———. 2001d. Perceptions of Relative Wealth in a Tibetan Community: A Note on Research Methodology. *Tibet Journal* 26 (2): 26–38.

———. 2003. Polyandry and Population Growth in a Historical Tibetan Society. *The History of the Family* 8 (3): 423–444.

———. 2004. How to Fund a Ritual: The Social Usage of the Kanjur (Bka'-'gyur) in a Tibetan Village. In *Tibetan Studies: Proceedings of the 8th Seminar of the International Association for Tibetan Studies,* ed. E. Sperling. Bloomington: Indiana University Press.

Childs, Geoff, and Michael Walter. 2000. Tibetan Natal Horoscopes. *Tibet Journal* 25 (1): 51–62.

Clarke, Graham. 1980a. A Helambu History. *Journal of the Nepal Research Centre* 4: 1–38.

————. 1980b. Lama and Tamang in Yolmo. In *Tibetan Studies in Honour of Hugh Richardson,* ed. M. Aris and A. Kyi, 79–86. Warminster, Eng.: Aris and Phillips.

————, ed. 1998. *Development, Society, and Environment in Tibet.* Vienna: Verlag der Österreichischen Akademie der Wissenschaften.

Combe, G. A. 1989 [1925]. *A Tibetan on Tibet.* Berkeley: Snow Lion Graphics.

Conboy, Kenneth, and James Morrison. 2002. *The CIA's Secret War in Tibet.* Lawrence: University of Kansas Press.

Cornu, Philippe. 1997. *Tibetan Astrology.* Boston: Shambhala.

Crook, John, and Stamati Crook. 1994. Explaining Tibetan Polyandry: Sociocultural, Demographic, and Biological Perspectives. In *Himayalan Buddhist Villages,* ed. J. Crook and H. Osmaston, 735–786. Bristol: University of Bristol Press.

Cuevas, Bryan J. 2003. *The Hidden History of the Tibetan Book of the Dead.* Oxford: Oxford University Press.

Dagyab Rinpoche. 1995. *Buddhist Symbols in Tibetan Culture: An Investigation of the Nine Best-Known Groups of Symbols.* Boston: Wisdom.

Dargyay, Eva. 1979. *The Rise of Esoteric Buddhism in Tibet.* Delhi: Motilal Banarsidass.

————. 1982. *Tibetan Village Communities.* New Delhi: Vikas.

Dawa Norbu. 1997. *Tibet: The Road Ahead.* New Delhi: HarperCollins.

Desjarlais, Robert R. 1992. *Body and Emotion: The Aesthetics of Illness and Healing in the Nepal Himalayas.* Philadelphia: University of Pennsylvania Press.

Diehl, Keila. 2002. *Echoes from Dharamsala: Music in the Life of a Tibetan Refugee Community.* Berkeley: University of California Press.

Diemberger, Hildegard. 1991. Lhakama *(lha-bka'-ma)* and Khandroma *(mkha'-'gro-ma):* The Sacred Ladies of Beyul Khenbalung *(sbas-yul mKhan-pa-lung).* In *Tibetan History and Language,* ed. E. Steinkellner, 137–153. Vienna: University of Vienna.

————. 1993. Gangla Tshechu, Beyul Khenbalung: Pilgrimage to Hidden Valleys, Sacred Mountains, and Springs of Life Water in Southern Tibet and Eastern Nepal. In *Anthropology of Tibet and the Himalaya,* ed. C. Ramble and M. Brauen, 60–72. Zurich: Ethnological Museum of the University of Zurich.

————. 1996. Political and Religious Aspects of Mountain Cults in the Hidden Valley of Khenbalung—Tradition, Decline, and Revitalisation. In *Reflections of the Mountain: Essays on the History and Social Meaning of the Mountain Cult in Tibet and the Himalaya,* ed. A. Blondeau and E. Steinkellner, 219–231. Vienna: Verlag der Österreichischen Akademie der Wissenschaften.

————. 1997. Beyul Khenbalung, the Hidden Valley of the Artemisia: On Himalayan Communities and Their Sacred Landscape. In *Mandala and Landscape,* ed. A. W. Macdonald, 287–334. New Delhi: D.K. Printworld.

Dobremez, Jean-François, ed. 1986. *Les collines du Népal central : Écosystèmes, structures sociales et systèmes agraires.* Paris : Institute National de la Recherche Agronomique.

Dobremez, Jean-François, and Corneille Jest. 1976. *Manaslu: Hommes et milieux des vallées du Népal central.* Paris: CNRS.

Dodin, Thierry, and Heinz Räther, eds. 2001. *Imagining Tibet: Perceptions, Projections, and Fantasies.* Boston: Wisdom.

Dowman, Keith, trans. 1973. *The Legend of the Great Stupa.* Berkeley: Dharma.

———. 1997. *The Sacred Life of Tibet.* London: Thorsons.

Downs, Hugh R. 1980. *Rhythms of a Himalayan Village.* San Francisco: Harper and Row.

Dudjom Rinpoche. 1991. *The Nyingma School of Tibetan Buddhism.* Boston: Wisdom.

Duncan, Marion H. 1964. *Customs and Superstitions of Tibetans.* London: Mitre Press.

Dunham, V. Carroll, Ian Baker, and Thomas L. Kelly. 2001. *Tibet: Reflections from the Wheel of Life.* New York: Abbeville Press.

Ehrhard, Franz-Karl. 1997. A "Hidden Land" in the Tibetan-Nepalese Borderlands. In *Mandala and Landscape,* ed. A. W. Macdonald, 335–364. New Delhi: D.K. Printworld.

———. 1999. Political and Ritual Aspects of the Search for Himalayan Sacred Lands. In *Sacred Space and Powerful Places in Tibetan Culture,* ed. T. Huber, 240–257. Dharamsala: Library of Tibetan Works and Archives.

Eimer, Helmut. 1992. *Ein Jahrzehnt Studien zur Überlieferung des tibetischen Kanjur.* Vienna: Arbeitskreis für Tibetische und Buddhistische Studien, Universität Wien.

Ekvall, Robert B. 1964. *Religious Observances in Tibet.* Chicago: University of Chicago Press.

———. 1968. *Fields on the Hoof: Nexus of Tibetan Nomadic Pastoralism.* New York: Holt, Rinehart and Winston.

———. 1976 [1952]. *Tibetan Sky Lines.* New York: Octagon.

Epstein, Lawrence. 1982. On the History and Psychology of the 'Das-log. *Tibet Journal* 7 (4): 20–85.

———. 1990. A Comparative View of Tibetan and Western Near-Death Experiences. In *Reflections on Tibetan Culture: Essays in Memory of Turrell V. Wylie,* ed. L. Epstein and R. Sherburne, 315–328. Lewiston, N.Y.: Edwin Mellen Press.

———, ed. 2002. *Khams pa Histories: Visions of People, Place, and Authority.* Leiden: E. J. Brill.

Ferrari, Alfonsa. 1958. *Mk'yen Brtse's Guide to the Holy Places of Central Tibet.* Rome: IsMEO.

Fields, Rick. 1992. *How the Swans Came to the Lake: A Narrative History of Buddhism in America.* Boston: Shambhala.

Filippi, Filippo de, ed. 1995 [1937]. *An Account of Tibet: The Travels of Ippolito Desideri, 1712–1727.* New Delhi: Asian Educational Services.

Fisher, James F., ed. 1978. *Himalayan Anthropology: The Indo-Tibetan Interface.* The Hague: Mouton.

———. 1986. *Trans-Himalayan Traders.* Delhi: Motilal Banarsidass.

———. 1990. *Sherpas.* Berkeley: University of California Press.

Forbes, Ann A. 1989. *Settlements of Hope: An Account of Tibetan Refugees in Nepal.* Cambridge, Mass.: Cultural Survival.

Fox, Jefferson. 1993. Forest Resources in a Nepali Village in 1980 and 1990: The Positive Influence of Population Growth. *Mountain Research and Development* 13 (1): 89–98.

Frank, Walter. 1974. *Ethnische Grundlagen der Siedlingstruktur in Mittelnepal unter besonderer Berücksichtigung der Tamang*. Innsbruck: Universitätsverlag Wagner.

Fremantle, Francesca, and Chogyam Trungpa. 1987. *The Tibetan Book of the Dead*. Boston: Shambhala.

Fricke, Tom. 1994. *Himalayan Households*. New York: Columbia University Press.

Fürer-Haimendorf, Christoph von. 1964. *The Sherpas of Nepal: Buddhist Highlanders*. Berkeley: University of California Press.

————. 1974a. The Changing Fortunes of Nepal's High-Altitude Dwellers. In *Contributions to the Anthropology of Nepal,* ed. Christoph von Fürer-Haimendorf, 98–113. Warminster, Eng.: Aris and Phillips.

————, ed. 1974b. *Contributions to the Anthropology of Nepal*. Warminster, Eng.: Aris and Phillips.

————. 1975. *Himalayan Traders: Life in Highland Nepal*. London: John Murray.

————, ed. 1981. *Asian Highland Societies in Anthropological Perspective*. New Delhi: Sterling.

————. 1989. *The Renaissance of Tibetan Civilization*. New York: Oxford University Press.

Gedün Chöpel. 1992. *Tibetan Arts of Love*. Ithaca, N.Y.: Snow Lion.

Germano, David. 1997. Dying, Death, and Other Opportunities. In *Religions of Tibet in Practice,* ed. D. Lopez, 458–493. Princeton: Princeton University Press.

Germano, David, and Helmut Eimer, eds. 2002. *The Many Canons of Tibetan Buddhism*. Leiden: E. J. Brill.

Goldstein, Melvyn C. 1971a. Stratification, Polyandry, and Family Structure in Central Tibet. *Southwest Journal of Anthropology* 27: 64–74.

————. 1971b. Taxation and the Structure of a Tibetan Tillage. *Central Asiatic Journal* 15 (1): 1–27.

————. 1973. The Circulation of Estates in Tibet: Reincarnation, Land, and Politics. *Journal of Asian Studies* 32 (3): 445–455.

————. 1976. Fraternal Polyandry and Fertility in a High Himalayan Valley in Northwest Nepal. *Human Ecology* 4 (2): 223–233.

————. 1981. New Perspectives on Tibetan Fertility and Population Decline. *American Ethnologist* 8 (4): 721–738.

————. 1989. *The History of Modern Tibet, 1913–1951: The Demise of the Lamaist State*. Berkeley: University of California Press.

————. 1990. Religious Conflict in the Traditional Tibetan State. In *Reflections on Tibetan Culture: Essays in Memory of T. V. Wylie,* ed. L. Epstein and R. Sherburne. Lewiston, N.Y.: Edwin Mellen.

————. 1997. *The Snow Lion and the Dragon: China, Tibet, and the Dalai Lama*. Berkeley: University of California Press.

Goldstein, Melvyn C., and Cynthia M. Beall. 1990. *Nomads of Western Tibet: The Survival of a Way of Life*. Berkeley: University of California Press.

————. 1997. Growing Old in Tibet—Tradition, Family, and Change. In *Aging: Asian Concepts and Experiences Past and Present*, ed. S. Formanek and S. Linhart, 155–176. Vienna: Verlag der Österreichischen Akademie der Wissenschaften.

Goldstein, Melvyn C., and Matthew T. Kapstein, eds. 1998. *Buddhism in Contemporary Tibet: Religious Revival and Cultural Identity.* Berkeley: University of California Press.

Goldstein, Melvyn C., William Siebenschuh, and Tashi Tsering. 1997. *The Struggle for Modern Tibet: The Autobiography of Tashi Tsering.* Armonk, N.Y.: M. E. Sharpe.

Goldstein, Melvyn, Ben Jiao (Benjor), Cynthia M. Beall, and Phuntsog Tsering. 2002. Fertility and Family Planning in Rural Tibet. *China Journal* 47 (1): 19–39.

Greenhalgh, Susan, ed. 1995. *Situating Fertility: Anthropology and the Demographic Inquiry.* Cambridge: Cambridge University Press.

Grunfeld, A. Tom. 1996. *The Making of Modern Tibet.* Armonk, N.Y.: M. E. Sharpe.

Guenther, Herbert V. 1996. *The Teachings of Padmasambhava.* Leiden: E. J. Brill.

Guillet, David W. 1983. Toward a Cultural Ecology of Mountains: The Central Andes and the Himalayas Compared. *Current Anthropology* 24 (5): 561–574.

Gurung, Nareswor J. 1976. An Introduction to the Socio-Economic Structure of Manang District. *Kailash* 4 (3): 295–308.

Gutschow, Kim. 1997. Unfocussed Merit-Making in Zangskar: A Socio-economic Account of Karsha Nunnery. *Tibet Journal* 22 (2): 30–58.

————. 2001. The Women Who Refuse to Be Exchanged: Nuns in Zangskar, Northwest India. In *Celibacy, Culture, and Society: The Anthropology of Sexual Abstinence*, ed. E. Sobo and S. Bell, 47–64. Madison: University of Wisconsin Press.

Gyatso, Janet. 1999. *Apparitions of the Self: The Secret Autobiographies of a Tibetan Visionary.* Princeton: Princeton University Press.

Haddix, Kimber. 2001. Leaving Your Wife and Your Brothers: When Polyandrous Marriages Fall Apart. *Evolution and Human Behavior* 22 (1): 47–60.

Hale, Austin. 1982. *Research on Tibeto-Burman Languages.* New York: Mouton.

Harris, Melissa, and Sidney Jones, eds. 2000. *Tibet since 1950: Silence, Prison, or Exile.* New York: Aperture and Human Rights Watch.

Harrison, Paul. 1992. Meritorious Activity or Waste of Time? Some Remarks on the Editing of Texts in the Tibetan Kanjur. In *Tibetan Studies*, ed. I. Shoren and Y. Zuiho, 77–91. Narita, Japan: Naritasan Shinshoji.

————. 1996. A Brief History of the Tibetan bKa' 'gyur. In *Tibetan Literature*, ed. J. Cabezon and R. Jackson, 70–94. Ithaca, N.Y.: Snow Lion.

Harvey, Peter. 2000. *An Introduction to Buddhist Ethics: Foundations, Values, and Issues.* Cambridge: Cambridge University Press.

Havnevik, Hanna. 1989. *Tibetan Buddhist Nuns.* Oslo: Norwegian University Press.

————. 1994. The Role of Nuns in Contemporary Tibet. In *Resistance and Reform in Tibet,* ed. R. Barnett and S. Akiner, 259–266. Delhi: Motilal Banarsidass.

———. 1999. *The Life of Jetsun Lochen Rinpoche (1865–1951) as Told in Her Autobiography. Acta Humaniora*, no. 50. 2 vols. Oslo: University of Oslo.

Heller, Amy. 2000. *Tibetan Art: Tracing the Development of Spiritual Ideals and Art in Tibet, 600–2000 A.D.* Milan: Jaca Books.

Hitchcock, John T., and Rex L. Jones. 1976. *Spirit Possession in the Nepal Himalayas.* Warminster, Eng.: Aris and Phillips.

Hodge, Stephen, and Martin Boord. 2000. *The Illustrated Tibetan Book of the Dead: A New Translation with Commentary.* New York: Sterling.

Höfer, András. 1979. *The Caste Hierarchy and the State in Nepal.* Innsbruck: Universitätsverlag Wagner.

———. 1981. *Tamang Ritual Texts.* Wiesbaden: Franz Steiner Verlag.

Holmberg, David H. 1989. *Order in Paradox: Myth, Ritual, and Exchange among Nepal's Tamang.* Ithaca: Cornell University Press.

Hopkins, Jeffrey. 2000. Reason and Orgasm in Tibetan Buddhism. In *Love, Sex, and Gender in the World Religions,* ed. J. Runzo and N. Martin, 271–286. Oxford: Oneworld.

Howell, Nancy. 1979. *Demography of the Dobe !Kung.* New York: Academic.

Huber, Toni. 1992. A Tibetan Map of lHo-kha in the South-Eastern Himalayan Borderlands of Tibet. *Imago Mundi* 44: 9–23.

———. 1994. Why Can't Women Climb Pure Crystal Mountain? Remarks on Gender, Ritual, and Space at Tsa-ri. In *Tibetan Studies,* ed. Per Kvaerne, 350–371. Oslo: Institute for Comparative Research in Human Culture.

———. 1997. Green Tibetans: A Brief Social History. In *Tibetan Culture in the Diaspora,* ed. Frank J. Korom, 103–119. Vienna: Verlag der Österreichischen Akademie der Wissenschaften.

———. 1999a. *The Cult of Pure Crystal Mountain: Popular Pilgrimage and Visionary Landscape in Southeast Tibet.* Oxford: Oxford University Press.

———, ed. 1999b. *Sacred Spaces and Powerful Places in Tibetan Culture.* Dharamsala: Library of Tibetan Works and Archives.

Ives, Jack D. 1987. The Theory of Himalayan Environmental Degradation: Its Validity and Application Challenged by Recent Research. *Mountain Research and Development* 7 (3): 189–199.

Ives, Jack, and Bruno Messerli. 1989. *The Himalayan Dilemma.* New York: Routledge.

Jackson, David P. 1984. *The Mollas of Mustang.* Dharamsala: Library of Tibetan Works and Archives.

———. 1996. *A History of Tibetan Painting: The Great Tibetan Painters and Their Traditions.* Vienna: Verlag der Österreichischen Akademie der Wissenschaften.

Jackson, David P., and Janice A. Jackson. 1999 [1984]. *Tibetan Thangka Painting: Methods and Materials.* Ithaca, N.Y.: Snow Lion.

Jamyang Norbu. 1987. *Warriors of Tibet: The Story of Aten and the Khampas' Fight for the Freedom of Their Country.* Boston: Wisdom.

———. 2001. Behind the Lost Horizon: Demystifying Tibet. In *Imagining Tibet: Perceptions, Projections, and Fantasies,* ed. T. Dodin and H. Räther, 373–378. Boston: Wisdom.

Jest, Corneille. 1975. *Dolpo: Communautés de langue tibétaine du Népal.* Paris: CNRS.

———. 1981. *Monuments of Northern Nepal.* Paris: UNESCO.

———. 1993. *Tales of the Turquoise: A Pilgrimage in Dolpo.* Kathmandu: Mandala Book Point.

Kapstein, Mathew. 1997. Turning Back Gossip. In *Religions of Tibet in Practice,* ed. D. Lopez, 527–537. Princeton: Princeton University Press.

———. 1998. A Pilgrimage of Rebirth Reborn: The 1992 Celebration of the Drigung Powa Chenmo. In *Buddhism in Contemporary Tibet: Religious Revival and Cultural Identity,* ed. M. Goldstein and M. Kapstein, 95–119. Berkeley: University of California Press.

Karma Thinley. 2001. *The History of the Sixteen Karmapas of Tibet.* Boston: Shambhala.

Karmay, Samten G. 1994. Mountain Cults and National Identity in Tibet. In *Resistance and Reform in Tibet,* ed. R. Barnett, 112–120. London: C. Hurst.

———. 1998. *The Arrow and the Spindle: Studies in History, Myths, Rituals, and Beliefs in Tibet.* Kathmandu: Mandala Book Point.

Kawakita, Jiro. 1957. *Ethno-geographical Observations on the Nepal Himalaya.* Vol. 3 of *Peoples of Nepal Himalaya,* ed. H. Kihara. Kyoto: Fauna and Flora Research Society, Kyoto University.

Kertzer, David I., and Tom Fricke, eds. 1997. *Anthropological Demography: Toward a New Synthesis.* Chicago: University of Chicago Press.

Kertzer, David I., and Dennis P. Hogan. 1989. *Family, Political Economy, and Demographic Change: The Transformation of Life in Casalecchio, Italy, 1861–1921.* Madison: University of Wisconsin Press.

Khangkar, Lobsang Dolma. 1986. *Lectures on Tibetan Medicine.* Dharamsala: Library of Tibetan Works and Archives.

Kikhang, Yangchen. 1997. Women Face Cultural Genocide on the Roof of the World. In *Gender and Catastrophe,* ed. R. Lentin, 110–116. London: Zed Books.

Kleiger, P. Christiaan. 1992. *Tibetan Nationalism: The Role of Patronage in the Accomplishment of a National Identity.* Berkeley: Folklore Institute.

———, ed. 2002. *Tibet, Self, and the Tibetan Diaspora: Voices of Difference.* Leiden: E. J. Brill.

Klein, Anne C. 1995. *Meeting the Great Bliss Queen: Buddhists, Feminists, and the Art of the Self.* Boston: Beacon Press.

Klimburg-Salter, Deborah, and Eva Allinger, eds. 2002. *Buddhist Art and Tibetan Patronage: Ninth to Fourteenth Centuries.* Leiden: E. J. Brill.

Knaus, John K. 1999. *Orphans of the Cold War: America and the Tibetan Struggle for Survival.* New York: Public Affairs.

Korom, Frank J., ed. 1997. *Tibetan Culture in the Diaspora.* Vienna: Verlag der Österreichischen Akademie der Wissenschaften.

Lama Kunga Rinpoche and Brian Cutillo, trans. 1995. *Drinking the Mountain Stream: Songs of Tibet's Beloved Saint, Milarepa.* Boston: Wisdom.

Lamb, Sarah. 2000. *White Saris and Sweet Mangoes: Aging, Gender, and Body in North India.* Berkeley: University of California Press.

Larsen, Knud, and Amund Sinding-Larsen. 2001. *The Lhasa Atlas: Traditional Tibetan Architecture and Townscape.* Boston: Shambhala.

Lazar, Edward, ed. 1994. *Tibet: The Issue Is Independence*. Berkeley: Parallax Press.

Levine, Nancy E. 1981. The Theory of Rü: Kinship, Descent, and Status in a Tibetan Society. In *Asian Highland Societies: Anthropological Perspective*, ed. C. von Fürer-Haimendorf, 52–78. New Delhi: Sterling.

———. 1987. Differential Child Care in Three Tibetan Communities: Beyond Son Preference. *Population and Development Review* 13 (2): 281–304.

———. 1988. *The Dynamics of Polyandry: Kinship, Domesticity, and Population on the Tibetan Border*. Chicago: University of Chicago Press.

Levine, Nancy E., and Joan Silk. 1997. Why Polyandry Fails: Sources of Instability in Polyandrous Marriages. *Current Anthropology* 38 (3): 375–398.

Lhalungpa, Lobsang P., trans. 1997. *The Life of Milarepa*. Delhi: Book Faith India.

Lhamo Pemba. 1996. *Tibetan Proverbs*. Dharamsala: Library of Tibetan Works and Archives.

Lhasang Tsering. 1993. Talks with Lhasang Tsering (Interviewed by Michel-Acatl Monnier). *Lungta* 7: 32–37.

Lopez, Donald S., ed. 1997. *Religions of Tibet in Practice*. Princeton: Princeton University Press.

———. 1998. *Prisoners of Shangri-La: Tibetan Buddhism and the West*. Chicago: University of Chicago Press.

Macdonald, Alexander. 1983a. *Essays on the Ethnology of Nepal and South Asia*. Kathmandu: Ratna Pustak Bhandhar.

———. 1983b. The Tamang as Seen by One of Themselves. In *Essays on the Ethnology of Nepal and South Asia*, 129–167. Kathmandu: Ratna Pustak Bhandhar.

———, ed. 1997. *Mandala and Landscape*. New Delhi: D.K. Printworld.

Macfarlane, Alan. 1976. *Resources and Population: A Study of the Gurungs of Nepal*. Cambridge: Cambridge University Press.

Maiden, Anne Hubbell, and Edie Farwell. 1997. *The Tibetan Art of Parenting: From before Conception through Early Childhood*. Boston: Wisdom.

Maki, Yuko, and T. Imanishi. 1957. The Ascent of Manaslu. *Himalayan Journal* 20: 11–25.

March, Kathryn S. 2002. *"If Each Comes Halfway": Meeting Tamang Women in Nepal*. Ithaca: Cornell University Press.

Martin, Dan. 1996. On the Cultural Ecology of Sky Burial on the Himalayan Plateau. *East and West* 46 (3–4): 353–370.

———. 1997. *Tibetan Histories: A Bibliography of Tibetan-Language Historical Works*. London: Serindia.

McGuckin, Eric. 1997. Tibetan Carpets: From Folk Art to Global Commodity. *Journal of Material Culture* 2 (3): 291–310.

McKay, Alex, ed. 1998. *Pilgrimage in Tibet*. Richmond, Eng.: Curzon.

Messerschmidt, Donald. 1976a. Ecological Change and Adaptation among the Gurungs of the Nepal Himalaya. *Human Ecology* 4 (2): 167–185.

———. 1976b. *The Gurungs of Nepal: Conflict and Change in a Village Society*. Warminster, Eng.: Aris and Phillips.

Michael, Franz H. 1982. *Rule by Incarnation: Tibetan Buddhism and Its Role in Society and State.* Boulder, Colo.: Westview Press.

Milarepa. 1985 [15th cent.]. *rJe-btsun Mi-la Ras-pa'i rdo-rje'i mgur-drug-sogs gsung-rgyung thor-bu* (A collection of various songs of spiritual insight by the venerable Milarepa). Delhi: Sonam Rabten.

Montgomerie, Capt. T. G. 1868. Report of a Route-Survey Made By Pundit ———, from Nepal to Lhasa, and Thence through the Upper Valley of the Brahmaputra to Its Source. *Journal of the Royal Geographic Society* 38: 129–218.

Moran, Emilio F. 2000. *Human Adaptability: An Introduction to Ecological Anthropology.* Boulder, Colo.: Westview Press.

Moran, Peter. 1998. Buddhism Observed: Western Travelers, Tibetan Exiles, and the Culture of Dharma in Kathmandu. Ph.D. diss., University of Washington.

Mullin, Glenn H. 1998. *Living in the Face of Death: The Tibetan Tradition.* Ithaca, N.Y.: Snow Lion.

Mumford, Stan R. 1989. *Himalayan Dialogue: Tibetan Lamas and Gurung Shamans in Nepal.* Madison: University of Wisconsin Press.

———. 1998. Tibetan Identity Layers in the Nepal Himalayas. In *Selves in Time and Place,* ed. D. Skinner, A. Pach, and D. Holland, 175–193. Lanham, Md.: Rowman and Littlefield.

Namkai Norbu. 1997. *Journey among the Tibetan Nomads: An Account of a Remote Civilization.* Dharamsala: Library of Tibetan Works and Archives.

Nebesky-Wojkowitz, Rene de. 1956. *Oracles and Demons of Tibet: The Cult and Iconography of the Tibetan Protective Deities.* The Hague: Mouton.

Netting, Robert M. 1981. *Balancing on an Alp: Ecological Change and Continuity in a Swiss Mountain Community.* New York: Cambridge University Press.

Ngawang Zangpo. 1997. *Enthronement: The Recognition of the Reincarnate Masters of Tibet and the Himalayas.* Ithaca, N.Y.: Snow Lion.

Norbu Chophel. 1983. *Folk Culture of Tibet.* Dharamsala: Library of Tibetan Works and Archives.

Novak, Margaret. 1984. *Tibetan Refugees: Youth and the New Generation of Meaning.* New Brunswick, N.J.: Rutgers University Press.

Obermiller, Eugene, trans. 1986 [1932]. *The History of Buddhism in India and Tibet.* Delhi: Sri Satguru.

Oppitz, M. 1968. *Geschichte und Sozialordnung der Sherpa.* Khumbu Himal, Band 8. Innsbruck: Universitätsverlag Wagner.

Orlove, Benjamin S., and David W. Guillet. 1985. Theoretical and Methodological Considerations on the Study of Mountain Peoples: Reflections on the Idea of Subsistence Type and the Role of History in Human Ecology. *Mountain Research and Development* 5 (1): 3–18.

Orofino, Giacomella. 1991. The Tibetan Myth of the Hidden Valley in the Visionary Geography of Nepal. *East and West,* n.s., 41: 239–271.

Ortner, Sherry B. 1975. Gods' Bodies, Gods' Food: A Symbolic Analysis of a Sherpa Ritual. In *The Interpretation of Symbolism,* ed. R. Willis, 133–169. New York: John Wiley.

———. 1978. *Sherpas through Their Rituals.* New York: Cambridge University Press.

————. 1989. *High Religion*. Princeton: Princeton University Press.

Osmaston, Henry, and Tashi Rabgyas. 1994. Weights and Measures Used in Ladakh. In *Himalayan Buddhist Villages*, ed. J. Crook and H. Osmaston, 121–138. Delhi: Motilal Banarsidass.

Pandey, Ram Niwas. 1997. *Making of Modern Nepal*. New Delhi: Nirala.

Pasang Wangdu and Hildegard Diemberger. 1996. *Shel dKar Chos 'Byung: History of the "White Crystal."* Vienna: Verlag der Österreichischen Akademie der Wissenschaften.

————. 2000. *dBa' bzhed: The Royal Narrative Concerning the Bringing of the Buddha's Doctrine to Tibet*. Vienna: Verlag der Österreichischen Akademie der Wissenschaften.

Paul, Robert A. 1976. The Sherpa Temple as a Model of the Psyche. *American Anthropologist* 3 (1): 131–146.

Peissel, Michel. 1972. *Cavaliers of Kham: The Secret War in Tibet*. London: Heinemann.

Pema Döndrup. 1979 [18th cent.]. *bDag bya-btang ras-pa Padma Don-grub-kyi chos byas-'tshul dang bka'-ba spyad-'tshul-rnams* (The manner in which I, Pema Döndrup, "The Cotton-Clad Forsaker of Deeds," practiced and obtained teachings and undertook austerities). In *Autobiographies of Three Spiritual Masters of Kutang*, 1–143. Thimphu: Kunsang Topgay and Mani Dorji.

Pema Lhundrup. 1979 [18th cent.]. *rNam-'byor ras-pa Padma Lhun-grub bsTan-'dzin rGya-mtsho'i gsung-pa'i rnam-mthar kun-bsal me-long* (The biography recited by Pema Lhundrup Tenzin Gyatso, "The Cotton-Clad Yogin," [entitled] *The Mirror Which Illuminates All*). In *Autobiographies of Three Spiritual Masters of Kutang*, 591–757. Thimphu: Kunsang Topgay and Mani Dorji.

Pema Wangdu. 1979 [18th cent.]. *mKha'-mnyams 'gro-ba'i rtsug-brgyan Padma Dbang-'dus-kyi rnam-par thar-pa gsal-bar bkod-pa-la rmongs-mun thib-po las-ba'i sgron-me* (The clearly written biography of Pema Wangdu, "Head-Ornament of Beings Limitless as the Sky," [entitled] *The Lamp Which Removes Dark Obscurities*). In *Autobiographies of Three Spiritual Masters of Kutang*, 145–495. Thimphu: Kunsang Topgay and Mani Dorji.

Petech, Luciano. 1973. *Aristocracy and Government in Tibet, 1728–1959*. Rome: IsMEO.

————. 1977. *The Kingdom of Ladakh, c. 950–1842 A.D.* Rome: IsMEO.

————. 1980a. The Mongol Census in Tibet. In *Tibetan Studies in Honour of Hugh Richardson*, ed. M. Aris and A. Kyi, 235–238. Warminster, Eng.: Aris and Phillips.

————. 1980b. Ya-ts'e, Gu-ge, Pu-rang: A New Study. *Central Asiatic Journal* 24 (1): 85–111.

————. 1988. The Tibet-Ladakhi-Moghul War (1679–1683). In *Selected Papers on Asian History*, Serie Orientale Roma 60: 19–44. Rome: IsMEO.

Pigg, Stacy L. 1997. "Found in Most Traditional Societies": Traditional Medical Practitioners between Culture and Development. In *International Development and the Social Sciences*, ed. F. Cooper and R. Packard, 259–290. Berkeley: University of California Press.

Pignède, Bernard. 1993 [1966]. *The Gurungs: A Himalayan Population of Nepal*. Kathmandu: Ratna Pustak Bhandar.

Planning Council. 2000. *Tibetan Demographic Survey 1998*. Dharamsala: Planning Council, Central Tibetan Administration, Gangchen Kyishong.

Pommaret-Imaeda, Françoise. 2002. *Lhasa in the Seventeenth Century: The Capital of the Dalai Lamas*. Leiden: E. J. Brill.

Powers, John. 1995. *Introduction to Tibetan Buddhism*. Ithaca, N.Y.: Snow Lion.

Prebish, Charles S., and Martin Baumann, eds. 2002. *Western Dharma: Buddhism beyond Asia*. Berkeley: University of California Press.

Prebish, Charles S., and Kenneth K. Tanaka, eds. 1998. *The Faces of Buddhism in America*. Berkeley: University of California Press.

Rahula, Walpola. 1967. *What the Buddha Taught*. New York: Grove Press.

Ramble, Charles. 1990. How Buddhists Are Buddhist Communities: The Construction of Tradition in Two Lamaist Villages. *Journal of the Anthropological Society of Oxford* 21 (2): 185–197.

———. 1993a. The Name Bhotey. *Himal* 6 (5): 17.

———. 1993b. Whither, Indeed, the Tsampa Eaters. *Himal* 6 (5): 21–25.

———. 1997. Tibetan Pride of Place: Or, Why Nepal's Bhotiyas Are Not an Ethnic Group. In *Nationalism and Ethnicity in a Hindu Kingdom: The Politics of Culture in Contemporary Nepal*, ed. D. Gellner, J. Pfaff-Czarnecka, and J. Whelpton, 379–413. Amsterdam: Harwood.

———. 2004. *The Navel of the Demoness: Tibetan Buddhism and Civil Religion in Highland Nepal*. New York: Oxford University Press.

Ramble, Charles, and Martin Brauen, eds. 1993. *Anthropology of Tibet and the Himalaya*. Zurich: Ethnological Museum of the University of Zurich.

Regmi, D. R. 1961a. *Medieval Nepal*. 2 vols. Calcutta: Mukhopadhyay.

———. 1961b. *Modern Nepal*. Calcutta: Mukhopadhyay.

Regmi, Mahesh C. 1978. *Thatched Huts and Stucco Palaces: Peasants and Landlords in 19th-Century Nepal*. New Delhi: Vikas.

Reinhard, Johan. 1978. Khembalung: The Hidden Valley. *Kailash* 6 (1): 5–35.

Rhie, Marylin M., and Robert A. F. Thurman. 1996. *Wisdom and Compassion: The Sacred Art of Tibet*. New York: Tibet House.

Rhoades, Robert G., and Stephan I. Thompson. 1975. Adaptive Strategies in Alpine Environments: Beyond Ecological Particularism. *American Ethnologist* 2 (3): 535–551.

Ricard, Matthieu, trans. 1994. *The Life of Shabkar: The Autobiography of a Tibetan Yogin*. Albany: State University of New York Press.

Richardson, Hugh. 1998a. Early Burial Grounds in Tibet and Tibetan Decorative Art of the Eighth and Ninth Centuries (1963). In *High Peaks, Pure Earth: Collected Writings on Tibetan History and Culture*, 219–233. London: Serindia.

———. 1998b. The Jo-khang "Cathedral" of Lhasa (1977). In *High Peaks, Pure Earth: Collected Writings on Tibetan History and Culture*, 237–260. London: Serindia.

———. 1998c. Memories of Tshurphu (1982). In *High Peaks, Pure Earth: Collected Writings on Tibetan History and Culture*, 730–733. London: Serindia.

————. 1998d. The Mgar Family in Seventh-Century Tibet (1989). In *High Peaks, Pure Earth: Collected Writings on Tibetan History and Culture*, 114–123. London: Serindia.

————. 1998e. The Rwa-sgreng Conspiracy of 1947 (1979). In *High Peaks, Pure Earth: Collected Writings on Tibetan History and Culture*, 714–721. London: Serindia.

Rigzen Gödem. 1983 [14th cent.]. *sBas-yul sKyid-mo-lung-gi lam-yig gags-sel* [The obstacle-removing guide to Kyimolung, the hidden land]. In *Collected Biographies and Prophesies of the Byang-gter Tradition*, 557–598. Gangtok: Sherab Gyaltsen and Lama Dawa.

Rinjing Dorje. 1997. *Tales of Uncle Tompa: The Legendary Rascal of Tibet*. Barrytown, N.Y.: Station Hill Arts.

Robinson, Richard H., and Willard L. Johnson. 1997. *The Buddhist Religion: A Historical Introduction*. Belmont, Calif.: Wadsworth.

Roerich, George N., trans. 1988 [1949]. *The Blue Annals*. Delhi: Motilal Banarsidass.

Róna-Tas, András. 1985. *Wiener Vorlesungen zur Sprach- und Kulturgeschichte Tibets*. Vienna: Arbeitskreis für Tibetische und Buddhistische Studien, Universität Wien.

Rose, Leo E. 1971. *Nepal: Strategy for Survival*. Berkeley: University of California Press.

Ross, J. L. 1984. Culture and Fertility in the Nepal Himalayas: A Test of a Hypothesis. *Human Ecology* 12 (2): 163–181.

Rustomji, N. K., and Charles Ramble, eds. 1990. *Himalayan Environment and Culture*. Shimla: Indian Institute of Advanced Study.

Samuel, Geoffrey. 1993. *Civilized Shamans: Buddhism in Tibetan Societies*. Washington, D.C.: Smithsonian Institution Press.

Schicklgruber, Christian. 1993. Who Marries Whom among the Khumbo. In *Anthropology of Tibet and the Himalayas*, ed. C. Ramble and M. Brauen, 343–353. Zurich: Ethnological Museum of the University of Zurich.

————. 1997. Gods and Sacred Mountains. In *Bhutan: Mountain Fortress of the Gods*, ed. C. Schicklgruber and F. Pommaret, 159–175. London: Serindia.

Schicklgruber, Christian, and Françoise Pommaret. 1997. *Bhutan: Mountain Fortress of the Gods*. London: Serindia.

Schuh, Dieter. 1988. *Das Archiv des Klosters bKra-shis-bsam-gtan-gling von sKyid-grong*. Bonn: VGH Wissenschaftsverlag.

Schuler, Sidney R. 1987. *The Other Side of Polyandry*. Boulder, Colo.: Westview Press.

Schwartz, Ronald D. 1994. *Circle of Protest: Political Ritual in the Tibetan Uprising*. New York: Columbia University Press.

Seager, Richard H. 1999. *Buddhism in America*. New York: Columbia University Press.

Sestini, Valerio, and Enzo Somigli. 1978. *Sherpa Architecture*. Paris: UNESCO.

Sever, Adrian. 1996. *Aspects of Modern Nepalese History*. New Delhi: Vikas.

Shakabpa, Tsepon W. D. 1988. *Tibet: A Political History*. New York: Potala.

Skorupski, Tadeusz. 1982. The Cremation Ceremony according to the Byang-gter Tradition. *Kailash* 9 (4): 361–376.

Snellgrove, David L. 1966. For a Sociology of Tibetan-Speaking Regions. *Central Asiatic Journal* 11 (3): 199–219.

———. 1987. *Indo-Tibetan Buddhism: Indian Buddhists and Their Tibetan Successors.* Boston: Shambhala.

———. 1989 [1958]. *Himalayan Pilgrimage.* Boston: Shambhala.

———, trans. 1992 [1967]. *Four Lamas of Dolpo.* Kathmandu: Himalayan Book Seller.

Snellgrove, David L., and Hugh Richardson. 1980. *A Cultural History of Tibet.* Boulder, Colo.: Prajna Press.

Sogyal Rinpoche. 1994. *The Tibetan Book of Living and Dying.* San Francisco: Harper.

Sørensen, Per K. 1994. *The Mirror Illuminating the Royal Genealogies.* Weisbaden: Harrassovitz.

Sperling, Elliot. 2000. Exile and Dissent: The Historical and Cultural Context. In *Tibet since 1950: Silence, Prison, or Exile,* ed. M. Harris and S. Jones, 30–37. New York: Aperture and Human Rights Watch.

———. 2001. "Orientalism" and Aspects of Violence in the Tibetan Tradition. In *Imagining Tibet: Perceptions, Projections, and Fantasies,* ed. T. Dodin and H. Räther, 317–330. Boston: Wisdom.

Stein, Rolf A. 1959. *Les tribus anciennes des marches Sino-Tibétans.* Paris: Bibliothèque de l'Institute des Hautes Études Chinoises.

———. 1972. *Tibetan Civilization.* Stanford: Stanford University Press.

Steinmann, Brigitte. 1987. *Les Tamang du Népal, usages et religion, religion de l'usage.* Paris: Éditions Recherche sur les Grandes Civilisations.

Stevens, Stanley F. 1993. *Claiming the High Ground: Sherpas, Subsistence, and Environmental Change in the Highest Himalaya.* Berkeley: University of California Press.

Stiller, Ludwig F. 1975. *The Rise of the House of Gorkha.* Kathmandu: Ratna Pustak Bhandar.

Sun Huaiyang and Li Xiru. 1996. The Evolution and Current Status of China's Tibetan Population. *Chinese Journal of Population Science* 8 (2): 221–229.

Surkhang, Wangchen. 1966. Tax Measurement and lag 'don Tax. *Bulletin of Tibetology* 3 (1): 15–28.

———. 1986. Government, Monastic, and Private Taxation in Tibet. *Tibet Journal* 11 (1): 31–39.

Takagi, M. 1954. Manaslu 8125 m. (26,650 ft.). In *Mountain World,* ed. M. Kurz, 63–70. London: George Allen and Unwin.

Taklha, Namgyal Lhamo. 2001. *Born in Lhasa.* Ithaca, N.Y.: Snow Lion.

Taylor, McComas, and Lama Choedak Yuthok, trans. 1996. *The Clear Mirror: A Traditional Account of Tibet's Golden Age.* Ithaca, N.Y.: Snow Lion.

Teichman, Eric. 1922. *Travels of a Consular Officer in Eastern Tibet.* Cambridge: Cambridge University Press.

Tenzin Gyatso. 1990. *Freedom in Exile: The Autobiography of the Dalai Lama.* New York: HarperCollins.

Thompson, Michael, and Michael Warburton. 1985. Uncertainty on a Himalayan Scale. *Mountain Research and Development* 5 (2): 115–135.

Thubten Jigme Norbu and Colin M. Turnbull. 1968. *Tibet*. New York: Simon and Schuster.

Thubten Legshay Gyatsho. 1979. *Gateway to the Temple: Manual of Tibetan Monastic Customs, Art, Building, and Celebrations*. Kathmandu: Ratna Pustak Bhandar.

Thubten Sangay. 1984a. Tibetan Rituals of the Dead. *Tibetan Medicine* 7: 30–40.

———.1984b. Tibetan Traditions of Childbirth and Childcare. *Tibetan Medicine* 7: 3–24.

Thurman, Robert A., trans. 1994. *The Tibetan Book of the Dead*. New York: Bantam Doubleday Dell.

Toffin, Gérard, ed. 1991. *Man and His House in the Himalayas: Ecology of Nepal*. New Delhi: Sterling.

Toffin, Gérard, Fernand Meyer, Corneille Jest, and Igor de Garine. 1986. Salme: Ethnologie et démographie d'un village Tamang. In *Les collines du Népal central*, 55–120. Paris: Institute National de la Recherche Agronomique.

Tsarong, Dundul Namgyal. 2000. *In the Service of His Country: The Biography of Dasang Damdul Tsarong, Commander General of Tibet*. Ithaca, N.Y.: Snow Lion.

Tsepak Rigzen. 1993. *Festivals of Tibet*. Dharamsala: Library of Tibetan Works and Archives.

Tsering Shakya. 1993. Whither the Tsampa Eaters? *Himal* 6 (5): 8–11.

———. 1999. *The Dragon in the Land of Snows: A History of Modern Tibet since 1947*. London: Pimlico.

Tsewang Norbu. 1990. *Bod-rje lha-btsad-po'i gdung-rabs mNga'-ris smad Gung-thang du ji-ltar byung ba'i tshul deb-ther dwangs shel-'phrug-gyi me-long* (The manner in which the divine emperors, Lords of Tibet, came to Gungtang in Lower Ngari, [entitled] *The Crystal Chronicle*). In *Bod-kyi lo-rgyus deb-ther khag-lnga,* ed. Chab-spel Tshe-brtan Phun-tshogs, Gangs-can rig-mdzod, 9:87–150. Lhasa: Bod-ljongs bod-yig dpe-rnying dpe-skrun-khang.

Tucci, Giuseppe. 1950. *The Tombs of the Tibetan Kings*. Rome: IsMEO.

———. 1956. *Preliminary Report on Two Scientific Expeditions to Nepal*. Rome: IsMEO.

Tulku Thondup. 1986. *Hidden Teachings of Tibet*. London: Wisdom.

———. 1996. *Masters of Meditation and Miracles: The Longchen Nyingthig Lineage of Tibetan Buddhism*. Boston: Shambhala.

Turner, Samuel. 1991 [1800]. *An Account of an Embassy to the Court of the Teshoo Lama in Tibet*. New Delhi: Asian Educational Services.

Turner, Victor. 1969. *The Ritual Process: Structure and Anti-Structure*. Chicago: Aldine.

Uray, Géza. 1960. The Four Horns of Tibet according to the Royal Annals. *Acta Orientalia Hungaricae* 10: 31–57.

———. 1980. *Khrom:* Administrative Units in the Tibetan Empire in the 7th–9th Centuries. In *Tibetan Studies in Honour of Hugh Richardson,* ed. M. Aris and A. Kyi, 310–318. Warminster, Eng.: Aris and Phillips.

van der Kuijp, Leonard W. J. 1996. Tibetan Historiography. In *Tibetan Literature: Studies in Genre*, ed. J. Cabezón and R. Jackson, 39–56. Ithaca, N.Y.: Snow Lion.

van Gennep, Arnold. 1960 [1909]. *The Rites of Passage*. Chicago: University of Chicago Press.

Vansina, Jan. 1985. *Oral Tradition as History*. Madison: University of Wisconsin Press.

van Spengen, Wim. 2000. *Tibetan Border Worlds: A Geohistorical Analysis of Trade and Traders*. New York: Kegan Paul International.

Vitali, Roberto. 1990. *Early Temples of Central Tibet*. London: Serindia.

———. 1996. *The Kingdoms of Gu.ge and Pu.hrang*. Dharamsala: Tho.ling gtsug.lag.khang lo.gcig.stong 'khor.ba'i rjes.dran.mdzad sgo'i go.sgrig tshogs.chung.

———. 1997. Nomads of Byang and mNga'-ris-smad: A Historical Overview of their Interactions in Gro-shod, 'Brong-pa, Glo-bo and Gung-thang from the 11th to the 15th Century. In *Tibetan Studies*, ed. H. Krasser, M. Much, E. Steinkellner, and H. Tauscher, 1023–1026. Vienna: Verlag der Österreichischen Akademie der Wissenschaften.

Watkins, Joanne C. 1996. *Spirited Women: Gender, Religion, and Cultural Identity in the Nepal Himalaya*. New York: Columbia University Press.

Weitz, Charles A., et al. 1978. Cultural Factors affecting the Demographic Structure of a High Altitude Nepalese Population. *Social Biology* 25 (3): 179–195.

White, Stephen. 1990. The Flowering of Tibetan Architecture. In *White Lotus: An Introduction to Tibetan Culture*, ed. C. Elchert, 139–154. Ithaca, N.Y.: Snow Lion.

Wiley, Andrea S. 1997. A Role for Biology in the Cultural Ecology of Ladakh. *Human Ecology* 25 (2): 273–295.

———. 1998. The Ecology of Low Natural Fertility in Ladakh. *Journal of Biosocial Science*, 30: 457–480.

Williams, Paul, and Anthony Tribe. 2000. *Buddhist Thought: A Complete Introduction to the Indian Tradition*. New York: Routledge.

Willis, Janice D. 1987. *Feminine Ground: Essays on Women and Tibet*. Ithaca, N.Y.: Snow Lion.

Winkler, Daniel. 1998. Deforestation in Eastern Tibet: Human Impact Past and Present. In *Development, Society, and Environment in Tibet*, ed. G. Clarke, 79–96. Vienna: Verlag der Österreichischen Akademie der Wissenschaften.

Wood, James W. 1994. *Dynamics of Human Reproduction: Biology, Biometry, Demography*. New York: Aldine De Gruyter.

Wylie, Turrell V. 1962. *The Geography of Tibet according to the 'Dzam-gLing-rGyas-bShad*. Rome: IsMEO.

———. 1964. Ro-langs: The Tibetan Zombie. *History of Religions* 4: 69–80.

———. 1970. Was Christopher Columbus from Shambhala? *Bulletin of the Institute of China Border Area Studies* 2: 24–33.

Yeshe Tsogyal. 1993. *The Lotus-Born: The Life Story of Padmasambhava*. Boston: Shambhala.

Index

Text: 10/13 Sabon
Display: Sabon
Compositor: TechBooks
Cartographer: Bill Nelson
Printer and Binder: Edwards Brothers, Inc.